State on Board!

"This book is a comprehensive reference full of important theoretical and empirical information for those who wish to gain an understanding of corporate governance of state-owned enterprises (SOEs), especially those with mixed ownership of state capital and private capital. It provides a new evidence-based framework that integrates agency and political economic theories for corporate governance of mixed ownership SOEs. This book adopts a pragmatic approach in its presentation and offers practical models for corporate practitioners, investors and academics to help them appreciate and navigate the intricacies of corporate governance of state ownership in emerging markets. This is an indispensable guide for those planning to or are engaged in emerging market business"

—Professor Iftekhar Hasan, E. Gerald Corrigan Chair in *Finance at the Gabelli School of Business, Fordham University, New York,* Scientific Advisor at the *Bank of Finland,* Managing Editor of the *Journal of Financial Stability*

"State-owned enterprises (SOEs) in Vietnam remain a major pillar of the Vietnamese economy—the government owns a significant level of assets of listed companies. This is despite the equitation programmes of the 1990's and 2000's. In recent times there has been a marked reform of SOE governance and performance in Vietnam in its search for economic growth and to achieve its goal of national middle income status by 2030. Such efforts are to be commended and this study supports such steps to reform. It informs the further reforms necessary to move to an even more to a market oriented economy, such as better transparency and disclosure in the governance of SOEs, and improved state ownership activities and state capital management. In SOEs it is important to prevent inefficiencies and misallocation of resources. The study reviews state-owned enterprises with mixed ownership—partially state-owned combined with private sector investors and uses the benchmarks and compares SOE practices in Vietnamese SOEs with those of Singapore, Malaysia and China. As a regular provider of corporate governance support in Vietnam, I am heartened to see this very good review of SOEs in Vietnam. The authors are to be complimented on their efforts."

—Ms. Anne Molyneux, Director of *CS International, Vice Chair of the International Corporate Governance Network (ICGN)*

"A timely discussion about corporate governance of state-owned companies with mixed ownership in Vietnam. The book offers a good theoretical lens to understand the state shareholder as well as empirical evidence of the impact of state ownership. The book is a good read for both academic and practitioner audience."

—Mr. Vu Bang, Economic Advisor to the Prime Minister, Chairman of *Council of Vietnam Corporate Governance Initiative*, Former Chairman of the *State Securities Commission of Vietnam*

"A surprisingly good read for investors and others doing business in Vietnam and other emerging markets. This book—the first of its kind—offers an insightful peek into the corporate culture and governance of listed state-owned enterprises (SOEs), which comprise about one-third of the aggregate market capitalisation of Vietnam's stock market. Many more SOEs set to be privatised over the decade, and the issue of corporate governance in SOEs is only going to become more important. The authors provide readers with a unique opportunity to gain a better understanding of the motivation and behaviour of the state shareholder, with useful takeaways derived from pragmatic and empirical research. I highly recommend it to anyone currently or considering investing in these companies."

—Ms. Thu Nguyen, CFA, Managing Director, *Head of Investment in Public Equities and Fixed Income, VinaCapital*

Nga Pham • Kok-Boon Oh

State on Board!

Navigating Corporate Governance in Emerging
Market Business

Nga Pham
Monash Centre for Financial Studies
Monash University
Melbourne, VIC, Australia

Kok-Boon Oh
Director
eGalaxy Solutions
Melbourne, VIC, Australia

ISBN 978-981-16-3524-3   ISBN 978-981-16-3525-0   (eBook)
https://doi.org/10.1007/978-981-16-3525-0

This Palgrave Macmillan imprint is published by the registered company Springer Nature Singapore Pte Ltd.
The registered company address is: 152 Beach Road, #21-01/04 Gateway East, Singapore 189721, Singapore

To our family,
whose love and support have always been with us
unconditionally in whatever we pursue.

PREFACE

The vexed issues of state-owned enterprises (SOEs) in global business compel an investigation in a theoretical context of the motivation of the state in business. Neither existent political-economic theories of SOEs nor agency theory of a public firm can adequately explain the behaviour, influence and propositions of the state as a shareholder in the business.

This book looks at the role of the state in the emerging market business. We provide a review of the literature relevant to the state as an interceding economic actor with a focus on business impacts. The gist of the book is to investigate the "non-traditional" role of the state as a shareholder from that of a policymaker and regulator. We discuss the impacts of this shifting role and how investors and firms should deal with the challenges that come with it.

We study the strategic behaviour of the state as a shareholder in business and the implications it has for the other shareholder(s) and business performance. In this non-traditional role, the State shares ownership; hence, it influences the strategic direction and operations of the business. This phenomenon is common in both listed firms and non-listed firms in emerging markets. Through these firms, the state could also exert its influence in both local and international business.

We analyse the institutional characteristics of state-linked firms, state-invested enterprises (SIEs), in emerging markets, using Vietnam as a case study, with a comparative analysis on China and selected ASEAN countries, Singapore and Malaysia. The choice of Vietnam is that it is one of the fastest-growing emerging markets in ASEAN and the world. It plays an increasingly important role in shaping and contributing to the development of the global supply chain as more multinational companies look to Vietnam as a key investment destination. In this context, this book is a useful reference for business, policymakers, practitioners, students and academics for understanding the non-traditional economic role and behaviour of the state in emerging markets.

The book adopts an evidence-based approach to explain the state's role as a shareholder in firms with mixed ownership. Mixed-ownership firms face unique corporate challenges in which state shareholder and private sector shareholders' objectives do not converge. This heterogeneity of ownership motives creates a principal-principal conflict between the state and other shareholders, putting the interest of minority shareholders at risk. Mixed-ownership firms also face a more severe agency problem when more agency layers are added to the ownership chain. The situation intensifies as state capital is represented and managed at various authority levels at and beyond the firm. Each link added weakens the ownership chain and leads to more agency costs.

Our study on the influence of the state as a shareholder is premised upon and consistent with the "path dependence" theory, which postulates that the initial and underlying structure of an economy influences its performance. As an emerging market with a "centrally-planned economy" heritage, state-related institutional factors are important in shaping the business landscape and firm behaviour. Particularly, the book presents the findings of an empirical study that explains how state ownership, state control via industry regulation and corporate governance structure of a firm, affect its M&A performance.

To sum up, this book focuses on the dynamics of corporate governance arising from interactions between the state and other shareholders, which has not yet been well addressed in the literature. Based on our findings, we propose a new paradigm for firms and investors intending to engage in business with SOEs in emerging markets.

Melbourne, VIC, Australia
Melbourne, VIC, Australia

Nga Pham
Kok-Boon Oh

ACKNOWLEDGEMENTS

Try to become a person of value.
—*Albert Einstein*

This book condenses our years of experience working in both emerging and developed markets. We have been fortunate to work with and learn from many great minds and kind supporters over those years. This book is our gratitude to them all.

We wish to thank our interview participants from companies in Vietnam who were willing to share their business insights.

We appreciate valuable suggestions from the book reviewers for our book proposals. We are also grateful to Mr Vu Bang, Economic Advisor to the Prime Minister, Former Chairman of the State Securities Commission of Vietnam; Professor Iftekhar Hasan at Fordham University; Ms Anne Molyneux at CS International and the International Corporate Governance Network; and Ms Thu Nguyen at VinaCapital for their endorsements.

We are indebted to our colleagues at the International Finance Corporation—a member of the World Bank Group in Vietnam, Hanoi University, La Trobe University, and Monash Centre for Financial Studies—Monash Business School for their support during the time we conducted the research and wrote the book.

We also want to express our thanks to the editorial and production team at Springer Nature for their helpful assistance.

Last but not least, this work would have been impossible without our family. Nga wants to send her heartfelt gratitude to her family for their unconditional love and tremendous encouragement for anything she does.

Nga especially thanks her mother, Le Thi Thanh Xuan; mother-in-law, Hoang Thuy Nga; and her husband, Nguyen Hoang, for their love and care. Nga thanks her kids, Tu Khue and Tung Lam, for their smiles that cheer her up after any day of hard work.

KB wishes to thank his family for their support, especially Sarah Guo, for her patience, and John Sturdy for his encouragement during challenging times.

For all the things we have gained, this book is our commitment to becoming persons of value that could make humble contributions to the world of knowledge.

CONTENTS

ABOUT THE AUTHORS

Dr. Nga Pham CFA is a research fellow at the Monash Centre for Financial Studies (MCFS), Monash Business School, Monash University, Australia. She works on issues related to pensions and corporate governance. She is also a member of the Disclosure and Transparency Committee of the International Corporate Governance Network (ICGN) and a member of the Advisory Board of the Mercer CFA Institute Global Pension Index.

Before joining Monash University, Pham was an academic at Hanoi University, where she served as the Dean of the Faculty of Management and Tourism. She was also the Executive Director of La Trobe–HANU joint programmes at Hanoi University.

Pham's industry experience includes three years of corporate governance consulting for the International Finance Corporation (a member of the World Bank Group). Her projects involved raising awareness, regulatory advisory and building market capacity in corporate governance for companies in Vietnam. She had also worked as an equity analyst in Vietnam.

Pham holds a Bachelor of Commerce from the University of Melbourne, an MBA and a PhD in Finance from La Trobe University, Australia. She is an alumnus of the Australian Government's AusAID Scholarship and the Australian Leadership Award.

Pham is a CFA Charterholder.

Dr. Kok-Boon Oh CPA has industry experience from working in corporate finance, international business and academia in the Asia-Pacific region for over a period of 40 years. He held senior management positions in US and Asian multinational corporations, including board directorships, chief executive officer, chief finance officer and general manager of a listed company on the Kuala Lumpur Stock Exchange. He is currently a Director at eGalaxy Solutions, a business consulting firm based in Mebourne, Australia.

He was the Honorary Regional Ambassador (South East Asia) for Aviation and Aerospace Australia's Trade and Export Network (AAA) and also represented AAA as a delegate on the Victorian Government trade missions to Mongolia and China in 2010, Super Trade Mission to China in 2012 and South East Asia Super Trade Mission in 2013.

Oh has taught accounting, finance, enterprise risk management, cybersecurity and international business at La Trobe University Graduate School of Management and School of Business. He was the Acting and Deputy Head and MBA Program Director of the Graduate School of Management. He has co-authored 11 reference books and over 70 refereed international conference papers and journal articles.

Abbreviations

AE	Advanced economies
ASEAN	Association of Southeast Asian Nations
BOD	Board of Directors
CEO	Chief executive directors
CIEM	Central Institute for Economic Management
CMSC	Commission for the Management of State Capital
COB	Chairman of the Board
CPC	Communist Party of China
EBRD	European Bank for Reconstruction and Development
EME	Emerging market economy
EMMA	Emerging market M&A model
FDI	Foreign direct investment
GDP	Gross domestic product
GLC	Government-linked company
GSM	General shareholders' meeting
GSO	General Statistics Office
HNX	Hanoi Stock Exchange
HSCCI	Hang Seng China-Affiliated Corporations Index
HSCEI	Hang Seng China Enterprises Index
HSX	Hochiminh City Stock Exchange
IFC	International Finance Corporation
IMF	International Monetary Fund
LIDC	Low-income developing economy
M&A	Mergers and acquisitions
MNE	Multinational enterprise
m-SOE	State-owned multinational enterprise
MXCN	MSCI China Index

MXEF	MSCI Emerging Markets Index
MXFEM	MSCI Frontier Emerging Markets Index
OECD	Organisation for Economic Co-operation and Development
OFDI	Outward foreign direct investment
RQ	Research question
SASAC	State-Owned Assets Supervision and Administration Commission of the State Council
SBV	State Bank of Vietnam
SCIC	State Capital Investment Corporation
SCMA	State capital management agencies
SEG	State Economic Group
SIE	State-invested enterprise
SME	Small- and medium-sized enterprise
SOE	State-owned enterprise
UNCTAD	United Nations Conference on Trade and Development
VND	Vietnam Dong
WB	World Bank
WEF	World Economic Forum
WTO	World Trade Organization

TECHNICAL TERMS

2SLS	Two-stage least squares regression
BAHR	Buy-and-hold returns
CAR	Cumulative abnormal returns
EBITDA	Earnings before interest, tax, depreciation and amortisation
EPSG	Earnings per share growth
IV	Instrumental variables
OCF	Operating cash flow
OLS	Ordinary least squares regression
PCA	Principal component analysis
PSM	Propensity score matching
QUAL	Qualitative
QUAN	Quantitative
ROA	Return on assets

List of Figures

LIST OF TABLES

LIST OF BOXES

CHAPTER 1

Introduction

The total asset value of state-owned enterprises (SOEs) all over the world in 2018 was US $45 trillion, which was equal to 50% of the global GDP. SOEs now represent 20% of total assets, 17% of total revenue and 14% of the total debt of the 2000 largest companies in the world (IMF, 2020). SOEs have grown in size and importance on all fronts, be it banking, listed equity, sovereign debt or corporate debt markets.

Over the last two decades, a large number of state-owned firms have emerged as new corporate giants in the global marketplace. SOEs have been back to the spotlight these days, not so much about their poor performance and inefficiency, as in the past, but more about their economic power. Mighty state-owned firms now have become state-owned multinationals. The scope and scale of their contribution and impact are no longer restricted to their home market. In many emerging markets, SOEs are considered the backbone of the economy as they contribute to the economic prosperity, employment stability and international trade of both the home and host countries.

SOEs make up a significant number and occupy key positions on all big business lists. There were 326 SOEs[1] in the Forbes' Global 2000 in 2015 (IMF, 2020) and 124 in the 2020 Fortune Global 500[2] (CSIS, 2020).

[1] Including 128 from Mainland and 13 from Hong Kong, China.
[2] Ninety-one of which were from China, according to CSIS (the Centre for Strategic and International Studies, Washington, DC).

© The Author(s), under exclusive license to Springer Nature Singapore Pte Ltd. 2021
N. Pham, K.-B. Oh, *State on Board!*,
https://doi.org/10.1007/978-981-16-3525-0_1

Among the 10,000 largest listed firms, representing 90% of the world's market capitalisation, surveyed by the OECD at the end of 2017, almost 10% were controlled by the public sector owners (De La Cruz et al., 2019). SOEs have accumulated massive assets over the years, both in the listed and in the unlisted markets.

The world is paying ever greater attention to SOEs. So much has been written about SOEs. A simple search by Google Scholar for articles published on "state-owned enterprises" (SOEs) resulted in more than 2 million items in 0.04 seconds.[3] About 22,000 of them have only appeared in the last two years. The topics appear to be endless, from SOEs' motivations, objectives to economic performance and efficiency. But do we fully understand SOEs? Does state ownership matter to firms' performance? How does the state influence corporate governance and to what consequences? Do public sector owners behave differently from private shareholders? Should private investors view the rise of state-owned firms as an opportunity or a challenge?

This book addresses the questions above. We eagerly join the renewed debate on SOEs with a unique theoretical perspective and share in this book an empirical study conducted to prove our view.

New wine is not good in old bottles as old bottles will break. SOEs of today are different in many aspects from what they used to be, so is their landscape. Nowadays, the majority of SOEs have some level of mixed private and public ownership. Many SOEs are listed on organised stock exchanges; therefore, they are expected to behave like a listed entity. SOEs have outgrown their theoretical space, calling for new theoretical perspectives.

1.1   DEFINITIONS

There are millions of things we want to unpack in this book. Let's start with the definition of an SOE. The term "state-owned enterprise" generally refers to an enterprise in which the state has significant control via ownership. According to the OECD's Guidelines on Corporate Governance of State-Owned Enterprises, an SOE is "any corporate entity recognised by national law as an enterprise, and in which the state exercises ownership", including joint-stock companies, limited liability companies and partnerships limited by shares (OECD, 2015c) (Page 14). An

---

[3] The search was conducted on 17 June 2020.

SOE is a distinct legal entity conducting commercial activity in competitive or non-competitive sectors of the economy. Apart from the commercial objectives, SOEs may also pursue a policy objective.

The OECD uses the term "state-invested enterprise" (SIE) to refer to an enterprise in which the state owns more than 10% of the equity or voting rights. SIEs can be classified into *"majority-owned SOEs"*, denoting SOEs in which the state owns over 50% of the shares, and *"partly state-owned enterprises"* (PSOEs)—companies with a significant government minority shareholding. Minority stakes are defined as at least 10% to less than 50% of the common stock or equivalent voting rights. There are, however, cases where minority-owned companies (under 50%) can be counted as majority-owned SOEs if the state can appoint more than half of board members or otherwise exercise effective control (OECD, 2016b). For entities in which the state ownership represents less than 10% of the voting rights, the state does not usually have effective control. In most cases, the state shares are held indirectly via asset managers such as pension funds or other agencies. These entities, therefore, are not considered SOEs by the OECD (2015c). Figure 1.1 illustrates different levels of state ownership.

In this book, we use the term "SOE" for general cases in which the state can, or could reasonably be expected to, have control over a firm, not necessarily by holding beyond the 50% equity threshold. The term

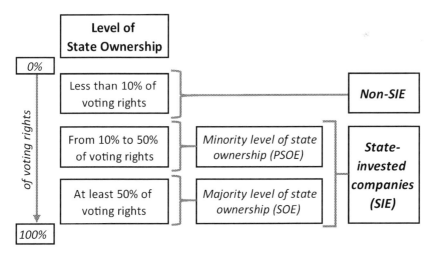

Fig. 1.1 Different levels of state ownership

"state-invested enterprise" (SIE) will be used when we need to emphasise that the information is relevant to both firms with minority and majority state ownership.

It is important to note that apart from the government, at both central and local levels, public sector shareholders can also be sovereign wealth funds, public pensions funds and other state-owned enterprises such as government-owned corporations and large economic groups. With the accumulation of pension assets over time, sovereign wealth funds and public pension funds, like the Government Pension Investment Fund (GPIF) of Japan or the Norwegian Government Pension Fund, are gigantic investors in the market now. These funds, however, invest differently from the government owner and SOE corporate owners and tend to be more passive with their holdings. Therefore, this book does not focus on them; nevertheless, they deserve a whole bookshelf to themselves.

This book is about SOEs in their new form with mixed ownership between the state capital and private capital. We also present an empirical study on how state ownership, state control and corporate governance could affect firm performance, using firms that have been through mergers and acquisitions (M&A) in Vietnam. The examination of mixed ownership and M&A in our study is important as they are common in many SOE privatisation, equitisation and amalgamation. Although the primary research context is in Vietnam, we will be discussing other markets such as China and, to a lesser extent, Singapore and Malaysia as well to provide a broader view on state ownership.

1.2   SOEs with Mixed Ownership: A Theoretical Perspective

The mixed-ownership structure of SOEs presents a unique challenge as existing theories fail to adequately explain the contemporary nexus between the state shareholder, other shareholders and management.

For mixed-ownership firms that are still substantially owned by the state, having multiple owners, including the state and private shareholders, these firms fundamentally differ from wholly state-owned firms of which the state is the single owner. Furthermore, these state-owned firms are also different from regular publicly listed firms. Normal firms have multiple shareholders with the same wealth maximisation objective, whereas for mixed-ownership SOEs, the state shareholder may have political, social and economic targets (OECD, 2015c; Shleifer & Vishny, 1994).

Agency theory about modern firms says that due to the conflict of interest, shareholders (*the principal in the agency relationship*) should monitor the firm's management (*the agent*) to ensure that managers maximise the firm's value in the best interest of shareholders.

In light of agency theory, the state shareholder is a principal of the firm. Will the state principal have the same motivations, ability, responsibility and accountability as other shareholders?

First, with the state shareholder, maximising the firm value may not serve their best interest if driven by political and social objectives. The political behaviour of the state theory (Shleifer, 1998; Shleifer & Vishny, 1994) suggests that politicians who control SOEs may pursue their own interests and objectives by practising cronyism, being driven by special interest groups or politicians in power and committing resources to pet projects rather than maximising shareholder wealth. State-owned firms tend to be less efficient due to overstaffing, excessive executive compensation and inefficient resources allocation.

When ownership is concentrated among large shareholders, including the state shareholder, there is potentially some level of heterogeneity in ownership motives. This principal-principal conflict inherent in partially state-owned firms is a new angle of agency theory, illustrated in Fig. 1.2.

Second, agency theory also emphasises the agency costs arising from the system shareholders devise to control and incentivise management.

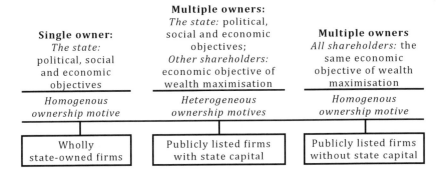

Fig. 1.2 Ownership motives in different types of firms

Does the state shareholder have the ability and willingness to act that part? What if there are costs involved for the firm to serve the interest of the state shareholder? If the state shareholder follows political and social interests at large at the expense of the firm, it could be detrimental to firm value. This could be seen as the root cause of the principal problem, resulting in costs to be borne by the firm as a collective representative of all other shareholders.

Our research indeed identifies such costs that manifest the principal-principal conflict between the state and other private shareholders in mixed-ownership SOEs. We, therefore, have developed the theoretical concept of principal costs. We define "principal costs" as (1) the negative impacts of the state, as a principal, deviating from the shareholder wealth maximisation objective and (2) the costs incurred by the firm in incentivising the principal (as the shareholder) to exercise their ownership rights and responsibilities effectively. We will also discuss the broader implications of principal costs for corporate governance in an institutionally transitioning market. We also provide empirical evidence that justifies this theorisation.

In a nutshell, although the political theory of state ownership still reflects the political interest of the state in owning and running a firm (Shleifer & Vishny, 1994), it seems to insufficiently capture the interest of other shareholders in the firm. Agency theory, on the other hand, fails to represent the set of ownership motives of the state shareholder. There is a need to integrate these theories to develop an adequate theoretical foundation to study the corporate governance and performance of emerging market firms.

Based on this observation, we devote much of the content of the book to explain how the state elements should be incorporated into agency theory to understand SOEs with mixed ownership. We identify multiple layers of agents involved with managing state capital between various authority levels and the firm. We also analyse how the presence of the state in the firm affects its corporate governance structure in practice. The new economic and political power of SOEs calls for a move towards a political theory of the firm (Zingales, 2017).

This is not simply an ownership puzzle. The state also seeks to control the firm via industry regulation, whereas the firm tries to avoid, or mitigate, the impact of being regulated. The OECD, World Bank and the International Finance Corporation (IFC) all call for strong separation between the state's ownership function and other functions. However, such separation requires high-level systematic solutions and the capacity to professionalise the management of state capital at enterprises. Not all emerging markets are capable at this stage. Our research shows that there are cost implications for firms that are regulated and, not surprisingly, firms with state capital bear less of such costs.

Our research also shows that the issues of ownership, control and governance become central to firm performance questions, at least, as evident from our research findings related to M&A in Vietnam. Research on emerging markets needs to address the special institutional features embracing emerging market firms, mostly associated with the state, and how it may affect corporate activities. Firms in emerging markets such as China and Vietnam are still heavily owned by the state. Given the relative size of public ownership to private ownership, how the state behaves as a shareholder may affect the wealth of public investors at large.

1.3   SOEs with Mixed Ownership in Emerging Markets: A Practical View

In the last two decades, due to the high level of state ownership retained in privatised enterprises, the state remains among the largest shareholders in a significant number of listed companies. SOEs own about US $10 trillion of the listed market, which is worth 14% of the global market capitalisation. The most popular government owners are the central and local governments. For example, 57% of state capital in listed firms worldwide is in the hands of the Chinese government investors (De La Cruz et al., 2019). In India, SOEs represent approximately 18% of market capitalisation (OECD, 2016a). Mixed ownership between state capital and private capital has become popular in most emerging markets. We will now discuss the progress of mixed ownership in Vietnam and China.

1.3.1   Vietnam

Vietnam has been among the strongest growing economies in the region, with an average gross domestic product (GDP) annual growth of 5.96% in the last ten years. The equitisation of state-owned firms in Vietnam started with a few pilot years after Doi Moi then went on full gear during the 1990s and 2000s. So far, almost 5000 state-owned enterprises have been fully or partially equitised. According to the General Statistics Office (GSO) the state-owned sector now comprises 1097 wholly state-owned enterprises, 1163 partially equitised SOEs, with the state retaining a controlling interest and 1125 joint-stock companies with the state capital at the minority level (GSO, 2019). The government owns a significant level of assets of listed companies, especially in the strategic sectors. Among the companies on the VN100 Index (100 largest listed firms in Vietnam), as of early 2021, there are 24 companies with state ownership, totalling almost US $82 billion of market capitalisation owned by the state. For 15 firms, the state's shareholding is larger than 50%. For these firms, the range of government ownership is from 50.46% to 95.76%, and, on average, the government owns 65.31%. The top three sectors that see substantial government ownership are Utilities, Materials and Energy, as shown in Fig. 1.3. The presence of these firms in the VN100 Index is strong evidence for the welcome of the capital market for mixed-ownership SOEs.

The equitisation process has slowed down significantly in the last few years, with much fewer SOEs equitised each year. The main reasons are the quality of the remaining unequitised SOEs, the delayed IPO preparation and critical performance and governance issues both before and after equitisation. Furthermore, unlike China, despite the impressive economic growth of Vietnam, there have not been many success stories of large Vietnamese SOEs investing overseas.

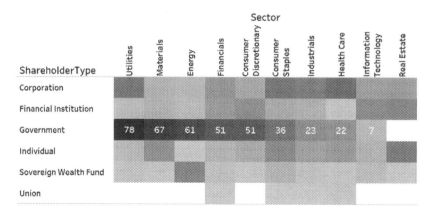

Fig. 1.3 State ownership (%) among VN100 Index firms by sector in 2021. (Data was obtained from Bloomberg in Feb 2021. The figure shows the distribution of ownership among various shareholder types as a snapshot. A higher level of holding is shown by a darker colour. Ownership ratio by government is provided in percentage.)

1.3.2   China

Central SOEs have long played a pillar role in China's economic development. The total assets of these enterprises reached 69.1 trillion yuan (about $10.71 trillion) by the end of last year, representing an annual growth rate of 7.7% during the 13th five-year plan period (2016–2020).

The mixed-ownership reform in China is swift and bold. SOEs have been asked to refocus on their core business by divesting off non-core and inefficient investment projects. They have also been restructured and regrouped. So far, with 41 central SOEs regrouped, the total number of central SOEs has reduced from 150 in 2008 to only 95 now, under the management of the State-Owned Assets Supervision and Administration Commission of the State Council (SASAC). Thousands of other state-owned companies are managed by the Ministry of Finance and line ministries and local governments.

Central SOEs are encouraged to invest in emerging technologies of strategic importance. Examples are 5G, industrial internet, artificial intelligence, big data and new infrastructure. SOEs are committed to the strategy of the government to modernise the economy with new business activities and new business models. New business models are defined as ways to integrate industries with the internet, focusing on one-stop services of consumption, entertainment and leisure.

To promote the mixing of public and private capital, China designs and implements a two-way strategy. On one way, SOEs are open to non-state capital, domestic or foreign alike. The Chinese government has welcome investors into such strategic sector as telecom (e.g., giant telco China Unicom), energy, aviation, public utilities, automobiles and railways. On the other way, SOEs can proactively invest in shares of private companies. According to the SASAC (2020),[4] since 2013, centrally administered SOEs have invested in more than 6000 private companies. SOEs are given autonomy in arranging mixed-ownership reform of subsidiaries. In 2020, centrally administered SOEs received $31 billion of non-State capital through mixed-ownership reform.

This "two-way strategy" is also reflected well in recent China's white paper, titled "China and the World in the New Era" by the State Council Information Office of the People's Republic of China (2019). As the Council describes it, from "*bringing in on a large scale*" to "*going out in*"

[4] http://en.sasac.gov.cn/2020/08/14/c_5380.htm

great strides" (page 8), this is how China interacts with the world. For more than 60 years, China's FDI has increased 140 folds in the non-financial sectors. During the last 40 years, China has attracted over US $2 trillion in non-financial FDI to set up nearly 1 million firms with foreign-invested capital. In terms of "going global", China's strategy has been *"going global faster, further, and more extensively"* (page 9). Since 2002, China's overseas investment has grown 53 times, at an annual rate of 28.2%, mainly through mergers and acquisitions, many of which were by SOEs. The massive outflow of capital has helped China's private and state-owned enterprises to own much of the world's assets. In 2018, China invested US $143 billion overseas.

The blending of state and private capital has helped China's economy to be more resilient throughout the pandemic. According to Xinhuanet, in 2020, despite the impact of the pandemic, the net profit of the central SOEs totalled 1.4 trillion yuan (about $217 billion), even higher than the previous year (Xinhuanet, 2021).

It seems that notwithstanding the similarities in political systems and the model for economic development, the two countries have gained different results in the mixed-ownership reform of SOEs. While Vietnam has under-delivered in its privatisation programme (Asian Development Bank Institute, 2020), China's proactive two-way strategy has shown positive, solid results for Chinese enterprises both at home and abroad. We will elaborate further on the equitisation progress and performance of SOEs in these two countries in Chaps. 2 and 3.

1.4   MIXED-OWNERSHIP SOEs: AN OPPORTUNITY OR THREAT?

As the governments in emerging markets are opening up the state-owned sector to private capital, should private investors view mixed-ownership SOEs as an opportunity of a threat? While there are issues of concern regarding fairness in competition due to preferential treatments of the state to SOEs, political motivations of state ownership and potential government intervention in management and governance at the firm, these SOEs present opportunities for investors to participate in sectors that are driving growth in emerging markets.

Both Vietnam and China's economies and stock markets have performed reasonably well compared to other emerging and frontier markets for the last few decades. The two countries have shown the willingness and

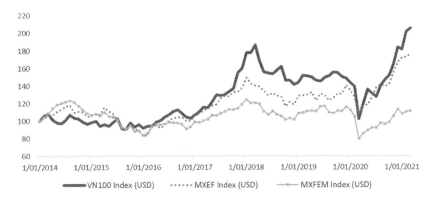

Fig. 1.4 The growth of the VN100 Index since inception

commitment to open doors to domestic private sector investors and foreign investors.

Vietnam has weathered the COVID-19 pandemic well, as the country has been relatively successful in keeping the virus at bay. The Vietnamese economy and its stock market have both recovered well since then, with the stock market gaining 43.6% just in the last year. As it can be seen from Fig. 1.4, the VN100 Index, comprising of 100 largest listed firms in Vietnam in terms of market capitalisation, has performed well compared to both the MSCI Emerging Markets Index (MXEF Index) and MSCI Frontier Emerging Markets Index (MXFEM Index) since its inception in 2014. Its average annualised returns are 17.23% and 11.34% for the last five and ten years, respectively. Vietnam has been on the watchlist of a number of index providers since 2018 to be reclassified from a Frontier to an Emerging Market. When that happens, listed firms, including listed SOEs, will benefit from a new influx of fresh capital from international investors.

There are also ample opportunities for investors in the list of future SOEs to be equitised and/or divested by the government.

Like Vietnam, with its economy back on track, China's stock market has been doing well through the COVID-19 pandemic, with the MSCI China Index for all China's shares (MXCN Index) gaining 43.5% this year, well above the MSCI Emerging Markets Index (MXEF Index) (see Fig. 1.5 and Table 1.1). Some Chinese SOEs have also been listed in Hong Kong; however, during the last ten years, both Hang Seng China

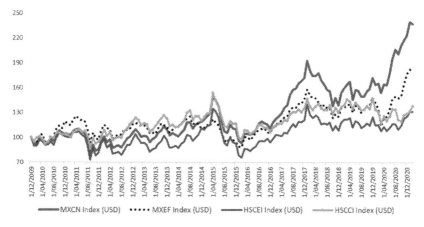

Fig. 1.5   Selected China's stock market indices

Table 1.1   Selected stock market indices in Vietnam and China

Stock market return (annualised) (%)

Index	1-Year	2-Year	3-Year	5-Year	10-Year
VN100	**43.61**	14.73	4.61	17.23	**11.34**
MXCN	43.49	**21.79**	**9.54**	**20.48**	8.74
HSCEI	13.54	3.34	0.68	11.61	2.75
HSCCI	4.9	-0.92	-0.1	7.05	3.23
MXEF	36.58	15.95	6.72	16.68	4.77
MXFEM	5.05	0.4	-3	5.03	2.14

Bold values showed the highest performance for each time window

Enterprise Index (HSCEI, covering China's H shares[5]) and Hang Seng China-Affiliated Corporations Index (HSCCI)[6] underperform the overall MSCI China Index.

[5] China's H shares are of companies incorporated in mainland China that are traded on the Hong Kong Stock Exchange.

[6] This index is a part of Hang Seng Indices. It covers the top 25 "red chip" stocks. [https://www.hsi.com.hk/static/uploads/contents/en/dl_centre/factsheets/redchipse.pdf]. (The information contained in this document is not intended to provide professional advice and should not be relied upon in that regard. Persons intending to use any information obtained from this document are advised to obtain appropriate professional advice.) As of 31 January 2021, there are 173 red chips with a total market cap of HK$4.7 trillion listed

Listing SOEs on major domestic and international stock exchanges, such as in Singapore, London and New York, has been seen as the Chinese government's commitment to reform the SOE sectors.

1.5   THE EMPIRICAL RESEARCH

The empirical research presented in this book illustrates how the level of state ownership, state control and corporate governance affect merger and acquisition (M&A) decisions and performance of firms in Vietnam, both SOEs and non-SOEs. As M&A represents a strategic business decision that requires shareholders' approval, it could be reasonably expected that if the state shareholder has political objectives that are different from the commercial motivation of the firm, the state shareholder may exercise its power to influence the firm towards the state's interest.

As an emerging market, Vietnam is experiencing strong economic growth as a result of a substantial surge in M&A activities over the last decade. Vietnam's M&A market has grown substantially since 2009, with a total deal value of US $10.2 billion in 2017. Secondly, the Vietnamese government holds significant stakes in various strategic industries for the national interest. The combination of these two factors enables us to examine how State ownership affects corporate governance and decisions. As a former centrally planned economy, Vietnam offers an opportunity to explore whether the state is motivated by economic incentives, as with other shareholders of the firm, or by political considerations.

The focus of the study is on how such heterogeneity of ownership motives affects organisational outcomes in the context of M&A. While many prior studies on M&A are grounded in the agency problem to explain M&A outcomes, none has considered the potential principal-principal problem and principal costs, especially those resulting from having a state shareholder. Although principal costs can exist in many situations, it is expected that they will be particularly prominent in firms undergoing M&A because this type of corporate restructuring decision involves the reallocation of resources in the economy, which could be well subject to political interference to serve the state's motivations and priorities (Li et al., 2014). The existence of a large number of partially equitised

in Hong Kong. Red chips are mainland *China government*-controlled companies incorporated outside the Mainland and listed in Hong Kong.

firms with different levels of state shareholdings in the listed stock market makes Vietnam an exciting context for this research.

The research followed an exploratory sequential mixed-methods design, with two components. The first component was a qualitative study to explore the factors affecting M&A motivations and performance of SOEs and non-SOEs in Vietnam. It was conducted with 31 in-depth interviews on M&A practitioners and corporate managers. The second component was a quantitative study on M&A of listed firms in Vietnam from 2004 to 2013. Chapter 5 of the book describes the interview sample, data collection and analysis in details.

The remainder of this chapter presents the structure of the book. Chapter 2 provides background information on the development of the state-owned sector in Vietnam and China, with some reference made to Singapore and Malaysia. Chapter 3 explains the increasingly important role of state-owned multinationals in the global economy. Next, Chap. 4 characterises the typical institutional governance features regarding the presence of the state shareholders and the management of state capital of mixed-ownership SOEs in Vietnam. From here, we present the research hypotheses which guided us in the empirical study of how state ownership and state control may impact corporate M&A outcomes. Chapter 5 explains in details the research questions and justifies the choice of the qualitative and quantitative methods employed. The qualitative study findings are presented in Chap. 6, followed by the insights gained from the quantitative study in two chapters, Chaps. 7 and 8. Here, we discuss the impact of state ownership, state control via industry regulation and corporate structure on firms' M&A performance, respectively. In Chap. 9 of the book, we integrate our findings to develop a theoretical model for mixed-ownership SOEs and a practical model for M&A decision-making for business and investors. Chapter 9 ends with some concluding thoughts for the book.

This book is an urge to rethink the corporate governance nature of SOEs, where state ownership is mixed with private capital. While the material in this book is based on rigorous academic research, the book is geared towards both academic audience and corporate managers, investors and practitioners. We also hope this book will help to bridge the gap between academic research and industry by our interpretation and presentation of the contents and findings in an applied approach.

REFERENCES

Asian Development Bank Institute. (2020). *State-owned Enterprise Reform in Vietnam: Progress and Challenges*, ADBI Working Paper Series, Asian Development Bank Institute, No. 1071, January.

Centre for Strategic and International Studies. (2020). The Biggest But Not the Strongest: China's Place in the Fortune Global 500. August 8. Retrieved February 25, 2021, from https://www.csis.org/blogs/trustee-china-hand/biggest-not-strongest-chinas-place-fortune-global-500

De La Cruz, A., Medina, A., & Tang, Y. (2019). Owners of the World's Listed Companies. OECD Capital Market Series, Paris. www.oecd.org/corporate/Owners-of-the-Worlds-Listed-Companies.htm

IMF. (2020). Chapter 3: State-Owned Enterprises: The Other Government, *Fiscal Monitor Series*, April. Retrieved February 27, 2021, from https://www.imf.org/en/Publications/FM/Issues/2020/04/06/fiscal-monitor-april-2020

Li, M. H., Cui, L., & Lu, J. (2014). Varieties in State Capitalism: Outward FDI Strategies of Central and Local State-owned Enterprises from Emerging Economy Countries. *Journal of International Business Studies, 45*(8), 980–1004.

OECD. (2015a). *State-Owned Enterprise Governance: A Stocktaking of Government Rationales for Enterprise Ownership*. OECD Publishing. https://doi.org/10.1787/9789264239944-en

OECD. (2015b). *State-Owned Enterprises in the Development Process*. OECD Publishing. https://doi.org/10.1787/9789264229617-en

OECD. (2015c). *Guidelines on Corporate Governance of State-Owned Enterprises*. OECD Publishing.

OECD. (2016a). *State-Owned Enterprises as Global Competitors: A Challenge or an Opportunity?* OECD Publishing.

OECD. (2016b). *Broadening the Ownership of State-Owned Enterprises: A Comparison of Governance Practices*. Organisation for Economic Co-operation Development.

SASAC. (2020). *New Industries, New Type of Business, New Business Model*. Retrieved February 02, 2021, from http://en.sasac.gov.cn/2020/08/14/c_5380.htm

Shleifer, A. (1998). State Versus Private Ownership. *Journal of Economic Perspectives, 12*(4), 133–150.

Shleifer, A., & Vishny, R. W. (1994). Politicians and Firms. *The Quarterly Journal of Economics, 109*(4), 995–1025.

The General Statistics Office. (2019). *The Statistical Yearbook 2019*. The Statistics Publishing House.

The State Council Information Office of the People's Republic of China. (2019) China and the World in the New Era, September 2019. Retrieved January 05,

2021, from http://english.www.gov.cn/archive/whitepaper/201909/27/content_WS5d8d80f9c6d0bcf8c4c142ef.html

Xinhuanet. (2020). China's Central SOEs Assets to Near 69 trln Yuan: Regulator. Retrieved February 28, 2021, from http://www.xinhuanet.com/english/2020-12/25/c_139618898.htm

Xinhuanet. (2021). Biz China Weekly: SOEs' Profit, Forex Market, Sharing Economy, Lottery Sales. Retrieved February 28, 2021, from http://www.xinhuanet.com/english/2021-02/28/c_139772811.htm

Zingales, L. (2017). Towards a Political Theory of the Firm. *The Journal of Economic Perspectives, 31*(3), 113–130. Retrieved March 3, 2020, from http://www.jstor.org/stable/44321282

CHAPTER 2

Changing Role of State-Invested Enterprises in Emerging Markets

There is a divergence of the intended *and the* realised, *the* ought *and the* is.
—James (1933)

The International Monetary Fund (IMF) indicated that state-owned enterprises play an increasing role in many countries worldwide in both emerging and advanced economies. In 2018, the IMF estimated that SOEs' assets are worth US $45 trillion, about half of the world's GDP (IMF, 2020). The past three decades have seen the emergence of privatisation as the modus operandi for emerging countries to achieve business efficiency at the expense of state ownership of the business enterprise. However, this may not necessarily have the intended outcome as expected. The rate of privatisation has slowed down somewhat in countries like Vietnam and China. At least there is advocacy for the state to maintain a role as a shareholder of enterprise business. Nowadays, many SOEs have mixed public and private ownership with a strong commercial focus. The state has always held ownership to varying degrees in many former SOEs that are publicly traded corporations. This type of holding remains prominent in many parts of the world.

State ownership has generally remained relevant across the globe, with policymakers opting to list SOE shares as an alternative to or act of privatisation. According to the IMF Fiscal Monitor data reported in 2020,

© The Author(s), under exclusive license to Springer Nature
Singapore Pte Ltd. 2021
N. Pham, K.-B. Oh, *State on Board!*,
https://doi.org/10.1007/978-981-16-3525-0_2

17

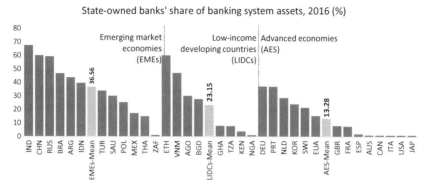

Fig. 2.1 State-owned banks' share of total assets by country. (Data: The IMF, Fiscal Monitor, Apr 2020)

state-owned banks occupy a large share of banking asset in emerging market economies and low-income developing countries. China's state-owned banks, for example, have a share of 60% (Country code—CHN in Fig. 2.1), much higher than the average level of 36.6% in emerging market economies (EMEs). Vietnam's state-owned banks make up 47% of total assets, compared to 23.2% of low-income developing countries (LIDCs) average. In advanced economies (AEs) where private sector firms play a more critical role, the share of state-owned banks is modest at around 13%. Apart from banks, other types of state-owned financial institutions such as sovereign wealth funds and state-owned investment funds and pension funds have grown substantially in size and importance.

Non-financial SOEs have also emerged as giants in the global marketplace during the last two decades. In 2018, they accounted for over 20% of the total assets and 16.62% of the total revenue of the world's 2000 largest firms, compared to the share of just around 5% in 2000 (see Fig. 2.2). Their growth results mainly from the expansion of China's SOEs (see Fig. 2.3).

Among the world's 2000 biggest firms, according to the IMF's Fiscal Monitor (IMF, 2020), the top three sectors dominated by SOEs are Financials, Industrial and Materials and Energy, with SOEs contributing a share of 84%, 16% and 7.5% of assets and 13% and 20% and 37% and 34.5% of revenue, respectively.

While SOEs operate in the same commercial space as privately owned enterprises in many industries, they are driven by different motivations and objectives that are more closely aligned with public service and national interests. There are also concerns about the need for

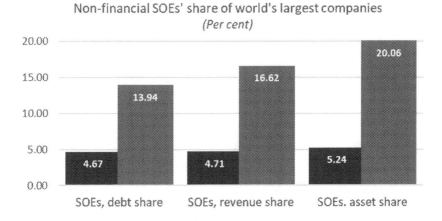

Fig. 2.2 Non-financial SOE's share of the world's 2000 largest firms. (Data: The IMF, Fiscal Monitor, Apr 2020)

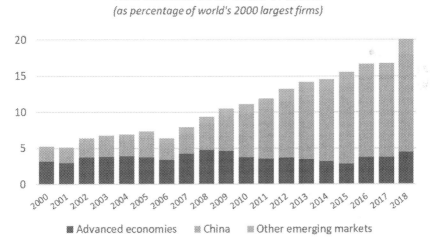

Fig. 2.3 Growth of non-financial SOEs' share of assets. (Data: The IMF, Fiscal Monitor, Apr 2020)

governments to subsidise SOEs in emerging markets, which compounds the problem of them being perceived as beholden to the state. These subsidies may include bank loans extended at preferential rates of interest to the SOEs, which is often seen as distorting the markets by discouraging investment and competition. As a result of any change in policies, there is always the risk that these SOEs may be responsible for a very high proportion of non-performing loans causing economic shocks to these countries. The traditional role of SOEs is to operate for the benefit of the state and the population as a whole, so the government must ensure that it is properly managed.

Therefore, there has been a persistent clarion call from external stakeholders for more accountable, transparent and responsible corporate governance of SOEs given their growing influence and importance in business, especially with their global reach nowadays. This requires a review of those factors such as ownership, board constitution, the role of the CEO and public policy consideration in their influence of SOEs' management, operations and strategic direction. Many state-invested enterprises are managed by people appointed by government leaders or their associates. Government leaders also sit on the boards of SOEs. The involvement of government leaders can create conflicts of interest between economic objective and political motivation or when such people stand to lose significant status if an SOE is sold off.

This chapter discusses the influence of the state in SOEs and their role in selected emerging markets in Asia, focusing on the two case studies of Vietnam and China. On the one hand, the two countries share some political resemblances and geographical proximity, leading to similarities in SOEs' structure and governance. On the other hand, due to the different levels of development between the two economies, there are interesting contrasts in the role that Chinese and Vietnamese SOEs play at home and abroad.

2.1   Economic Reform in Vietnam and the Changing Role of the State

Vietnam is a rising economic power in Southeast Asia, with a population of 97 million people. From 2011 to 2020, Vietnam achieved average annual GDP growth of 5.96% despite the impact of the COVID-19 pandemic (General Statistics Office, 2020). Significant milestones of Vietnam's development include joining ASEAN[1] in 1995, accession into the World Trade Organization (WTO) in 2007 and the recent Trans-Pacific Partnership, the EU-Vietnam Free Trade Agreement (EUVFTA) in 2020. Economic growth and international integration have led the Vietnamese government to improve the regulatory framework and market institutions to prepare the country for a stable transformation into a full market economy.

The 13th National Congress of the Communist Party of Vietnam in early 2021 put forward a roadmap for socio-economic development with clear targets and milestones.[2] Vietnam aims to become an industrialised developing economy within the upper-middle-income group by 2030 and a developed economy of the high-income group by 2045. Vietnam lags behind its 2020 goal of becoming a high-tech industrialised economy, with high-tech products contributing to 45% of GDP due to the slow progress in equitisation in recent years (Lye & Ha, 2020).

In order to achieve the new targets, Vietnam needs new growth drivers as traditional growth drivers are losing steam. Vietnam's economic growth in the past 35 years since Doi Moi has been fuelled by the structural transformation from agriculture to industry and trade, the promotion of export-driven sectors based on cheap labour and the fast development of the private sector. Current challenges are low demographic dividends due to diminishing advantages of low-skilled labour and undercapitalised enterprises in need of capital to realise their economies of scale. Additionally, the exporting sectors of the economy are vulnerable to external shocks to the global supply chain, as evidenced throughout the COVID-19 pandemic. Lastly, being among the countries most affected by climate change, Vietnam also needs to rethink its dependence on natural resources, especially coal, oil and gas.

2.1.1   SOEs in the Economy of Today

According to the path dependence theory (Bebchuk & Roe, 2000), the popular corporate structures of an economy partly stem from the structure with which its economy started. Basically, this means that what is observed

---

[1] ASEAN is the Association of Southeast Asian Nations with the total population of more than 600 million people of ten member countries. ASEAN's combined GDP in 2013 was $2.4 trillion. ASEAN is in free trade agreements with China, Japan, Korea, India, Australia and New Zealand (Mahbubani & Severino, 2014).

[2] https://vov.vn/chinh-tri/nghi-quyet-dai-hoi-xiii-xac-dinh-3-moc-muc-tieu-den-nam-2045-834591.vov

today in the economy in terms of corporate ownership structure and governance practice is deeply rooted in the past economic setting of the country. Up until Doi Moi (Reform) in 1986, Vietnam followed a centrally planned economic system in which the state owned and controlled resources and the firms' output. The 30-year transition process since Doi Moi has transformed Vietnam from a centrally planned economy to a socialist-oriented market economy in which the commercialised state-owned sector and the private sector co-exist. In the 1990s, with the Reform, the government restructured a number of SOEs and merged them into state general corporations. Later in the years leading to Vietnam's accession into the World Trade Organization in 2007, SOEs were restructured into large and diversified state economic groups. These general corporations and economic groups were created to develop strategic industries and assume social responsibilities of economic stability and employment. However, SOEs of those decades were known to be inefficient. SOEs caused bad debt for banks due to the directed lending practice. As SOEs could also borrow capital from other SOEs, they were caught in a "maze of cross-subsidisation and indebtedness" (Sjöholm, 2006). Ten state economic groups exist until now with full state ownership.[3] Even though the economy has gradually opened to international integration and competition, the majority of Vietnamese listed firms originated from wholly state-owned enterprises or spin-offs of SOEs, with the state retaining significant ownership in critical sectors. This is similar to what is observed in most other transitioning markets.

Since the pilot privatisation programme in 1992, almost 5000 state-owned enterprises have been fully or partly equitised. The equitisation process accelerated at the beginning of the new century then slowed down significantly from the onset of the global financial crisis in 2007 (see Fig. 2.4). However, it should be noted that the average size of equitised enterprises of recent years is substantially higher than those equitised in the early years. The average charter capital of equitised business was VND 400 billion in 2016, VND 2000 billion in 2017 and VND 800 billion in 2018.

According to the General Statistics Office of Vietnam, in 2018, there were 2260 state-owned enterprises, of which 1097 were wholly state owned. The other 1163 companies were partially equitised SOEs, with

---

[3] These are EVN, PVN, Viettel, Petrolimex, Vinacomin, VNPT, Vinachem, VN Rubber, Bao Viet and Vinatex in order of revenue rank reported in 2017.

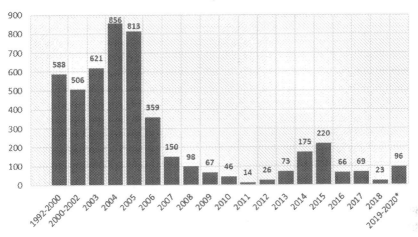

Fig. 2.4 Equitisation progress in Vietnam. (Data source: From CIEM (2019) and Vu Thanh Tu Anh (2012), Restructuring of SOEs in Viet Nam, Fulbright Economics Teaching Program, Vietnam Program, Harvard Kennedy School, 14 March 2012, Hanoi)

the state retaining a controlling interest of at least 50% of equity. There were also 1125 joint-stock companies with the state capital of less than 50% of equity (GSO, 2019a). Among the largest 500 enterprises in Vietnam, SOEs still contribute 52% of the total revenue[4] (VNR500, 2017).

From 2000, as can be seen from Fig. 2.5, in contrast to the growth of private firms, the number of SOEs has shrunk from approximately 13.6% of all enterprises (5759 SOEs) to only 0.37% (2260) in 2018. During that period, the number of employees, fixed assets and total net revenue of SOEs all reduced significantly from 59% to 8%, 56% to 23% and 55% to 14%, respectively (see Chapter Appendix 1—*Key indicators of the state-owned sectors over the last 20 years*).

According to the GSO Statistical Yearbook (GSO, 2019b), as of 31 December 2018, 95% of businesses in Vietnam have less than 50 employees (see Fig. 2.6), primarily due to the small size of private businesses. Among the various types of SIEs, the most popular group is small- to

---

[4] https://vnr500.com.vn/Charts/Index?chartId=1

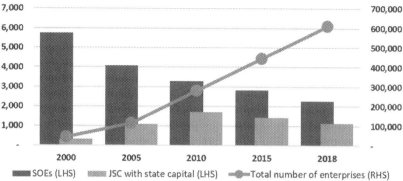

Fig. 2.5 Number of SOEs and joint-stock companies with state capital

medium-sized enterprises with from 50 to 199 employees. About 59.5% of SOEs are classified as SMEs.[5] More information is provided in Appendix 2.

Over the years, the economic significance of the state-owned sector has also reduced substantially in terms of its contribution to GDP, share in the state budget revenue and capital investments, as shown in Appendix 3. In 2019, the SOE sector accounted for 27.06% of GDP and only 10.6% of the state budget. While capital investments by SOEs declined from 59% in 2000 to 31% in 2019, employment in the sector just reduced slightly from 11.8% to 7.7% of labour of at least 15 years old (GSO, 2020).

The government still maintains significant ownership in strategic sectors of the economy, considered as "sensitive sectors" or those with the national interest, therefore requiring government control. The Prime Minister decides the sectors that the government retains full ownership of and the target state ownership ratio for other sectors.[6] In general, the state

---

[5] As per SME Law 04/2017/QH14 effective from 2018, SMEs are micro-, small- and medium-sized enterprises having no more than 200 employees, total capital below VND 100 billion or total revenue below VND 300 billion.

[6] See Decision No. 26/2019/QD-TTg ("Decision 26") of the Prime Minister of Vietnam dated 15 August 2019 on the list of State-owned enterprises ("SOEs") lists 93 SOEs to be equitized by the end of 2020: the state will hold (i) more than 65%, (ii) from 50% to 65% or (iii) less than 50% of the charter capital. Four SOEs (Agribank, Vinacomin, Vinafood 1 and Thua Thien Hue Minerals Co. Ltd.) are in group (i), 62 SOEs (e.g. VNPT, VICEM,

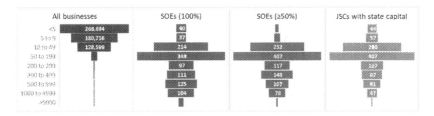

Fig. 2.6 Distribution of SOEs by size

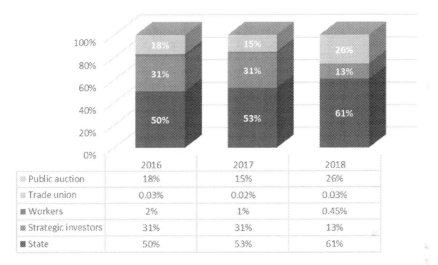

	2016	2017	2018
▨ Public auction	18%	15%	26%
▨ Trade union	0.03%	0.02%	0.03%
▨ Workers	2%	1%	0.45%
▨ Strategic investors	31%	31%	13%
▨ State	50%	53%	61%

Fig. 2.7 Shareholder structure upon equitisation in Vietnam. (Data source: Pham and Mai (2020))

continues to hold full ownership in electricity, air traffic services, aeronautical information services, rescue services, public postal services, lottery, publishing (excluding printing and publication), notes printing, social credit and credit system security. As Fig. 2.7 shows, on average, after

MobiFone, Transerco, UDIC, Vinachem) in group (ii) and 27 other SOEs (EVN's Genco 1, Genco2, HUD, among others) in group (iii). Decision No. 58/2016/QD-TTg with a list of 103 SOEs in which the state plans to retain 100% ownership is still in place.

equitisation, the state still holds more than 50% of the equity in newly equitised firms in recent years.

To fulfil the commitment to the World Trade Organization, the Vietnamese government has been relaxing state ownership and protection by encouraging firms in other sectors to be privatised and listed on the stock market. Although the government has reduced state ownership in areas of financial risk such as securities, investment fund, insurance, banks and real estate, finance is still among the sectors with the most significant state ownership. According to the Vietnam Enterprise Survey 2016 (OECD, 2020), other sectors with substantial state presence are water supply and waste management, mining, agriculture, entertainment and electricity and gas provision (Fig. 2.8).

Approximately only 10% of the 5000 equitised firms have been listed on the national stock markets. The two stock exchanges in Vietnam are the Ho Chi Minh City stock exchange (HSX), established in 2000, and the Hanoi Stock Exchange (HNX) in 2005. Despite their short history, both stock markets have grown in terms of the number of listed firms, with a total market capitalisation of US $47 billion for HSX[7] and US $11.4 billion for HNX in 2021.[8] The stock markets have become an

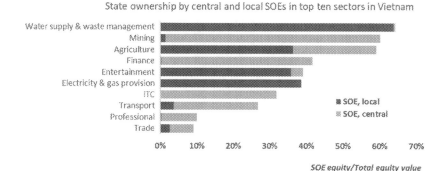

Fig. 2.8 Top sector with state ownership in Vietnam. (Data source: OECD (2020), based on the Vietnam Enterprise Survey 2016)

---

[7] https://www.hsx.vn/Modules/Listed/Web/ListingSummary/153?fid=a1b2850 9a59441f28d508074c0a72aad

[8] https://hnx.vn/vi-vn/hnx.html

essential channel for listed firms to access capital. On the broad market, there are 29 large SOEs with majority state ownership and 20 with significant minority state ownership, making up approximately 40% of the total market capitalisation (OECD, 2020). Among the 100 largest firms that are constituents of the VN100 Index (as of early 2021[9]), 15 SOEs are controlled by the government, with an average shareholding of 65.31%.

SOEs, however, do not perform well in terms of profitability and efficiency, especially when compared to their private counterparts and FDI firms. In 2018, among all types of SOEs, wholly state-owned enterprises had the lowest profit margin (4.95%). Other SOEs with state capital at the controlling level earn a profit margin of 6.54%, whereas SIEs in which state capital is reduced to minority level achieve 8.05%. Foreign-invested joint ventures, in contrast, have their highest profit margin (9.19%). For better performance, SOEs will need to be more efficient. Currently, SOEs pay the highest average monthly income per worker. The average monthly income per SOE employee is VND 12.6 million, 42% higher than the overall average and 30% more than the FDI's figure. SOEs also have the highest value of fixed assets per employee, over three times the FDI's value. In contrast, SOEs contribute only 21% of the total profits of all enterprises, whereas FDI firms' share is 42.6% (see Appendix 5 for detailed information). It is imperative that SOEs are better managed to enhance the productivity of state capital.

State capital can be managed by various levels of authority. Large economic groups and general corporations belong to the central government, under the ultimate responsibility of the Prime Minister. The central government could delegate its ownership responsibility to the Commission for the Management of State Capital (CMSC). State-owned banks, financial institutions and other SOEs are under local governments, relevant ministries, the State Bank of Vietnam, other SOEs or the State Capital Investment Corporation (SCIC) as an agency of the government. According to the Guidelines of OECD for corporate governance of SOEs, for better separation between ownership and regulating functions, state capital should be managed by professional state investment agencies such as CMSC and SCIC.

2.1.2   A Quest for New Growth

To achieve the vision of becoming a developed market by 2045, Vietnam has invested in a new growth model. Vietnam expects its new growth

---

[9] Data obtained from Bloomberg in February 2021.

drivers to be the development of innovation capital and human capital to support high-tech industries. The government is committed to further unleashing SOEs, speeding up the equitisation process of large SOEs and focusing on efficiency after equitisation.

SOEs are under pressure to be more innovative, productive and upscaled to realise their economies of scale. Needed fuel for the new growth calls for more private capital as the state capital is limited. Over the last 15 years, several sectors, namely cement, steel production and sugar, have been opened up and witnessed a significant reduction in SOEs' contribution to the total output of all enterprises from 64% to 31%, 33% to 11% and 46% down to almost 0% respectively. The government could open up to encourage more private capital into lucrative sectors such as post and telecommunication, airlines, shipping, pharmaceutical, electricity production, coal and chemicals.[10] Currently, SOEs still account for 99% of coal production, 91% of chemical fertilisers and 81% of electricity (see Appendix 4).

While domestic and international private sector investors may eagerly welcome equitised enterprises newly to the capital market, they are concerned about if and when these businesses can really become good investment candidates. The long delay from equitisation to listing of equitised firms has lowered investors' confidence to participate in IPOs due to liquidity risk. For example, at the end of 2018, the Ministry of Finance named 667 equitised enterprises with a significant delay in the listing process,[11] including 372 enterprises managed by local governments and 295 by ministries and state corporations. The Unlisted Public Company Market (UPCoM) was established as an over-the-counter market in 2009 to improve the liquidity of unlisted stocks and ease their access to capital.[12]

---

[10] Large state-owned economic groups and general corporations dominate these sectors. For example, Viettel (owned by the Ministry of Defense) (almost VND 250 trillion in revenue and VND 44 trillion in profit in 2017) and Vietnam Post and Telecommunication (VNPT) (the Ministry of Post and Telecommunication) (almost VND 56 trillion; VND 5156 billion) are the two largest telecommunication companies in the sector. Other examples are Vietnam Airlines, Vietnam National Chemical Group (Vinachem), Vietnam Cement Industry Corporation, Vietnam Pharmaceuticals and Vietnam Rubber Corporation. All have large revenues and fixed assets.

[11] https://vietnamfinance.vn/vi-sao-667-doanh-nghiep-nha-nuoc-co-phan-hoa-nhung--chua-len-san-chung-khoan-20180504224216270.htm

[12] As at early 2021, there are 908 stocks traded on UPCoM, more than 500 of which were admitted to trading from 2016 to 2018. New admissions were low in the years prior to 2016 and were halved in 2019 and 2020, compared to 2018. Since 2009, less than 5% of securities

Despite the existence of the UPCoM, preparing for listing on an organised exchange is still a challenge for many firms with inadequate capital and an insufficient number of shareholders to be qualified as a public company.

Additional barriers to the listing of equitised firms are poor financial performance and weak corporate governance after equitisation. An example was Vinafood2 (Ticker VSF on UPCoM) which had a long-awaited IPO in 2018. A private investor, T&T Group, invested VND 1.2 trillion for 25% of equity as a strategic investor at IPO. By the end of June 2020, Vinafood2 reported an accumulated loss of VND 2188 billion[13] and traded at 30% lower than its IPO price. Another 180 companies on UPCoM reported negative earnings in 2020. On average, the return on equity (ROE) of UPCoM companies was 7.35% in 2020, much lower than 9.33% of HNX-listed companies and 12.92% of those on HSX. UPCoM companies' ROE was just less than half of that of the top 30 listed companies, VN30.[14]

Corporate governance of newly equitised companies is another area of concern for private sector investors. Frequent conflict of interest arises due to weak oversight of related party transactions and the effectiveness of the state capital representative. Mixed ownership between state and private investors in equitised enterprises in Vietnam poses unique corporate governance challenges, which will be elaborated further in Chap. 4.

2.2   ECONOMIC REFORM IN CHINA AND THE CHANGING ROLE OF THE STATE

The literature on Chinese state-owned enterprises and privatised enterprises began after China's opening up of its economy in 1978. In the 1990s, as a centrally planned economy, the Chinese government directly controlled and made commercial decisions for the SOEs in annual output targets, finance, production and pricing, leaving little autonomy for the SOEs. SOEs provided lifetime employment, known as the "iron rice bowl" (铁饭碗), and essential social services for employees and their families.

---

on UPCoM have moved to the main exchanges. (https://hnx.vn/en-gb/cophieu-etfs/chung-khoan-uc.html)

[13] https://thanhnien.vn/tai-chinh-kinh-doanh/hau-co-phan-hoa-thua-lo-trien-mien-mat-von-nha-nuoc-1289454.html

[14] Authors calculated based on statistics for 2020, obtained from cafeF.vn and vndi-rect.com.vn.

Hence, Chinese SOEs were inefficient prior to market reforms in the 1980s before loosened government control giving SOEs more decision-making power and profit-sharing incentives.

Fast forward to today, one of the significant developments of Chinese SOEs is the role they play in extending the presence of the Chinese enterprise on a global scale. China is a developing country with the world's second-largest economy in which the state sector plays a major role in contributing to its growth over the last four decades. Many Chinese SOEs first appeared in the market during the import-substituting industrialisation period after 1978 when China opened up to the world.

China has the highest number of state-invested enterprises, and they make up the highest number of multinational state-owned enterprises (Jefferson, 2016). The expansion of China's SOEs size is reflected both by their share of assets and revenue of the 2000 largest companies (see Fig. 2.9, Panel A) and their growing presence in the Fortune 500 list (Panel B).[15] In 2017, non-financial SOEs from China represented 11.3% of the 2000 largest firms' total assets, three times the share of those from advanced economies. Among 500 Fortune companies, there were 75 Chinese SOEs, almost three times larger than the total number of SOEs from other markets (27). That number in 2005 was just 14. In the world's league of top 50 SOEs, there are 23 Chinese SOEs. The top three positions all belong to China, namely China Petrochemical, China National Petroleum and State Grid China (IMF, 2020).

The Chinese SOEs at the central and local government levels account for 40%[16] of all enterprises and contribute between 23% and 28% to its GDP in sectorial value-added and 43% of profits (Zhang, 2019; Holz, 2018). Profits made by SOEs contribute to the revenue of the state. The traditional role of SOEs is to operate for the benefit of the state and the population as a whole, so the government must ensure that it is properly managed.

The growth in the size of Chinese SOEs in recent years is magnificent. By the same token, one of the most significant challenges for Chinese SOEs in international business is managing the negative perception of

---

[15] Data in Panel A from the IMF represent a share of China's non-financial SOEs whereas Fortune 500 list includes both financial and non-financial companies.

[16] China Briefing, "China SOE reforms: What the latest round of reforms means for the market", China's SOE Reforms: Assessing Their Impact on the Market (china-briefing.com).

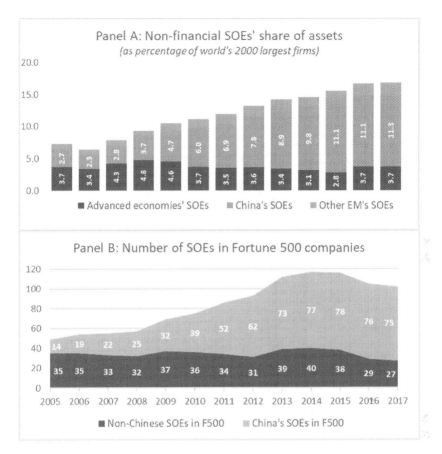

Fig. 2.9 China's SOEs in the world. (Data for Panel A: IMF (2020) Fiscal Monitor, Apr 2020, Data for Panel B: Fortune 500 annual list and Lin et al. (2020))

these entities acting proxies of the state and thus working as an arm of the state in advancing its political influence.

The crucial economic role of SOEs has also raised the need to monitor the performance and introduced needed enterprise reform in the state sector. The 1990s saw the emergence of a large number of Chinese SOEs that were transformed from government agencies into business enterprises as part of its economic modernisation strategy (Lin, 2001). Through its privatisation programme, many of these government agencies were listed. By the end of September 2011, there were 1047 former SOEs listed on the Shanghai and Shenzhen stock markets (Gang & Hope, 2012). China's SOEs account for near 40% of its stock market capitalisation.[17]

Chinese SOEs can be classified into four groups based on their regulators. They are the central industrial SOEs supervised by the central State-Owned Assets Supervision and Administration Commission of the State Council (SASAC); local industrial SOEs managed by local SASACs; financial institutions controlled by Central Huijin Investment Co., Ltd.; and entities under the Ministry of Finance (MOF).

The SASAC oversees the central and local industrial SOEs. SASAC, an institution directly under the control of the State Council, is the central holding company of Chinese SOEs and is considered the largest controlling shareholder in the world. The Central Huijin Investment Company Limited, an investment company owned by the Chinese government, essentially controls state-owned financial institutions. Finally, the Ministry of Finance (MOF) regulates enterprises created by central administrative institutions or have economic relations with MOF.

While China has reduced the total number of companies under central government control, their assets have grown to Yuan58.2 trillion (US $8.2 trillion) in 2018, up from Yuan 54.5 trillion in 2017. The net profits of those companies meanwhile jumped 15.7% from 2017 to Yuan1.2 trillion last year. China's state-owned enterprises employed between 5% and 16% of its workforce in 2017 (Zhang, 2019).

The current Chinese government encourages mixed ownership in an effort to reform the massive state sector of the economy by injecting private capital into SOEs to improve their management and much-needed market discipline (Ruan & Yin, 2018, Milhaupt & Pargendler, 2017). China's earlier attempt at reforming SOE ownership happened under the slogan "grasping the large and letting the small go" (抓大放小) in 1996 with the privatisation of some of the largest SOEs. This industrial Reform resulted in the "privatised" SOEs becoming firms with a mixed-ownership structure. Mixed ownership is regarded as a transitional means to the Reform of state-owned enterprises and economic transformation to a market economy (Ruan & Yin, 2018). While mixed ownership allows the introduction of modern corporate governance structure and system, it has also

---

[17] MAN Institute, "Low historical correlation to both DM and EM, along with a high retail investor base, may provide an opportunity in China's state-owned enterprises", The Value in China's SOEs | Man Institute | Man Group, https://www.man.com/.

exacerbated other corporate governance challenges such as the state versus non-state ownership agency problem. Ruan and Yin (2018) highlight other ambiguities such as investment strategy, state authority and the devolvement of the SASAC to state capital management in these hybrid SOEs.

Aharoni (1986) discusses the existence of SOEs as a major business player and those issues associated with them, such as government influence on them, management behaviour and their performance vis-à-vis private sector companies. In addition, Aharoni (1986) alludes to multinational SOEs as being subject to state control and are, therefore, other than focusing on achieving commercial objectives, operating in a multiple-goal setting also to promote political and social goals.

Historically, the SOEs were established by the state to mainly conduct business at home and at times to take on international business by exporting to provide foreign exchange to the home governments (Vernon, 1979; Aharoni, 1986). In the last two decades, many of these SOEs began expanding abroad by embarking on outward foreign direct investment (OFDI). The purpose is either to source resources as part of their upstream global supply chain activities (Liu & Qiao, 2013) or to distribute their products or services in downstream activities in their global value chain. Vernon (1979) and Aharoni (1986) study the collaborative relationship between multinationals and state-owned firms in the early days of state-owned firms involved in international projects.

It has been over four decades since China's opened up its market to the world and its embrace of a market economy. However, even with these developments, we witness the continued existence of the Chinese SOEs, not only domestically but also internationally. This can be attributed to the socialist market economy introduced by Jiang Zemin during the 14th National Congress of the Communist Party of China in 1992. It describes a system that has predominant public ownership and state-owned enterprises within a market economy. The Central Committee of the CPC and State Council issued a guideline in September 2015 on deepening SOE reforms by classifying SOEs into two categories: a public category (*gongyilei*) for entities in the public welfare sector and a commercial category (*shangyelei*) for those firms seeking profit. This classification is a new reform initiative aimed at instilling good corporate governance to foster efficiency. It also allows SOEs' performance to be measured differently (the so-called dual-track approach) with the former group to be measured by political metrics rather than market-based ones. However, commercial firms are still required to support the government in its economic initiatives[18] and maintain social cohesion. The ramifications of the dual-track approach are greater oversight by the state of corporate governance and performance.

The changing role of Chinese SOEs from import-substituting industrialisation to global commodity sourcing and consumer competition can be defined by the convergence of economic and political interests or the reality of the global political economy. The international political economy looks at how political forces influence global economic interactions. The COVID-19 pandemic is an example of how this has panned out, with the US and its allies blaming China for "knowingly responsible" for the contagion, creating an increasingly adversarial global environment. The US probably sees this as an extension to the US-China trade war and an opportunity to gain the upper hand in the current presidential election cycle by ramping up political pressure and threatening economic sanctions against China. This led President Xi Jinping to say that China should be ready for unprecedented external adversity and challenges in the long run, suggesting that China is prepared to face greater uncertainty of its long-term economic growth.[19]

Schweiger (2014) suggests that state ownership and influence continues to exist, leading to an ambiguity between private and state ownership and the emergence of the "hybrid organisations" (Bruton et al., 2015). These are organisations of which the state can be an owner or a strategic supporter. Many observers see this description apply to many private-owned Chinese companies.

2.3   Discussion

Similar to Vietnam and China, we witnessed the emergence of several Asian tigers from ASEAN countries in the past, where the state played a developmental role in the economy. That role by state-owned firms has survived and thrived to this present day in countries like Singapore and Malaysia, albeit with differing governance and performance results. The success of Singapore's state sector has provided an attractive model for China to replicate in mixed enterprises (Milhaupt & Pargendler, 2017), corporate governance and strategic direction.

Singapore's SOEs or "government-linked corporations" (GLCs) first emerged after the country independence from Malaysia in 1965. The

---

[18] Such as the "2025 Plan" for China to become a technology-intensive powerhouse and the Belt and Road Initiative (BRI).

[19] Xi Jinping's warning in April 2020 during the COVID-19 pandemic when China was facing an unprecedented challenge to its Belt and Road Initiative and longer-term economic growth in a century.

purpose of the SOEs at that time was to provide leadership and resources to reform, rejuvenate and grow the economy, a necessity without having the benefit of Malaysia's resources and value chain.

Singapore's early GLCs are Neptune Orient Lines (shipping), Development Bank of Singapore (banking) and Keppel/Jurong Shipyards/Sembawang (shipbuilding and repair). These GLCs provided the foundations for rebuilding Singapore's economy. They were later joined by other GLCs like Petrochemical Corporation of Singapore (1977), Singapore Refining Company (1979), CapitaLand (2000), Singtel (1992) and Singapore Airlines (1972). These GLCs formed successful strategic partnerships with foreign companies to gain expertise and foreign direct investment. These industries are those that define the Singaporean economy today. The growth of Singapore's Sovereign Wealth Funds, which are also regarded as very successful SOEs, is the driving force behind Singapore's greater presence in global business.

Singapore SOEs have always prided themselves as professionally managed, independent from political intervention and intensely commercially oriented. Singapore's UK-inspired Code of Corporate Governance guides listed companies on best practices for corporate governance stipulates strict regulatory safeguards to ensure that SOEs are commercially rather than politically driven. Regulatory safeguards include measures to prevent power abuse by the controlling shareholder by imposing legal constraints on the rights of the government as a shareholder, such as the need for the President of Singapore's approval to appoint or remove directors and disposition of investment assets at fair market value. Additionally, the Code stipulates that the board of a listed company should have at least one-third of its board represented by independent directors and increasing to one half where the chairman is not independent of management.

Malaysia is another ASEAN economy with a large state-owned sector. Malaysian SOEs play a prevalent role in protecting and advancing industries regarded as of national interest. These industries include utilities, aviation, postal services, public transport, water and sewerage and financial services. SOEs account for 41% of the market capitalisation of 4% of the total listed companies on the Kuala Lumpur Stock Exchange (Bhatt, 2016). There are also other companies directly controlled by the government that are not listed on the stock exchange, such as Khazanah Nasional, the sovereign wealth fund and Petronas. Leading the state-owned sector are the "G-15" firms, a collection of the "significantly large" GLCs[20] of

---

[20] They include Maybank, Telekom Malaysia Berhad, BIMB Holdings Berhad, Sime Darby Berhad, Bumiputra-Commerce Holdings Berhad, Golden Hope Plantations Berhad,

the Putrajaya Committee for GLC High Performance controlled by the federal government-linked investment companies.[21] The G15 firms account for 65% of the market capitalisation of all listed GLCs.[22]

The Malaysian SOEs play a crucial part in the government industrialisation programme as well as in the redistribution of wealth to the poorer "bumiputra" (indigenous) populace to further the affirmative action policy. The government appoints the company's board members and senior management in GLCs, and in some cases, it would make commercial decisions on strategy, M&A, financing and awarding contracts. However, the weak corporate governance of Malaysian SOEs has negatively affected their performance since the 1980s. Major SOEs, such as Perwaja Steel Berhad, Malaysian Airlines System Berhad, Sime Darby Berhad and Port Klang Free Zone, have been criticised for low valuation, conflict of interest, corruption and corporate failure (Norwani et al., 2010) despite their significant operations and size. They suffer from the agency problem arising from the lack of internal control and strategic direction (Norhayati & Siti-Nabiha, 2009, Ling & Lim, 2015). To overcome these governance challenges, the government launched the "Green Book: Enhancing Board Effectiveness (2006)"[23] emphasising board independence and effectiveness. State-owned companies are also encouraged to adopt the Malaysian Code on Corporate Governance issued by Securities Commission Malaysia in 2017.

2.4   Conclusion

While SOEs in Vietnam and China significantly differ in size and their global presence, the critical similarity permeating the Vietnam and China state sectors is their structural and commercial approach to embrace and accommodate the principles of market capitalism. The state sector plays an essential role in supporting the industrial development and economic growth of these countries. Therefore, the political governance in these countries is predicated on its performance and contribution to economic success.

Malaysian Airline System Berhad, Proton Holdings Berhad, Guthrie Berhad, Boustead Holdings Berhad, UEM Holdings Berhad, Affin Holdings Berhad, Malaysian Resources Corporation Berhad, Tenaga Nasional Berhad and Malaysian Building Society Berhad.
    [21] The GLICs are EPF, Khazanah, KWAP, LTAT, LTH, MKD and PNB.
    [22] Catalysing GLC Transformation to Advance Malaysian Development, March 2006, Putrajaya Committee for GLC High Performance, Malaysian Government. (summary-of-transformation-manual-eng.pdf (pcg.gov.my))
    [23] Ditto.

State ownership continues to play a crucial part in the economy of many emerging markets, including China. According to Yu (2013) as a "higher level of state ownership is superior to a dispersed ownership structure due to the benefits of government support and political connections". The sustainability of both the Chinese and Vietnamese economies is a case in point where both countries still experienced positive GDP growth throughout the COVID-19 pandemic in 2020.

Singapore is a successful model in which the management of state capital at SOEs is placed in the hands of large sovereign wealth funds and professional government agencies. Unlike Singapore, management in the state sectors in Vietnam and China is not totally independent and free from government policy intervention. SOE business decisions in Singapore are largely market-driven, while those in Vietnam and China may be influenced by party policy (Aharoni, 1986). Like European state sectors, state ownership and influence continues to exist, resulting in the emergence of the "hybrid organisations" (Schweiger, 2014) with different ownership structures and management systems. The Vietnamese and Chinese SOEs would consult with the party apparatus to appoint corporate personnel within the state-owned entities, including the rotation of key managers.

Singapore and China and, to a lesser extent, Vietnam are also cognizant of the conflict of interest and ambiguous corporate governance between shareholder and regulator posed by state ownership and have centralised SOE share ownership through a holding company structure as a means of separating the state's distinct roles (Milhaupt & Pargendler, 2017). A regulatory ownership change that had a positive outcome for corporate governance and performance is the Split Share Structure Reform in 2005 in China (Beltratti et al., 2012), which reduced the conflicts of interests between state and private shareholders and information asymmetry and made state shareholders' wealth reflective of market value (Hou et al. 2012).

With the changing strategic direction of SOEs of "growing large and going global" after consolidation and restructuring (Song, 2018), new corporate governance challenges have emerged with a significant impact on SOEs' operation and performance. With reforms, Chinese SOEs have created the scale perceivably needed for global expansion (Milhaupt & Pargendler, 2017). However, there is a need to revisit the implications of state ownership in the global marketplace in the light of the recent US-China trade war, where the sensitivity of state interests in SOEs has come under the spotlight. Better corporate governance of SOEs would encourage private capital investment and greater acceptance of Chinese SOEs globally.

Key indicators of State-owned sector over the last 20 years

Indicators	2000	2005	2010	2015	2018	2000	2005	2010	2015	2018
Total number of enterprises	42,288	112,952	279,360	442,485	610,637	100.0%	100.0%	100.0%	100.0%	100.0%
SOEs—total	5759	4086	3281	2835	2260	13.6%	3.6%	1.2%	0.6%	0.37%
State capital = 100%	—	—	1801	1315	1097	—	—	0.6%	0.3%	0.18%
State capital ≥ 50%	—	—	1480	1520	1163	—	—	0.5%	0.3%	0.19%
Private (domestic) enterprises	35,004	105,169	268,831	427,710	591,499	82.8%	93.1%	96.2%	96.7%	96.87%
Of which JSC with state capital	305	1096	1710	1416	1125	0.7%	1.0%	0.6%	0.3%	0.18%
Foreign-invested enterprises	1525	3697	7248	11,940	16,878	3.6%	3.3%	2.6%	2.7%	2.76%
Number of employees ('000)										
Total number of employees	3537.00	6240.6	9741.80	12,856.9	14,817.8	100.0%	100.0%	100.0%	100.0%	100.0%
SOEs—total	2088.53	2040.9	1602.7	1371.6	1126.7	59.0%	32.7%	16.5%	10.7%	7.6%
SOEs state capital = 100%	—	—	1078.0	779.1	669.7	—	—	11.1%	6.1%	4.5%
SOEs state capital ≥ 50%	—	—	524.7	592.5	457.0	—	—	5.4%	4.6%	3.1%
Private (domestic) enterprises	1040.90	2979.1	5983.0	7712.5	8977.2	29.4%	47.7%	61.4%	60.0%	60.6%
Of which JSC with state capital	61.87	280.8	505.5	353.8	295.3	1.7%	4.5%	5.2%	2.8%	2.0%
Foreign-invested enterprises	407.57	1220.6	2156.1	3772.7	4714.0	11.5%	19.6%	22.1%	29.3%	31.8%
Fixed assets and investments '000 billions (trillion)										
Fixed assets and investments—all enterprises	411.71	953.09	4658.9	10466.8	14109	100.0%	100.0%	100.0%	100.0%	100.0%
SOEs—total	229.86	487.21	1758.9	4599.7	3301.6	55.8%	51.1%	37.8%	43.9%	23.4%

SOEs state capital = 100%	—	—	*1140.9*	*3173.4*	2374.6	—	—	*24.5%*	*30.3%*	*16.8%*
SOEs state capital ≥ 50%	—	—	*618.0*	*1426.3*	927	—	—	*13.3%*	*13.6%*	*6.6%*
Private (domestic) enterprises	33.92	196.20	2129.7	3862	7909.6	8.2%	20.6%	45.7%	36.9%	56.1%
Of which JSC with state capital	2.95	25.08	*179.5*	*252.2*	484.2	0.7%	2.6%	*3.9%*	*2.4%*	*3.4%*
Foreign-invested enterprises	147.94	269.68	770.3	2005.1	2897.8	35.9%	28.3%	16.5%	19.2%	20.5%
Total net revenue '000 billions (trillion)										
Total net revenue—all enterprises	809.79	2158	7487.7	14,949.2	23,637.6	100.0%	100.0%	100.0%	100.0%	100.0%
SOEs—total	444.67	838	2033.5	2722.2	3413.8	54.9%	38.9%	27.2%	18.2%	14.4%
SOEs state capital = 100%	—	—	*1517.6*	*1666.0*	2079.2	—	—	*20.3%*	*11.1%*	*8.8%*
SOEs state capital ≥ 50%	—	—	*515.9*	*1056.2*	1334.6	—	—	*6.9%*	*7.1%*	*5.6%*
Private (domestic) enterprises	203.16	851	4068.2	8075.1	13,410.6	25.1%	39.4%	54.3%	54.0%	56.7%
Of which JSC with state capital	10.28	104	*432.9*	*474.0*	575.1	1.3%	4.8%	*5.8%*	*3.2%*	*2.4%*
Foreign-invested enterprises	161.96	468	1386.0	4151.9	6813.2	20.0%	21.7%	18.5%	27.8%	28.8%

Data source: Authors compiled from the annual Vietnam's GSO's Statistical Yearbooks from 2000 to 2018

APPENDIX 2: SIEs IN VIETNAM, BREAKDOWN BY SIZE

Number of enterprises by size based on number of employees

As at 31 December 2018	Total	<5 employees	5 to 9	10 to 49	50 to 199	200 to 299	300 to 499	500 to 999	1000 to 4999	>5000
Total number of all enterprises	610,637	268,694	180,716	128,599	23,074	3120	2645	2039	1532	218
SOEs—Total	2260	56	67	466	**755**	214	259	232	182	29
SOEs State capital = 100%	*1097*	*40*	*37*	*214*	***348***	*97*	*111*	*125*	*104*	*21*
SOEs State capital ≥ 50%	*1163*	*16*	*30*	*252*	***407***	*117*	*148*	*107*	*78*	*8*
Private JSCs with state capital	1125	44	57	280	**407**	107	97	81	47	5

Number of enterprises by size based on the total net revenue (in Vietnam Dong)

As at 31 December 2018	Total	<0.5 billion	0.5 to 1 b	1 to 5 b	5b to 10b	10 to 50b	50 to 200b	200b to 500b	>500b
Total number of all enterprises	610,637	58,997	57,152	237,045	94,262	115,826	31,930	233	7192
SOEs—Total	2260	11	10	93	89	456	572	358	**671**
SOEs State capital = 100%	*1097*	*7*	*8*	*59*	*47*	*210*	*247*	*150*	***369***
SOEs State capital ≥ 50%	*1163*	*4*	*2*	*34*	*42*	*246*	***325***	*208*	*302*
Private JSCs with state capital	1125	7	1	45	40	249	**319**	196	268

Data source: The General Statistics Office's Statistical Yearbook 2019

Bold values were the one with the largest number in each category of SOEs

APPENDIX 3: VIETNAMESE SOEs IN THE ECONOMY FROM 2000 TO 2019

A. Vietnam's GDP by types of ownership (at current prices)

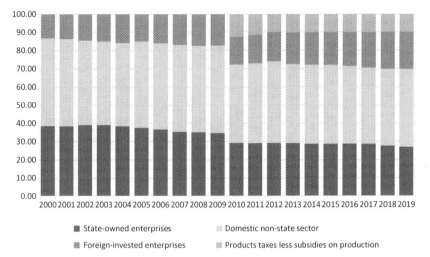

- State-owned enterprises
- Domestic non-state sector
- Foreign-invested enterprises
- Products taxes less subsidies on production

B. Vietnam's State budget revenue structure 2000 - 2019

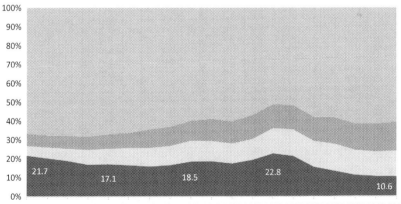

- Oil revenues, import export duties and other taxes
- Revenue from domestic non-state sector
- Revenue from foreign invested enterprises
- Revenue from state owned enterprises

C. Investment by type of ownership in Vietnam

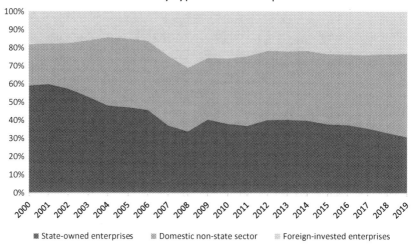

■ State-owned enterprises   ▩ Domestic non-state sector   ▨ Foreign-invested enterprises

D. Labour of at least 15 years of age

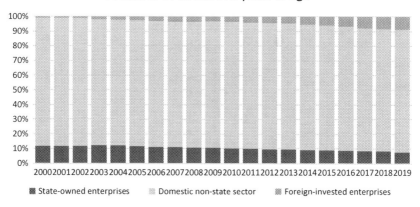

■ State-owned enterprises   ▨ Domestic non-state sector   ▩ Foreign-invested enterprises

Data source: General Statistic Office's Statistical Yearbooks various years

APPENDIX 4: VIETNAMESE SOEs' CONTRIBUTION TO THE TOTAL OUTPUT BY SECTOR

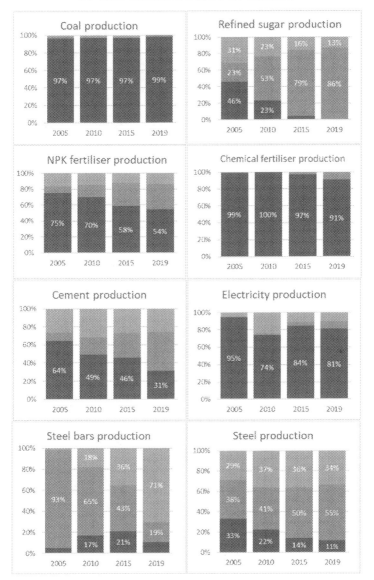

State ■ Non-State ■ Foreign invested sector

Data source: General Statistic Office's Annual Statistical Yearbooks 2005–2019

Appendix 5: Other Vietnamese SOE's Indicators

	2010	2015	2016	2017	2018
Average monthly income of workers (VND '000)					
Average of all enterprises	4124	6966	7514	8269	8816
SOEs—total	6553	9509	11,411	11,887	12,556
SOEs state capital = 100%	*6900*	*9083*	*11,260*	*11,343*	*12,043*
SOEs state capital ≥ 50%	*5839*	*10,075*	*11,620*	*12,652*	*13,309*
Private (domestic) enterprises	3420	6225	6405	7369	7868
Of which JSC with state capital	*4575*	*7958*	*8754*	*10,834*	*10,970*
Foreign-invested enterprises	4252	7502	8504	9035	9702
Foreign capital = 100%	*3852*	*7244*	*8256*	*8806*	*9488*
Joint ventures	*7170*	*10,448*	*11,316*	*11,860*	*12,374*
Profit before tax (billion VND)					
Total of all enterprises	356,301	552,747	711,975	877,534	895,560
SOEs—total	115,193	157,064	197,253	200,866	190,357
SOEs state capital = 100%	*79,973*	*59,703*	*113,458*	*124,845*	*103,014*
SOEs state capital ≥ 50%	*35,220*	*97,361*	*83,795*	*76,021*	*87,343*
Private (domestic) enterprises	115,654	150,528	188,092	291,388	323,637
Of which JSC with state capital	*34,164*	*33,688*	*36,460*	*49,334*	*46,279*
Foreign-invested enterprises	125,454	245,155	326,630	385,280	381,566
Foreign capital = 100%	*40,832*	*170,641*	*226,862*	*307,749*	*298,069*
Joint ventures	*84,622*	*74,514*	*99,768*	*77,531*	*83,497*
Profit margin (%)					
Total of all enterprises	4.53	3.63	3.99	4.25	3.79
SOEs—total	5.31	5.57	6.62	6.43	5.58
SOEs state capital = 100%	*5.27*	*3.46*	*6.04*	*6.13*	*4.95*
SOEs state capital ≥ 50%	*6.83*	*8.87*	*7.61*	*6.98*	*6.54*
Private (domestic) enterprises	2.71	1.84	1.88	2.48	2.41
Of which JSC with state capital	*7.55*	*6.91*	*7.59*	*8.81*	*8.05*
Foreign-invested enterprises	8.84	5.80	6.68	6.64	5.60
Foreign capital = 100%	*4.22*	*4.79*	*5.52*	*6.07*	*5.05*
Joint ventures	*18.77*	*11.22*	*12.89*	*10.63*	*9.19*
Fixed assets per employee (million VND)					
Average of all enterprises	253.9	286.5	297.7	338.3	357.0
SOEs	530.0	732.2	1053.6	1123.8	1155.0
Private (domestic) enterprises	186.2	208.6	175.6	221.8	247.4
Foreign-invested enterprises	209.3	275.7	302.4	348.8	369.7

Data source: General Statistic Office's Annual Statistical Yearbooks 2005–2019

REFERENCES

Aharoni, Y. (1986). *The Evolution and Management of State-Owned Enterprises.* Ballinger Publishing.

Bebchuk, L. A., & Roe, M. J. (2000). A Theory of Path Dependence in Corporate Ownership and Governance. *Stanford Law Review, 52*(1), 127.

Beltratti, A., Bortolotti, B., & Caccavaio, M. (2012). The Stock Market Reaction to the 2005 Split Share Structure Reform in China. *Pacific-Basin Finance Journal, 20*(4), 543–560.

Bhatt, P. R. (2016). Performance of Government-linked Companies and Private-owned Companies in Malaysia. *International Journal of Law and Management, 58*(2), 150–161.

Bruton, G. D., Peng, M. W., Ahlstrom, D., Stan, C., & Xu, K. (2015). State-owned Enterprises Around the World as Hybrid Organisations. *Academy of Management Perspectives, 29*, 92–114. https://www.adb.org/sites/default/files/publication/562061/adbi-wp1071.pdf

Central Institute for Economic Management. (2019). Vietnam's Economic Restructure: Ten-Year Review and Direction for 2021–2025. Issue 7/2019. Hanoi.

Gang, F., & Hope, N. (2012). The Role of SOEs in the Chinese Economy (Chapter 16). Retrieved January 1, 2021, from https://www.chinausfocus.com/2022/wp-content/uploads/Part+02-Chapter+16.pdf

Holz, C. A. (2018). The Unfinished Business of State-owned Enterprise Reform in the People's Republic of China. https://ssrn.com/abstract=3392986 or https://doi.org/10.2139/ssrn.3392986.

Hou, W. X., Kuo, J. M., & Lee, E. (2012). The Impact of State Ownership on Share Price Informativeness: The Case of the Split Share Structure Reform in China. *The British Accounting Review, 44*(4), 248–261.

IMF. (2020). Chapter 3: State-Owned Enterprises: The Other Government, *Fiscal Monitor Series*, April. Retrieved February 27, 2021, from https://www.imf.org/en/Publications/FM/Issues/2020/04/06/fviscal-monitor-april-2020

James, Daniel. (1933). The Modern Corporation and Private Property, by Adolf A. Berle Jr. and Gardiner C. Means. *Indiana Law Journal, 8* (8 Article 11).

Jefferson G. H. 2016, "State-owned Enterprise in China: Reform, Performance, and Prospects", *Working Paper Series* No. 2016/109, Brandeis University, (https://www.brandeis.edu/economics/RePEc/brd/doc/Brandeis_WP109R.pdf - accessed 28 April 2020).

Lin, C. (2001). Corporatisation and Corporate Governance in China's Economic Transition. *Economics of Planning, 34*(1–2), 5–35.

Lin, K. J., Lu, X., Zhang, J., & Zheng, Y. (2020). State-owned Enterprises in China: A Review of 40 years of Research and Practice. *China Journal of Accounting Research, 13* (1), 31–55, ISSN 1755-3091. https://doi.org/10.1016/j.cjar.2019.12.001

Ling, L. B., & Lim, S. Y. (2015). Board Mechanisms and Performance of Government-Linked Companies on Bursa Malaysia. *Procedia Economics and Finance, 31,* 399–417. www.elsevier.com/locate/procedia

Liu, H. & Qiao, X. (2013). Failure Cause Analysis on Overseas M&A of China Enterprises, *Contemporary Logistics,* Journal Homepage. www.seiofbluemountain.com

Lye, L. F., & Ha, H. H. (2020). Vietnam's 13th Party Congress: Document Preparation, and Personnel Line-up, Perspective, Issue No. 84, ISEAS—YUSOF ISHAK INSTITUTE, https://www.iseas.edu.sg/wp-content/uploads/2020/07/ISEAS_Perspective_2020_84.pdf

Mahbubani, Kishore, & Severino, Rhoda. (2014). ASEAN: The way forward: McKinsey & Company.

Milhaupt, C. J., & Pargendler, M. (2017). Governance Challenges of Listed State-Owned Enterprises around the World: National Experiences and a Framework for Reform, Working Paper N° 352/2017, European Corporate Governance Institute (ECGI) Working Paper Series in Law, April 2017.

Norhayati, M. A., & Siti-Nabiha, A. K. (2009). A Case Study of the Performance Management System in a Malaysian Government Linked Company. *Journal of Accounting and Organisational Change, 5*(2), 243–276.

Norwani, N. M., Mohamad, Z. Z., & Chek, I. T. (2010). Corporate Governance Failure and its Impact on Financial Reporting Within Selected Companies. *International Journal of Business and Social Sciences, 2*(21), 205–213.

OECD. (2020). *Multi-dimensional Review of Viet Nam: Towards an Integrated, Transparent and Sustainable Economy.* OECD Development Pathways, OECD Publishing, Paris. https://doi.org/10.1787/367b585c-en

Pham, T. T. V., & Mai, T. H. (2020). Cổ phần hóa doanh nghiệp nhà nước giai đoạn 2016–2020: Thực trạng và một số khuyến nghị. *Finance Magazine.* Retrieved February 15, 2021, from https://tapchitaichinh.vn/tai-chinh-kinh-doanh/co-phan-hoa-doanh-nghiep-nha-nuoc-giai-doan-2016-2020-thuc-trang-va-mot-so-khuyen-nghi-323115.html

Ruan, L., & Yin, M. (2018). A Study on Corporate Governance of Mixed Ownership Enterprises. *Advances in Economics, Business and Management Research, 56,* 104–107.

Schweiger, C. (2014). *The EU and the Global Financial Crisis: New Varieties of Capitalism.* Edward Elgar Publishing.

Sjöholm, F. (2006). *State-Owned Enterprises And Equitization In Vietnam.* EIJS Working Paper Series 228, Stockholm School of Economics, The European Institute of Japanese Studies.

Song, L. (2018). State-owned Enterprise Reform in China: Past, Present and Prospects. Retrieved February 15, 2021, from State-owned enterprise reform in China: Past, present and prospects (anu.edu.au).

The General Statistics Office. (2019a). *Dynamics and the Current Economic-Social Status of Vietnam 2016–2018.* The Statistics Publishing House. Retrieved January 05, 2021, from https://www.gso.gov.vn/du-lieu-va-so-lieu-thong-ke/2020/11/dong-thai-va-thuc-trang-kinh-te-xa-hoi-viet-nam-2016-2018/

The General Statistics Office. (2019b). *The Statistical Yearbook 2019.* The Statistics Publishing House.

The General Statistics Office. (2020). Kinh tế Việt Nam 2020: Một năm tăng trưởng đầy bản lĩnh. Retrieved February 15, 2021, from https://www.gso.gov.vn/du-lieu-va-so-lieu-thong-ke/2021/01/kinh-te-viet-nam-2020-mot-nam-tang-truong-day-ban-linh/

Vernon, R. (1979). The International Aspects of State-owned Enterprises. *Journal of International Business Studies, 10*(3), 7–15.

VNR500. (2017). https://vnr500.com.vn/Charts/Index?chartId=1

Vu Thanh Tu Anh. (2012). *Restructuring of SOEs in Viet Nam,* Fulbright Economics Teaching Program, Vietnam Program, Harvard Kennedy School, 14 March 2012, Hanoi.

Yu, M. (2013). State Ownership and Firm Performance: Empirical Evidence from Chinese Listed Companies. *China Journal of Accounting Research, 6*(2), 75–87.

Zhang, C. (2019). *How Much Do State-owned Enterprises Contribute to China's GDP and Employment?* World Bank. Retrieved May 11, 2020, from http://documents.worldbank.org/curated/en/449701565248091726/pdf/How-Much-Do-State-Owned-Enterprises-Contribute-to-China-s-GDP-and-Employment.pdf

CHAPTER 3

Beyond the Local Economy

The growth of global SOEs has been primarily driven by Chinese SOEs playing an increasingly dominant role, fuelled by the rise of China's economy and other emerging market economies. There were 124 companies from China mainland in the *2020 Fortune Global 500* of which 91 were Chinese SOEs, an increase from 75 in 2017 (CISC, 2020).[1] Until recently, multinational companies from industrialised countries were the main sources of outward foreign direct investment. The IMF (2020)[2] says that SOEs operate in virtually every country and providing goods and services in almost all sectors of the economy. The last two decades also witness the rise of state-owned multinationals from emerging markets as new players in the global marketplace.

The World Investment Report 2017 by the United Nations Conference on Trade and Development (UNCTAD) in (UNCTAD, 2017) published data that demonstrate the remarkable growth of state-owned multinationals in the world economy. Among a total of 100,000 operating in 2017, UNCTAD identified close to 1500 state-owned multinationals, with 86,000 affiliates, ten times bigger than the number reported in 2011.

UNCTAD (2017) defines state-owned multinationals (m-SOEs) as "entities" that have a commercial activity where the government has a

---

[1] CSIS: Centre for Strategic and International Studies, Washington, DC.
[2] IMF Fiscal Monitor Series, Chap. 3 State Owned Enterprises, April 2020.

State ownership of state-owned multinations in the world
(2017)

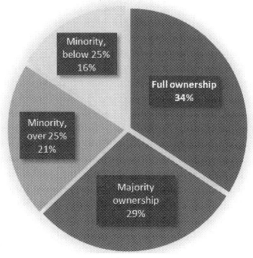

Fig. 3.1 State ownership at multinational SOEs in the world. (Data source: Kalotay (2017), based on data from UNCTAD's World Investment Report in 2017)

controlling interest (full, majority or significant minority ownership) whether listed on the stock exchange or not. They have to be conducting foreign direct investment (FDI) operations by way of having affiliates abroad or engaging in non-equity modes of international production. The "controlling interest" of the government is specified as an equity stake of at least 10% by the government or a governmental entity, such as a central bank, state property agency, a national investment fund (such as a Sovereign Wealth Fund) (but not a pension fund) or having the state shareholder as the largest shareholder, or shareholder with a "golden share"—the share that gives the government control of at least 51% of the voting rights. According to UNCTAC (2017), 34% of m-SOEs were wholly state-owned and 29% were with majority state ownership (Fig. 3.1).

This chapter examines the global business of SOEs from emerging markets, generally in Asia, in terms of their nationalities, the target countries, organisational characteristics and target industries of OFDI. It specifically addresses the role of the state in corporate governance as a shareholder in influencing outward FDI (OFDI).

The focus is on China, the second biggest economy after the US, because of its growing role in the world economy. From the literature and statistics, we discuss the inferences of corporate governance, business strategy, global value chain, motivation for foreign expansion and roles the Chinese SOEs play in international business. The discussion on Chinese SOEs' corporate governance vis-à-vis global business is an extension of the contents in Chap. 2 on the four important emerging Asian economies of Vietnam, China, Singapore and Malaysia. The foreign business expansion of the SOEs from these economies frequently appears in the news nowadays. Their foreign forays have altered the traditional dominance of Western multinational enterprises (MNEs) in global business. In some host countries, concerns have been raised about Chinese SOEs about the underlying motivations of their OFDI. We will conduct a comparative analysis on the influence of the state on the motivation, investment patterns and corporate governance of these m-SOEs and the implications to the host countries.

3.1   EMERGING MARKET M-SOES

The following sections compare the differences in the role of the state, governance, motivation and investments of m-SOEs to deduce the underpinning management styles and business patterns of the m-SOEs from these countries. The understanding of the idiosyncrasies of state influence will enable firms and policymakers to prepare for addressing these players in the global market.

According to the survey by UNCTAD, while m-SOEs are headquartered in 103 countries, typically emerging markets, China is home to 17.5% of them. The next biggest home countries of m-SOEs are Malaysia (5%), India (4%) and South Africa (4%) (Kalotay, 2017).

SOEs are an integral part of their home country institutions (Cui & Jiang, 2012) in which the government is a shareholder through its equity investment in them. The institutional theory of the state-owned sector and international business strategy explains the differences in firm strategy by exploring the role of the state, institutional framework and environment that influence strategic choices (Deng & Yang, 2015; Du & Boateng, 2015; Estrin et al., 2016; Peng et al., 2016; Huang et al., 2017; Zhou et al., 2017). Different institutional conditions and transitions create different strategic choices and impacts on the performance of international businesses (Peng et al., 2008; Cui et al., 2011).

State-owned enterprises in many Asian countries continue to play a significant economic role in economic growth and competitiveness. Similarly, SOEs are vital economic drivers in countries like Vietnam, China, Singapore and Malaysia. Their domestic and international business focuses mainly on large-scale industries such as public utilities, banking, telecommunications, mining, oil and gas and infrastructure projects. The globalisation of SOEs is primarily driven by the need to access scarce resources (e.g. natural resources, supply chain and technology) and markets and overcome regulatory constraints (e.g. trade barriers).

3.1.1   China

China's OFDI
Over the last 60 years, China has developed into the second biggest economy in the world, with nearly 1.4 billion people and a GDP of US $16.49 trillion, only after the US (US $21.92 trillion), based on GDP reported in 2020. According to the State Council Information Office of the People's Republic of China (2019), from 1952 until now, China has reported impressive growth in all aspects. Remarkably, GDP increased by 174 folds, per capita GDP by 70 folds, trade in goods 2380 folds and industrial added value 970 folds. China has occupied an essential role in the world supply chain. It has built a comprehensive economy with production covering all sections in the United Nations' International Standard Industrial Classification of All Economic Activities. China ranks first in the world in terms of the output of many industrial products.

China has become a major global player in outward foreign direct investments (OFDI) in the last two decades through its SOEs and involvement in the biggest infrastructural investment project in the world, the Belt and Road Initiative (BRI). Chinese SOEs' fundamental OFDI business strategy is aligned with the host nation's strategic priority.

The emergence of Chinese m-SOEs is a relatively new phenomenon, many of which operated as domestic entities initially and subsequently expanded into OFDI. These SOEs have ventured offshore seeking resources and markets. The Chinese m-SOEs operate predominantly in banking and insurance telecommunications, aviation, oil and gas (energy), manufacturing, agriculture, construction, railroad, consumer goods, mining and logistics. Chinese m-SOEs include China National Petroleum (China's largest non-financial SOEs) and Lenovo Group Ltd., a telecommunication and software company, which is a spin-off of the Chinese Academy of Science and remains a state-owned enterprise. Lenovo successfully acquired the personal computing division of IBM Corporation for $1.75 billion. There are also private-owned Chinese companies that are perceived to have strong state influence (Musacchio et al., 2015), including companies like Huawei, Alibaba and TikTok. They are all prominent in the global markets.

In general, Chinese companies tend to acquire foreign targets with lower profitability, larger size, higher debt levels and more patents. However, private-owned Chinese MNCs differ from m-SOEs with regard to their "preferences for location in offshore financial centres, industry diversification, natural resources and technology" (Fuest et al., 2019). This may be evidence of the Chinese government influence on m-SOEs governance to direct their activities to align with government political and economic interests. Fuest et al. (2019) mentions the BRI and Made in China 2025 as government interests that may influence m-SOEs investment decisions.

The growing support from the central government for the internationalisation of SOEs is also evident in China's "Going Global" policy. These Chinese state-owned firms would work closely with the home government in their OFDI (Child & Rodrigues, 2005; Cui & Jiang, 2012) to support the interests of the state.

UNCTAD (2017) reports that governments prefer majority ownership of m-SOEs. Full control is the most prevalent, with full ownership and majority control accounting for just over 60% of all multinational state-owned firms. In the case of China, the government is highly represented on the board. M-SOEs are closely connected to various ministries.

The expanding presence of Chinese m-SOEs globally has raised contentious issues in the West, especially those countries with vastly different political systems from China, due to state ownership, motivation and the lack of transparency. Recently, some Chinese m-SOEs have attracted much attention and negativity from host governments because of concerns that these m-SOEs help carry out their home government political and economic agendas. The BRI is arguably the most controversial projects despite its positive developmental impacts in the host countries. One of the main concerns of countries along the new BRI "silk road" is the level of state ownership of the participants, engineering companies and banks, in the construction of the BRI infrastructure. In addition, the BRI has been dragged into geopolitics as the superpowers jostle for regional influence.

China's Standing in the Global Supply Chain

China has been regarded as a global economic powerhouse and the "world's factory" in the last two decades. The state has always supported strategic outbound foreign investment aimed at acquiring expertise, advanced technology and resources in order to sustain its economic development. This stance is consistent with the country's "Go Global", BRI and "Made in China 2025" programmes that the state hopes will help China continue to advance the global manufacturing value chain and its international standing.

The recent US-China trade war will probably see a change in global economic structures. This change is fundamentally driven by the power conflict between these two countries. According to observers, the US is ready to decouple its economy from China. On the other hand, China is looking at increasing trade and investment outside of North America to avoid being dependent on the US as links in their supply chains. Such strategic considerations have seen some of China's SOEs securing access to resources in foreign countries. In particular, the increasing involvement of m-SOEs' in Greenfield projects suggests that they will remain an essential player in the world economy in the foreseeable future. The m-SOEs tend to be involved in fewer deals than Chinese private acquirers, but they are engaged in undertaking larger deals (Fuest et al., 2019). However, host countries do practise screening of foreign investments in industries that are considered by the home countries as having a strategic national interest and would bar foreign SOEs from controlling them.[3]

3.1.2   Vietnam's OFDI

Vietnam is still relatively new to SOE's OFDI activity, compared to China and other emerging markets in Asia such as Singapore and Malaysia. The government reported recently that Vietnamese firms invested US $528.78 million in 172 projects in 33 countries and territories in 2019,

---

[3] While Chinese software giant Lenovo succeeded in the acquisition of the personal computing division of IBM Corporation for $1.75 billion in 2005, the deal resulted in a backlash over the transaction's national security implications from Congress and the Pentagon.

representing a year-on-year increase of 10.7%. Recent OFDI activities are undertaken by both SOEs and private companies.

At the end of 2019, Vietnamese firms have invested a total of US $20.6 billion in 1321 projects in 78 countries and territories. These countries include Russia ($2.8 billion), Cambodia ($2.7 billion), Venezuela ($1.8 billion), Myanmar ($1.3 billion), Algeria ($1.2 billion), the US ($690 million) and Australia ($400 million). These OFDI investments are mainly in mining (US $3.5 billion), telecommunications (US $1.61 billion), agriculture (US $1.56 billion), electricity production (US $809 million), financial and banking (US $787 million) and real estate (US $384 million).

SOEs are typically geared to invest US $13.8 billion abroad, of which US $6.7 billion have been completed. PetroVietnam is the leading m-SOE investor with offshore projects totalling US $7.1 billion,[4] followed by Viettel with US $2.13 million and VN Rubber with US $1.412 million. Nevertheless, Viettel is the only Vietnamese company with more than USD 1.0 billion of revenue generated from overseas as it recorded US $1.25 billion of revenue from overseas markets in 2017.[5]

Figures reported by m-SOEs regarding their OFDI investments, however, are not promising. In 2018, based on a report on 114 projects overseas of 19 SOEs, while the total profit earned on profitable projects was US $187 million, 24% lower than the previous year, the total loss reported was US $367 million, 265% higher than the loss in 2017.[6] Profitable projects for Vietnamese m-SOEs overseas were in telecommunication, construction, oil and gas services and hospitality, whereas OFDI in oil exploration and mining was loss-making. The reasons for the poor performance of m-SOEs overseas include increasing competition and inflation in the host market, foreign exchange rate fluctuation and lack of experience in managing OFDI.

These 19 m-SOEs still have another committed US $6.15 billion abroad to executive, which is about 51% of the total registered capital for OFDI. Vietnam's Ministry of Finance is studying legal amendments on State capital at enterprises towards tighter regulation of SOE overseas investment to improve efficiency.

---

[4] Vietnam News, July 2020. Vietnamese firms increase overseas investment-Economy-Vietnam News | Politics, Business, Economy, Society, Life, Sports-VietNam News.

[5] https://emime.vn/tin-emime/toan-canh-doanh-thu-va-loi-nhuan-cua-10-tap-doan--kinh-te-nha-nuoc-lon-nhat-viet-nam-159.html

[6] https://dantri.com.vn/kinh-doanh/mang-hang-ty-usd-dau-tu-ra-nuoc-ngoai-doanh-nghiep-nha-nuoc-lo-nang-20191018093040394.htm

3.2   State Influence of m-SOEs' OFDI
and Governance

3.2.1   Concerns of State Influence on m-SOEs

Much of the global expansion of public and private Chinese enterprises has been the outcome of the Chinese government's proactive stance in encouraging and facilitating its leading domestic firms to go global in recent years. China's expansion was influenced by its official "Go Global" (走出去战略 or *Zǒuchūqū Zhànlüè*) policy first introduced in 1999. The policy was followed by a series of transformative reforms and institutional transitions or factors to facilitate Chinese firms' investment abroad (Redding et al., 2018; Milhaupt, & Pargendler, 2017; Ren et al., 2012; Child & Rodrigues, 2005).

The state, as a shareholder, commits resources,[7] such as capital, favourable policy and subsidy, to their pursuit of business internationalisation. Globerman (2015) observes that many governments provide direct or indirect support for their multinationals, especially m-SOEs, for offshore investment. For instance, Qingdao Haier Group, the global Chinese white goods manufacturer, had access to preferential treatments by the government that was not offered to other Chinese private companies (Holtbrugge & Kreppel, 2012). Therefore, government, through its involvement, has a strong influence on international expansion. The nature of impact is determined by the size of state ownership and the level of affiliation with the home country government (Meyer et al., 2014), putting these firms under ever closer host government's scrutiny and greater control (Li et al., 2014).

On the state's influence in OFDI, at the official policy level, in 2017, the Chinese government announced a set of codified rules for OFDI in three categories—banned, restricted and encouraged. The encouraged sectors are infrastructure projects connected to the BRI initiative, high-tech and advanced manufacturing businesses, oil and gas, mining, agriculture, forestry and service sector. The "negative list" ban investments in property, hotel, films, entertainment and sports. According to the Guideline jointly developed by several government authorities,[8] the OFDI

---

[7] See Peng (2001) for the resource-based view of business internationalisation.

[8] They are the National Development and Reform Commission, Ministry of Commerce, People's Bank of China and Ministry of Foreign Affairs.

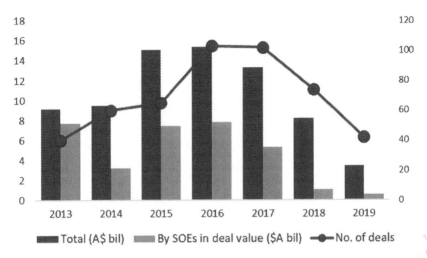

Fig. 3.2 China's OFDI into Australia. (Data collected from the Demystifying Chinese Investment in Australia series by KPMG and the University of Sydney in various years (KPMG & the University of Sydney (2013 to 2020))) (LHS: A$ bil; RHS: Number of deals)

made by Chinese enterprises must avoid investments in these sectors and cooperate with the relevant local authorities.

From a host country's perspective, state-invested multinationals are coming under greater scrutiny as they are treated with suspicion about their business motives. M-SOEs are subject to more stringent evaluations than privately owned multinationals. Take Australia for example, the flow of China's OFDI into Australia peaked in 2016 with 103 deals valued at a total of A$ 15.36 billion, of which 51% was from Chinese SOEs (Fig. 3.2). In recent years, China's OFDI into Australia has declined significantly, partly due to the impact of the overall redirection of China's OFDI from developed markets to BRI projects and partly because of the increased scrutiny of the Australian government.

The transparency of m-SOEs in their relationships and dealings with the authorities poses a challenge for many host governments. In the absence of transparent disclosure, the host country would always perceive state-owned entities as being beholden to the state and would bid home government interests. Tingley et al. (2015) studied Chinese M&A attempts with US firms and found that restrictions were often imposed on security-sensitive industries, economically distressed industries and sectors that US companies faced restrictions in China's M&A markets.

In recent years, Chinese m-SOEs have encountered national security issues in host countries where host governments have imposed restrictions or outright rejections of M&A proposals. The main reason is to refrain m-SOEs from investing in ventures that may raise sensitive sociopolitical issues. One of the underlying factors creating this impasse is political or geopolitical issues between home and host countries. Many Chinese SOEs have been prevented from M&A activities in Western countries due to their state ownership concerns. In Australia and the US, for example, they attract strong political opposition. Table 3.1 presents selected Chinese SOEs' M&A proposals that have been rejected by host governments across the world.

State-invested multinationals are usually welcomed in a host economy if the home country is a close ally. Still, due to government ownership and influence, they are considered a threat to the host country's security if the home country is regarded as unfriendly. Therefore, many criticise China for not committing to reforming the state sector to allow the private sector to play a more prominent role in the economy and open industries dominated by state-owned firms to foreign companies to alleviate state-induced security concerns.

Table 3.1 Selected rejected M&A projects of Chinese m-SOEs

Date	Chinese company	Target	Host
2002	CNPC	Slavic oil companies of Russian	Russia
2004	China Minmetals Corporation	Noranda Pty Ltd	Australia
2005	Qingdao Haier Group	Maytag Corporation	US
2005	China National Offshore Oil Corporation	Unocal Corporation	US
2008	China Minmetals Corporation	Gaby Copper	Chile
2009	Aluminum Corporation of China Limited	Rio Tinto	Australia
2016	CK Infrastructure Holdings Ltd	Ausgrid	Australia
2018	CK Infrastructure Holdings Ltd	APA Group	Australia
2019	Huawei	5G mobile network	Australia
2020	Mengniu Dairy Company	Lion Dairy & Drinks	Australia
2021	China State Construction Engineering Corp	Probuild	Australia

3.2.2   Governance Concerns of m-SOEs

Governance Interference and the Agency Problem
While state support may be critical for the success of SOEs in their internationalisation development, it also comes about with severe agency problem challenges. Chinese government involvement in SOEs may include appointing politicos to serve as board members. The Communist Party of China (CPC) evaluates the performance of corporate executives. CEOs of the largest 53 national SOEs are appointed directly by the Party's Organizational Department (Morck et al., 2007). The Chinese government is also highly represented on the board of many m-SOEs, and they are closely connected to various ministries.

Government influence is not limited to firms that it has a controlling interest but also those where it is a minority shareholder. There are situations when the state shareholder has "golden shares" that give them the veto power over changes to the company's charter. Although golden shares are now limited in most countries in the European Union, they are still available in other markets. OECD recommends against the existence of golden shares after privatisation (OECD, 2019). OECD advises that governments should disclose the existence of any shareholders' agreements that allow the state shareholder to have more control over the corporation disproportionate to their equity ownership in the enterprise (OECD, 2015).

It should also be noted that apart from direct state ownership, financial subsidies and political and bureaucratic interventions are other aspects of government influence on SOEs. A recent study by Cong et al. (2020) finds that "changes in the function, state control and structure of governance" in SOEs are influenced by political ideology and institution. Also, government interventions are for "political interests rather than for firms' effectiveness" (Cong et al., 2020). There is a need for Vietnam to define and disclose a transparent state ownership policy and financial and non-financial performance objectives for all SOEs (OECD, 2020).

Malaysia is another example when it comes to direct state intervention and opaque corporate governance (Huang et al., 2004), especially in the state sector. Malaysian OFDI increased in the 1990s with investments mainly in oil and gas, financial services, tourism and manufacturing. Malaysian GLCs make up a large proportion of OFDI from Malaysia. The seven government-linked investment companies control 35 public listed companies, which means about 42% of the entire Bursa Malaysia. However, over the years, markets have seen large GLC-related scandals both at home and overseas. Examples are National Feedlot, Felda Global Ventures Holdings, East-Coast Rail Link project, Tabung Haji and KWAP, among others.[9] In contrast to Singapore, political interventions by party politicians and ministers in Malaysia, a democratic country, has negatively impacted the performance of many of its SOEs, both at home and abroad. This is further complicated by affirmative regulations that favour the indigenous population.

Singapore is consistently ranked highly as a country for good SOE governance for transparency, accountability, anti-corruption and performance. Countries in the region have looked to Singapore to emulate its approach to mixed enterprises. Singapore's Temasek Holdings Pte Ltd (Temasek) offers an exemplar for sound m-SOE corporate governance. The government kept an arm's length relationship to prevent commercial decision-making from political influence. While the government, as the shareholder of Temasek, has the right to appoint or remove board members and the CEO, there is no government or ministerial representative on the board. Board members are highly qualified and experienced professionals with non-political orientation. The board typically comprises a majority of independent and private sector directors, including foreign nationals. In turn, Temasek manages its portfolio of companies by acting as an active investor by increasing, holding or decreasing the investment holdings without interference in the management of commercial decision-making. Temasek restricts its role to promoting corporate governance within the portfolio companies by fostering talent development and board diversity to support management leadership. Temasek avoids leadership duality by separating the positions of CEO and Chairman, with the Chairman being a non-executive director independent of Temasek's management. Temasek defines itself as having a strictly commercial orientation and a high degree of management independence to pursue commercial objectives. These values are reinforced in the Temasek Charter[10] as follows:

> *"As an active investor, we shape our portfolio by increasing, holding or decreasing our investment holdings. These actions are driven by a set of commercial principles to create and maximise risk-adjusted returns over the long term."*

[9] https://cilisos.my/these-7-companies-own-almost-half-of-all-malaysian-stocks-lets-see-how-this-happened/
[10] Source: https://www.temasek.com.sg/en/who-we-are/our-purpose

"Our portfolio companies are guided and managed by their respective boards and management; we do not direct their business decisions or operations."

"Similarly, our investment, divestment and other business decisions are directed by our board and management. Neither the President of Singapore nor our shareholder, the Singapore Government, is involved in our business decisions."

Singapore's SOE corporate governance is a model worth replicating by other Asian emerging markets. However, the diversity of political systems, populations, cultures and regulatory and institutional environments in different emerging markets may pose a challenge to successfully emulate the Singapore model.

The Organisation for Economic Co-operation and Development (OECD) published an essential reference entitled "SOEs Operating Abroad: An application of the OECD Guidelines on Corporate Governance of State-Owned Enterprises to the Cross-border Operations of SOEs" (OECD, 2009). This document contains critical recommendations for policymakers on SOE good governance in OFDI, which are:

- to provide transparency on public ownership policy and clarity of objectives to be pursued;
- to establish a central ownership function to ensure that SOEs are corporate entities separated from the governmental ones;
- to ensure a clear separation between the State ownership role and other State functions;
- to set an exclusive board of directors for SOEs, with full autonomy and responsibility for the corporate mandate, and to protect SOE board members from undue political influence;
- to promote regular financial and non-financial disclosures, consistent with international reporting standards for listed companies, undertaken by independent, external auditors.

3.3   CONCLUSION

The global growth of m-SOEs has raised many governance challenges for both the state-owned enterprises themselves and host countries. They include concerns about the influence of home country governments on the m-SOEs and their business motivations. State ownership has also raised issues about whether m-SOEs are competing on a level playing field in international business because of government subsidies and preferential treatment, not only to foreign firms but also to other SOEs companies. Some of China's biggest trade partners argue that state subsidies for and intervention in SOEs are distorting markets. Other host governments perceive m-SOEs as agents of their home country and are reluctant to accommodate their business initiatives to protect national security and industrial interests. The factors that can affect the levels of OFDI, therefore, are geopolitics, national security concerns, economic uncertainty and stricter regulatory control. We will continue to elaborate on the agency problem and other corporate governance challenges of SOEs in the coming chapter.

Despite these concerns, the growing expansion of m-SOEs in the world and their contribution to the development of regions that are most in need of capital and know-how is applaudable.

References

Centre for Strategic and International Studies. (2020). The Biggest But Not the Strongest: China's Place in the Fortune Global 500. August 8. Retrieved February 25, 2021, from https://www.csis.org/blogs/trustee-china-hand/biggest-not-strongest-chinas-place-fortune-global-500

Child, J., & Rodrigues, S. (2005). The Internationalisation of Chinese Firms: A Case for Theoretical Extension. *Management and Organization Review, 1*, 381–410.

Cong, P. N., Dinh, K. N. T., & Phuoc, V. H. (2020). Politics and Institution of Corporate Governance in Vietnamese State-owned Enterprises. *Managerial Auditing Journal, 35*(5), 667–684. https://doi.org/10.1108/MAJ-02-2018-1810

Cui, L., & Jiang, F. (2012). State Ownership Effect on Firms' FDI Ownership Decisions under Institutional Pressure: A Study of Chinese Outward Investing Firms. *Journal of International Business Studies, 43*, 264–284.

Cui, L., Jiang, F., & Stening, B. (2011). The Entry-Mode Decision of Chinese Outward FDI: Firm Resources, Industry Conditions, and Institutional Forces. *Thunderbird International Business Review, 53*(4), 483–499.

Deng, P., & Yang, M. (2015). Cross-border Mergers and Acquisitions by Emerging Market Firms: A Comparative Investigation. *International Business Review, 24*(1), 157–172.

Du, M., & Boateng, A. (2015). State Ownership, Institutional Effects and Value Creation in Cross-border Mergers & Acquisitions by Chinese Firms. *International Business Review, 24*(3), 430–442.

Estrin, S., Meyer, K. E., Nielsen, B. B., & Nielsen, S. (2016). Home Country Institutions and the Internationalisation of State Owned Enterprises: A Cross-country Analysis. *Journal of World Business, 51*(2), 294–307.

Fuest, C., Hugger, F., Sultan, S., & Xing, J. (2019). Chinese Acquisitions Abroad: Are they Different?. CESifo and Center for Economic Studies, University of Munich. Retrieved May 6, 2020, From http://eenee.org/DocDL/wp-2019-fuest-etal-chinese-acquisitions-abroad.pdf

Globerman, S. (2015). Host Governments Should Not Treat State-owned Enterprises Differently than Other Foreign Investors. *Columbia FDI Perspectives*, No. 138., Columbia Centre for Sustainable Investment.

Holtbrugge, D., & Kreppel, H. (2012). Determinants of Outward Foreign Direct Investment from BRIC Countries: An Explorative Study. *International Journal of Emerging Markets, 7*, 4–30.

Huang, Y., Morck, R., & Yeung, B. (2004). ASEAN Countries, External Threat, FTAA, and Internal Institutional Weaknesses. *Business and Politics, 6*(1), 1–45.

Huang, Y., Xie, E., Li, Y., & Reddy, K. S. (2017). Does State Ownership Facilitate Outward FDI of Chinese SOEs? Institutional Development, Market Competition, and the Logic of Interdependence between Governments and SOEs. *International Business Review, 26*(1), 176–188.

IMF. (2020). Chapter 3: State-Owned Enterprises: The Other Government, *Fiscal Monitor Series*, April. Retrieved February 27, 2021, from https://www.imf.org/en/Publications/FM/Issues/2020/04/06/fiscal-monitor-april-2020

Kalotay, K. (2017). Kyoto, Japan State-owned Multinationals: an Emerging Market Phenomenon?, Kyoto International Conference on *The Future of Transition Economics: Emerging Multinationals and Historical Perspective*, December 9. https://www.researchgate.net/publication/322378298_State-Owned_Multinationals_An_Emerging_Market_Phenomenon

KPMG & The University of Sydney. (2013 to 2020). Demystifying Chinese Investment in Australia. Sydney, Australia.

Li, M. H., Cui, L., & Lu, J. (2014). Varieties in State Capitalism: Outward FDI Strategies of Central and Local State-owned Enterprises from Emerging Economy Countries. *Journal of International Business Studies, 45*, 980–1004.

Meyer, K., Ding, Y., Li, J., & Zhang, H. (2014). Overcoming Distrust: How State-owned Enterprises Adapt Their Foreign Entries to Institutional Pressures Abroad. *Journal of International Business Studies, 45*, 1005–1028.

Milhaupt, C. J., & Pargendler, M. (2017). Governance Challenges of Listed State-Owned Enterprises around the World: National Experiences and a Framework for Reform. Working Paper N° 352/2017, European Corporate Governance Institute (ECGI) Working Paper Series in Law, April 2017.

Morck, R., Yeung, B., & Zhao, M. (2007). Perspectives on China's Outward Foreign Direct Investment. Retrieved February 20, 2021, from https://web2-

bschool.nus.edu.sg/wp-content/uploads/media_rp/publications/ W2Xvh1392617897.pdf

Musacchio, A., Lazzarini, S., & Aguilera, R. (2015). New Varieties of State Capitalism: Strategic and Governance Implications. *Academy of Management Perspectives, 29*(1), 115–131.

OECD. (2009). *SOEs Operating Abroad: An application of the OECD Guidelines on Corporate Governance of State-Owned Enterprises to the Cross-border Operations of SOEs*, OECD Publishing, Paris.

OECD. (2015). *OECD Guidelines on Corporate Governance of State-Owned Enterprises* (2015 Edn). OECD Publishing. Retrieved December 01, 2020, from https://doi.org/10.1787/9789264244160-en

OECD. (2019). *A Policy Maker's Guide to Privatisation*. OECD Publishing. Retrieved January 15, 2021, from https://www.oecd.org/ corporate/a-policy-maker-s-guide-to-privatisation-ea4eff68-en.htm

OECD. (2020). *Multi-dimensional Review of Viet Nam: Towards an Integrated, Transparent and Sustainable Economy*. OECD Development Pathways. OECD Publishing. Retrieved January 15, 2021, from https://doi. org/10.1787/367b585c-en

Peng, M., Sunny, L. S., Pinkham, B., & Chen, H. (2008). The Institution-based View as a Third Leg for a Strategy Tripod. *Academy of Management Perspectives, 23*(3), 63–81.

Peng, M. W. (2001). The Resource-based view and International Business. *Journal of Management, 27*(6), 803–829.

Peng, M. W., Bruton, G. D., Stan, C. V., & Huang, Y. (2016). Theories of the (State-owned) Firm. *Asia Pacific Journal of Management, 33*(2), 293–317.

Redding, K. S., Xie, E., & Tang, Q. (2018). The Transformational Dynamics and Outward Foreign Direct Investment of State-owned Enterprises. *International Journal of Public Sector Management, 31*(2), 241–264.

Ren, B., Liang, H., & Zheng, Y. (2012). An Institutional Perspective and the Role of the state for Chinese OFDI. In I. Alon, M. Fetscherin, & P. Gugler (Eds.), *Chinese International Investments* (pp. 11–37). Palgrave Macmillan.

The State Council Information Office of the People's Republic of China. (2019). China and the World in the New Era, September. Retrieved January 5, 2021, from http://english.www.gov.cn/archive/whitepaper/201909/27/content_ WS5d8d80f9c6d0bcf8c4c142ef.html

Tingley, D., Xu, C., Chilton, A., & Milner, H. (2015). The Political Economy of Inward FDI: Opposition to Chinese Mergers and Acquisitions. *The Chinese Journal of International Politics, 8*, 27–57.

UNCTAD. (2017). *World Investment Report 2017: Investment and the Digital Economy*. United Nations, New York and Geneva.

Zhou, K. Z., Gao, G. Y., & Zhao, H. (2017). State Ownership and Firm Innovation in China: An Integrated View of Institutional and Efficiency Logics. *Administrative Science Quarterly, 62*(2), 375–404.

CHAPTER 4

Corporate Governance of State-Invested Enterprises

State-owned enterprise: An agent without a principal
—Aharoni (1982)

This chapter reviews the literature on State ownership and its implications for corporate governance and business performance in emerging markets to understand the significance of the state as an economic actor.

We argue that there is a need for a new theoretical paradigm to reflect the different motivations of state-invested enterprises in business, whether at home or abroad. The discussion in previous chapters has alluded us to the potential agency problems of having the state shareholder. This chapter will highlight how the state-related agency problem is unique, totally different from that of other blockholders who are commercial, institutional investors. A review of the literature on agency theory is where we shall start.

4.1   THE LITERATURE ON STATE OWNERSHIP
AND CORPORATE GOVERNANCE

4.1.1   The State as a Shareholder: A New Perspective
of Agency Theory

The State Shareholder and Managers: The Principal-Agent Relationship
The agency problem arises from conflicts of interests between the owners
of the business and the professionally hired managers when ownership and
management of companies become separated in a modern corporation.

Armour et al. (2009) identify three generic agency problems in business firms: the conflict between the firm's owners and its hired managers,
the majority and the minority owners and the firm and other parties con-
tracted by the firm. While resolving all three problems is equally crucial to
the firm's success in achieving its strategic direction, this book focuses on
the first two problems. These problems are intensified when the state has
a controlling interest or holds an equity stake at a significant minority
level. However, the complexity of the issues depends on the motivation
and behaviour of the state (Milhaupt & Pargendler, 2017).[1]

Since the early years of the twentieth century, a survey of the top 20
largest non-financial firms in the US showed that the shareholding structures of these firms were so scattered that they were not controlled by the
stock owners. In the evolution of the corporate system, the shareholders
have lost control of their property (Berle & Means, 1932).

The agency problem was further described by Jensen and Meckling
(1976) as a contract in which shareholders—the principal—delegate the
decision-making power to the manager—the agent—to perform a service
on their behalf. The central assumption is that both parties in the relationship are utility maximising, and therefore, it is likely that the agent will not
always act in the best interests of the principal. Typical agency problems
are managerial entrenchment (Walsh & Seward, 1990) and perquisite
consumption (Gedajlovic & Shapiro, 1998), making value-destroying
acquisitions (Martynova & Renneboog, 2008).

---

[1] Milhaupt, C. J. & Pargendler, M. 2017, "Governance Challenges of Listed State-Owned
Enterprises around the World: National Experiences and a Framework for Reform", Working
Paper N° 352/2017, European Corporate Governance Institute (ECGI) Working Paper
Series in Law, April 2017.

To converge the interests of the principals and agents, the former has to establish appropriate incentives for the agent and monitor the agent's activities, which leads to positive monitoring and bonding costs to reduce the agency problem and possible residual loss, the so-called agency costs. Jensen and Meckling (1976) argue that the magnitude of the agency problem and, hence, agency costs depend on the ease with which managers can exercise their own preferences as opposed to value-maximising decisions, the costs of monitoring and bonding activities, measuring and evaluating managers' performance, compensating managers and replacing the agent. The key to the agency problem is the incentive alignment between the principal and the agent (P-A) and the effective monitoring of the agent, the solutions of which rely on an efficient governance context prevalent in most developed economies. In emerging markets, the unique set of agency concerns arising from having the state as the shareholder makes these suggested solutions ineffective, and the agency problem thus remains intensive.

There are several aspects of the role of the state as a shareholder that intensify the firm's agency problem. Firstly, as a shareholder of the firm, the state is likely to have a weak ability to exercise monitoring on corporate managers due to the lack of motivation and expertise in directly managing the state capital and the bureaucratic structure of decision-making. The state capital is typically represented and managed by state employees in ministries, provincial government and central government offices, other state-owned enterprises or state capital management agencies (SCMA). In China, for example, more than 70% of listed companies are ultimately owned by the state. Within this group, 72% are ultimately controlled by local governments, 23% by the central government and 4% by research institutions (Wang & Xiao, 2009). The agencies or offices in charge of managing state capital are, in many cases, under personnel constraints and a lack of financial expertise. They are found to be less effective in managing state shares in listed firms than legal person shareholders (Sun & Tong, 2003).

Additionally, as a shareholder, the state has layers of decision-makers, which increases coordination costs. In China, 88% of the listed firms ultimately owned by the state are controlled through two or three layers (Wang & Xiao, 2009).

Lastly, the incentive for monitoring is weak as there are no individual owners (Gupta, 2005). There is a low motivation for state employees who manage state capital as they are remunerated at the state employees' salary level. If the investment is profitable, the person in charge has no reward. However, in cases of severe loss of the state capital, the person in charge would have to face disciplinary charges.

As information asymmetry is the root of the agency problem, when it is difficult for the principal to reduce information asymmetry and exercise effective monitoring to validate the agent's behaviour, the agency problem becomes more severe.

Another critical issue about the state as a shareholder is the lack of strong incentives for active ownership. Jensen and Meckling (1976) discuss that the agency problem could be constrained by the market for the firm itself, which means that the owners always have the option to sell the firm. State shares and assets, however, are not transferred freely in the market due to possible government restrictions on transferring state ownership to the private sector (Fan et al., 2011), making the threat to exit (Hill & Snell, 1989) a less effective monitoring tool for the state shareholder.

The presence of the state as a shareholder also intensifies the agency problem of a firm by weakening the monitoring capacity of debt in the firm. Debt represents a way to mitigate the agency problem by restricting free cash flow and constraining managerial discretion (Jensen, 1986; Phan & Hill, 1995; Wu et al., 2011). Firms ultimately controlled by the government enjoy the status of a state-owned company, which provides easier access to banking financing, especially from state-owned banks. SOEs enjoyed a lower cost of capital due to the preferential interest rate from state-owned banks. On average, over the last two decades, interest rates paid by private borrowers have been 4.3% higher than those paid by SOEs (IMF, 2020). Allen et al. (2005) find that in China, most of the bank credit is to serve the state sector rather than the private sector. China banks favour industrial state-owned firms (Wei & Wang, 1997) and state-owned banks, which are found to be inefficient (Allen et al., 2009) and tend to provide easy credit when they lend to firms with greater state ownership (Firth et al., 2008). This could potentially create a moral hazard problem for both lenders and borrowers, which is the root of bad debt. The inadequacy of debt and bankruptcy mechanisms in some emerging markets coupled with moral hazard issues in lending to firms with state-owned status (Wei & Wang, 1997) impairs the capacity of debt as an effective mechanism to mitigate the agency problem.

Overall, due to weak monitoring ability and ownership incentive of the State shareholder, SOEs are considered an agent without a principal

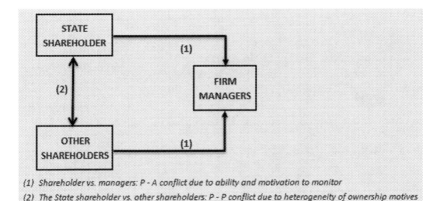

(1) Shareholder vs. managers: P - A conflict due to ability and motivation to monitor
(2) The State shareholder vs. other shareholders: P - P conflict due to heterogeneity of ownership motives

Fig. 4.1 The state shareholder agency model

(Aharoni, 1982). Consequently, we argue that there is potentially a severe agency problem between the state shareholder and firm managers, as illustrated by the arrow (1) in Fig. 4.1.

The State Shareholders and Other Shareholders:
The Principal-Principal Conflict
The classic agency theory focuses on the principal-agent conflict when the shareholding of the company is so dispersed that shareholders cannot effectively exercise their corporate control rights (Berle & Means, 1932). This is mainly from the perspective of the Anglo-Saxon system.

In many other markets, it seems that ownership is more concentrated. For example, firms in the European markets are typically majority controlled. The largest shareholders are banks, institutional investors, family and corporate shareholders (Barca & Becht, 2001; Goergen et al., 2005; Gugler & Yurtoglu, 2003). Firms in the East Asian markets tend to be family-owned (Claessens et al., 2000).

Large shareholders typically have adequate capacity to control managers (La Porta et al., 1999) as they cooperate closely with management, exercise voting rights and ensure a good voice on the board of directors of the firm (Claessens et al., 2000; Yeh & Woidtke, 2005). Blockholders can also use voting and the threat to exit for monitoring (Hill & Snell, 1989). Therefore, having large shareholders may reduce the traditional principal-agent problem between shareholders and managers of a modern firm.

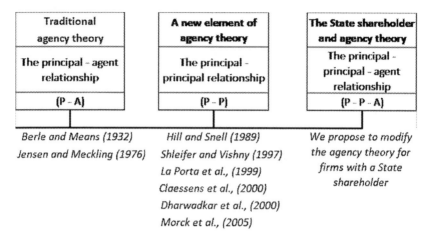

Fig. 4.2   Agency theory developments

The concentration of ownership, however, introduces the so-called Type 2 conflict between the large shareholder and minority shareholders, the expropriation of minority shareholders' interests (Claessens et al., 1999, 2000; Lins, 2003; Shleifer & Vishny, 1997; Yeh & Woidtke, 2005) or "the double principal-agent problem" (Gugler & Yurtoglu, 2003).

Figure 4.2 explains the evolution of agency theory in the literature:

As the government is among the large shareholders of publicly listed firms in many economies around the world, its presence in the firm not only intensifies the traditional principal-agent agency problem between shareholders and managers but also introduces a *unique* form of Type 2 agency problem, the principal-principal conflict between the state as a shareholder versus other non-state shareholders of the firm (Chen et al., 2011).

Coase (1937) describes the firm as a nexus of contracting relationships based on divisible residual claims of the assets and cash flows of the organisation, which can generally be sold without the other contracting parties' permission. The state's presence as a shareholder of the firm raises a crucial set of questions about the implications of these contractual relations between the state and the firm for other shareholders and how these relationships are affected by the changes exogenous to the organisation.

As shareholders of the firm are individuals and parties with conflicting objectives, firm behaviour is the outcome of a complex equilibrium process interacting with the different motivations and intentions of various shareholders (Coase, 1937). Corporate strategic decisions are essentially the outcome of a negotiation process among different shareholders, often favouring large shareholders. According to the theory of political behaviour of state firms (Shleifer & Vishny, 1994), the state shareholder may have complex objectives driven by government socio-economic preferences. The Chinese government, for instance, is particularly concerned about employment, capital market and foreign exchange market stability and international trade (Firth et al., 2012). As these objective functions are imposed on government-controlled firms (Bai et al., 2006), these firms may engage in projects that are not economically desirable (Chen & Young, 2010). Specifically, these firms may conduct M&A projects that serve the purpose of restructuring the state-owned sector, stabilising a particular industry, controlling unemployment or maintaining ownership of national brands, which is unlikely to be in the other shareholders' best interests of these firms. In cases of poor M&A decisions, managers can point to being directed by the government's socio-economic objectives as an excuse for failure (Firth et al., 2012). It is, therefore, plausible to expect that M&As conducted by state-invested firms are not value-maximising. Other firms are subject to more market disciplinary forces and are therefore less likely to conduct M&As with poor prospects.

The autonomy between executive management and the board of directors could be compromised when management has a solid link to state ministries. There are also cases in which the ministers appoint CEOs, bypassing the board (OECD, 2019) and undermining other shareholders' rights. Such politically motivated ownership interference could lead to unclear lines of responsibility and hence weak accountability.

The link between concentrated ownership and firm performance, that is, whether principal-principal conflict exists and matters, depends on the national context (Gedajlovic & Shapiro, 1998). In the US, Holderness and Sheehan (1988) do not agree with the argument that large shareholders expropriate corporate wealth. Similarly, in the Swiss market, despite the high level of pyramids and cross-holding, no evidence of minority shareholder expropriation is found in the M&A context (Holmén & Knopf, 2004) because, according to the authors, the extra-legal institutions offset weak corporate governance. Therefore, legal institutions may constrain potential expropriation problems (Jiang & Peng, 2011). Stan et al. (2014) argue that the degree to which SOEs' resources, such as slack, can be used towards political or economic purpose depends on the transitioning institutional context.

It is surprising to see that the principal-principal conflict of having the state shareholder has been largely neglected in emerging market literature, despite its economic significance. It is not just a P-A problem or P-P problem, but the interaction between the two issues that also matter, which we call "the P-P-A problem". P-P-A also captures the new essence of the agency relationship when its nature has shifted from dichotomy to triangulation, as argued earlier.

The nature of each problem is summarised in Table 4.1. Knowing that the financial performance of the state shareholder is subject to less scrutiny, managers of SOEs may invest in non-profitable projects for personal interests, which is an example of the P-P-A problem. As Shleifer and Vishny (1994) argue in their bargaining model between politicians and managers, bribes from managers to politicians emerge naturally. Another example of the P-P-A problem could be that managers know how to "win" the state shareholder's vote for self-serving proposals. The book sheds light on this P-P-A problem of SOEs in emerging markets.

4.1.2   *The State as an Industry Regulator*

Emerging markets also see the heavy influence of the state on business via industry regulations. Government regulations are relevant for corporate strategy formulation because they are related to products, production, prices, taxes, industry entries and exits (García-Canal & Guillén, 2008). Generally, regulations constrain firms, leading to inefficient production at greater than minimum cost, higher prices and slower technological progress than would occur without regulations (Joskow & Noll, 1981).

According to the Global Competitiveness Report 2019 issued by the World Economic Forum (WEF),[2] Vietnam is number 67 (out of 141 countries covered) for its general business environment and number 79 for the burden of government regulation regulatory environment. Some other countries in the region, such as China (19), India (26), Thailand (50), Indonesia (29) and Cambodia (66), all score better in terms of the regulatory environment, as they are more congenial to trade. Singapore is the world's best performer in terms of the regulation burden score. Over the last ten years, compared to 2010, Vietnam's regulation score has not improved, while China's rank was up by 19 steps and Indonesia 20. This

---

[2] The report available at http://www3.weforum.org/docs/WEF_TheGlobal CompetitivenessReport2019.pdf

Table 4.1 An agency perspective of state ownership

	The traditional agency problem	The new agency problem	The State shareholder agency problem
	Principal-agent conflicts (P-A)	Principal-principal conflicts (P-P)	Principal-principal-agent conflicts (P-P-A)
Ownership	Widely dispersed shareholding	Concentrated shareholding	Concentrated shareholding by the state
Managers	Assumed to be opportunistic. Weakly monitored due to information asymmetry between managers and owners	Assumed to be opportunistic. Well monitored due to power to vote and threat to exit of large shareholders	Assumed to be opportunistic. Weakly monitored due to the capacity and motivation of the state shareholder
Environment	Strong protection of minority interest	Weak protection of minority interest	Weak protection of minority interest
P-A conflict	High	Low	High
Agency costs (P-A)	High	Low	High
Shareholders' ownership motive	Homogeneous (to maximise return)	Homogeneous (to maximise return)	Heterogeneous motives between the state shareholder and non-state shareholders
Residual claim preferences	Homogeneous	Heterogeneous (large shareholders may differ from other shareholders in terms of preference for dividends, financing choices, BOD, compensations, R&D, etc.)	Heterogeneous (the state shareholder may differ from other shareholders in terms of preference for dividends, financing choices, BOD, R&D, compensations, etc.)
P-P conflicts	Low	High	Very high
Expropriation of minority interest	None	High	Very high
Nature of agency problem	Perquisites, self-dealing, entrenchment	Expropriation of minority interests	Both
Principal costs	None	Yes	Yes

shows that the regulatory environment in Vietnam is still very restrictive. The level of regulatory control of a country over its industries affects its overall productivity and competitiveness. According to the WEF (2019), the most problematic factors for doing business are policy instability, regulations (especially tax, labour and foreign exchange) and inefficient government bureaucracy.

In a recent move, according to the new Law on Investment (LOI) 2020, No. 61/2020/QH14, Vietnam has classified eight business activities as prohibited and 227 as conditional business activities, down from 267 in the previous law. It signals that the regulatory environment is becoming less restrictive. However, there are other specific issues relating to regulatory control that the Global Competitive Report has pointed out.

It appears that the heavy level of government regulation poses a business burden, and the assessment criteria include long and complicated business procedures, trade barriers and tariffs, bureaucratic customs procedures and restrictive regulations on capital flows and securities exchanges. As a result, although Vietnam scores high in terms of the domestic market size and foreign market size, the WEF's report scored Vietnam low on other criteria, including the soundness of banks, irregular payments and bribes, investor protection and intellectual property protection. Based on the current ranking, much further improvement of the regulatory environment for Vietnamese businesses is needed.

For firms in emerging markets, a high regulation level means more bureaucracy and longer regulatory delay, which potentially results in high business transaction costs, high capital raising costs and heavy lobbying costs (Fan et al., 2011). The more regulated an industry is, the more transaction costs firms belonging to that industry likely have to bear, which reduces their value.

Our arguments lead to the model illustrated in Fig. 4.3 to explain the state's influence on firms' corporate actions and performance via its role as a shareholder and an industry regulator. In this model, we integrate the agency theory of the firm (Jensen & Meckling, 1976) and the theory of political behaviour of state firms (Shleifer & Vishny, 1994) in explaining firm performance. The model also considers the possible impact of the regulatory environment of the industry on the firm.

First, the weak ability of the state shareholder to monitor company management resulting from the issue of low ownership motivation and constrained resources makes the agency problem among these firms potentially more severe.

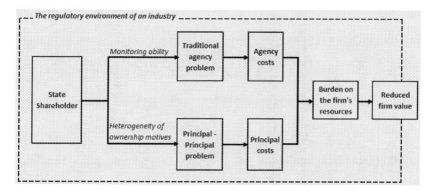

Fig. 4.3   An agency model of the state shareholder in emerging market firms

Second, the heterogeneity of ownership motives between the state shareholder and other shareholders creates a unique principal-principal problem. As the state shareholder may pursue political and economic objectives, it may not exercise active ownership effectively, leading to the firm's principal costs. These two issues are costly and place a burden on the firm's resources, which could negatively affect firm value.

4.2   CORPORATE CHALLENGES OF SOEs IN PRACTICE

In emerging markets, various agencies can manage state capital at different levels of government, including central government, local (provincial) government, relevant ministries, other SOEs or subsidiaries of SOEs. While the following section of the chapter discusses how state capital is managed in Vietnam as a case study, we have also seen similar arrangements of state capital management in China and other markets.

In Vietnam, the state capital of SOEs owned by the central government is typically transferred to the State Capital Investment Corporation (SCIC). SOEs are supervised mainly by central and local government bodies, and the state-owned corporations only manage 10.42% of equitised SOEs, as in Table 4.2.

Figure 4.4 illustrates the various types of state shareholders among major listed firms in Vietnam's pharmaceutical industry as an example. It shows that SCIC had significant holdings in some listed pharmaceutical firms, including 34.71% of Domesco, 43.31% of DHC Pharma and 31.82%

Table 4.2 Supervision of equitised SOEs in Vietnam by type of SCMA

Percentage	1992–2000	2001–2011
Central government/ministry	31.29	31.79
Local government	63.44	57.79
State-owned economic groups	5.27	10.42
Total	100%	100%

Source: Vu Thanh Tu Anh (2012)

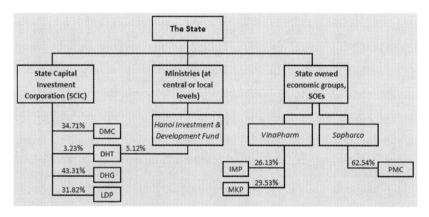

Fig. 4.4 An illustration of SIEs in the pharmaceutical industry in Vietnam. (All firms are listed on HOSE or HNX. Data reported as at December 2014, except for MKP, which was delisted in 2012)

of Lam Dong Pharma. Other firms such as Imexpharm (IMP) and Mekophar[3] (MKP) were held by large state-owned pharmaceutical groups VinaPharm and Sapharco.

In the banking sector, by the end of 2020, the State Bank of Vietnam, which regulates commercial banks, still held 74.8% of Vietcombank (VCB) and 64.46% of Vietinbank (CTG).

The state appoints the state capital management agency (SCMA), which then delegates the responsibility to the state capital representative in a firm to be involved with corporate management and directorship. Consequently, SCMA, the state shareholder, the principal in the relationship with the investee firm, is indeed an agent of the state.

[3] This firm was delisted in 2012.

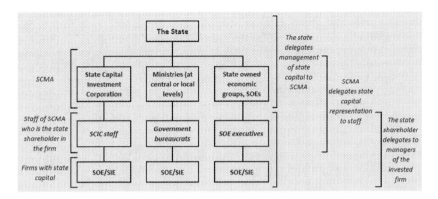

Fig. 4.5 State capital management model in listed SIEs in Vietnam—multilayers of delegation and agency

As Fig. 4.5 illustrates, there are, effectively, at least two layers of delegations between the state and its representative of state capital at firms. Who represents state capital in a firm?

The answer depends on the type of agency employed to manage state capital. If the agent is SCIC, SCIC appoints their staff or an executive member of the investee firm to represent state capital in the firm. In 2012, there were approximately 500 representatives of state capital in 420 firms held by SCIC.[4] In 2020, there were about 150. For firms with state capital under the management of local departments or central ministries, the state capital is typically represented by a government bureaucrat or an in-house executive, for example, the CEO. For firms with state capital under the management of a large state-owned economic group, the state shareholder in the firm is usually an executive director appointed by the group. The quality of state ownership thus depends much on the quality of the state capital management agency.

A vertical cut of the model allows us to see the agency relationship between the state, the SCMA and the firm more clearly, as in Fig. 4.6. This is an extension of Fig. 4.3 to highlight the double levels of agency of having the state shareholder in a Vietnamese firm. On the one hand, the SCMA is an agent in its *backward* agency relationship with the state,

[4] http://www.scic.vn/index.php?option=com_content&view=article&id=46:quyn-va-ngha-v-ca-tng-cong-ty&catid=10:cac-cau-hi-thng-gp&Itemid=9 (Accessed 16 Jan 2015)

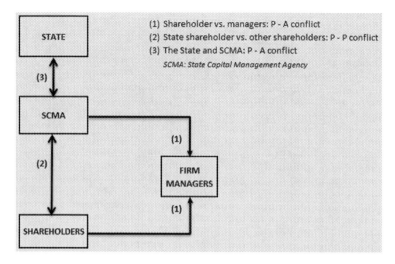

Fig. 4.6   The double agency model of the SCMA as the state shareholder

illustrated by the arrow (3); on the other hand, it is a principal in its *forward agency* relationships with the firm (1) and other shareholders (2).

We will now see how the backward agency problem intensifies the forward agency conflict regarding ownership motivation and autonomy.

4.2.1   The Backward Agency Relationship

The first issue is that although the SCMA is the state shareholder in a firm, it is a relatively lowly motivated shareholder. Taking the SCIC as an example, its mission as prescribed by the state is "to preserve and grow state capital". This could be interpreted as to preserve and, if possible, grow state capital. In cases of substantial state capital loss, the firm managers and the representatives of state capital in an SOE will face severe economic consequences to compensate for the loss.[5] Depending on whether the loss is due to external factors or opportunistic behaviour, weak management capability, legal or illegal transactions, the penalties range from a warning, demotion, dismissal to legal charges. This performance appraisal system is

---

[5] According to the Government Decree No. 66/2011/ND-CP and Circular No. 03/2012/TT-BNV.

skewed towards penalties rather than reward, which is less likely to motivate the state shareholder to effectively engage in the firm. The second issue is that the SCMA is not given full autonomy in managing the investment of state capital. On the one hand, its investment decisions have to comply with the state's policies on investment in the prioritised sectors driven by the overall socio-economic considerations. On the other hand, the state agent is restricted in the ways of and conditions to exit as it is bound by the need to preserve state capital and maintain the stability of business sectors. When market conditions are good, exiting a profitable investment does not pose a problem for the SCMA. However, during a difficult time of the stock market, it will be challenging for the SCIC and state-owned economic groups to exit their unprofitable investment.

The situation is further illustrated here. The Prime Minister specifies the conditions for SCMA to divest and the necessary approval procedures that the SCMA has to follow under each condition. For example, if the SCIC wants to exit an investment in a firm at a price lower than par value and book value, it has to obtain approval from the Ministry of Finance. Furthermore, when a state-owned economic group sells the state shareholding in a firm, it can no longer enjoy the capital gain of the investment. Instead, the entire proceeds of the investment return to the state budget and the Business Arrangements Support Fund[6] of the State. Essentially, SCMAs are not empowered to make effective investment decisions, and they are restricted in using the threat of exit strategy as a monitoring tool for firms in their portfolio. From 2012 to 2015, the SCIC had to divest approximately 500 million state shares of its portfolio of listed and unlisted firms. Many auctions that SCIC held to sell state shares were cancelled because of insufficient subscribers. The SCIC needs to obtain approval for most of its investment and divestiture activities from the Prime Minister or the Ministry of Finance.

SCIC has to preserve and grow state capital. Therefore, SCIC tends to prefer firms that pay high dividends, including Vinamilk, FPT Telecom, VNR and Hau Giang Pharma. This group collectively pays SCIC about VND 2000 billion in dividends annually. SCIC tends to vote for higher dividend payment and against share issues to avoid dilution of state capital, which contradicts the other shareholders who want the firm to grow in many cases by increasing equity. Examples include the cases of Vinamilk's ESOP (employee stock ownership plan) proposal (at some annual

---

[6] Quỹ Hỗ trợ sắp xếp và phát triển doanh nghiệp

shareholder meetings) and the business plan proposal of Sotran (STG) and Bao Bi My Chau (MPC) in the shareholders' meeting of 2012.[7]

As of February 2021, SCIC manages VND 37 trillion of state capital in 145 listed and unlisted enterprises in its portfolio (SCIC, 2021). The current portfolio is relatively modest compared to what used to be under its management, both in terms of the number of securities and capital share. SCIC ownership ratio ranges from as low as 0.02% to 100% of owners' equity. On average, for listed firms in the portfolio, SCIC holds 36%, whereas, for unlisted firms, it holds 47% of equity.

In December 2020, the market value of the listed firms in SCIC's portfolio was US $5.1 billion (see Table 4.3), over 10% of the total market capitalisation of the VN Index.[8] By industry sector, SCIC's listed portfolio was predominantly occupied by investments in Consumer Staples (71.7%). Other important sectors were Financials, Communications and Healthcare. In the last five years, SCIC's largest increase was in Consumer Staples while its largest decrease was in Materials.

The state also transferred state capital in equitised businesses managed by state-owned economic groups to SCIC. In 2020, SCIC received VND 8185.6 billion of the state capital of such transfer.[9] However, SCIC plans to divest more than half of its current portfolio as directed by Notice 281/TB-VPCP. SCIC will retain 39% in the short term and the remaining 5% for the long term (see Fig. 4.7, Panel B).

Table 4.3   SCIC's listed portfolio by sector (as of the end of 2020)

Sector breakdown	Market value of holdings (US$)	Weight in portfolio (%)
Consumer staples	3.6 billion	71.7
Financials	378.7 million	7.6
Communications	327.4 million	6.6
Healthcare	315.7 million	6.3
Consumer discretionary	200.6 million	4
Technology	147.6 million	3
Materials	22.0 million	0.4
Industrials	17.6 million	0.4
Total	**5.1 billion**	**100%**

[7] http://www.baomoi.com/Dai-hoi-co-dong-vuong-ham-ca-map/127/8509990.epi (Accessed date 1 December 2014)
[8] Based on the market value of SCIC's portfolio of listed securities, extracted from Bloomberg as of 31 December 2020.
[9] https://vneconomy.vn/co-phan-hoa-doanh-nghiep-con-cham-20201020110028514.htm

a

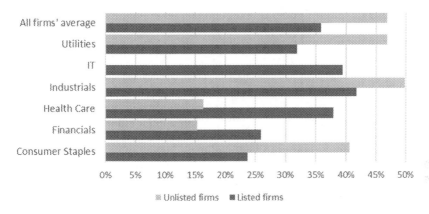

b

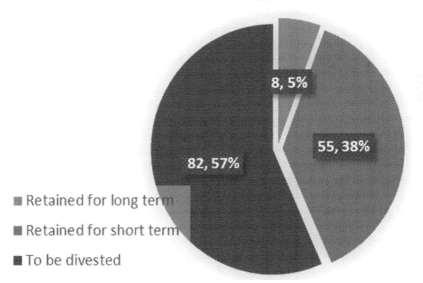

Fig. 4.7   (Panel A): SCIC's portfolio in 2021. (Panel B): SCIC's portfolio struc-ture by investment plan. (Data source. SCIC Website 2021)

In 2018, the government set up the Commission for the Management of State Capital at Enterprises in charge of wholly state-owned enterprises and state capital at other SOEs. CMSC is now managing VND 5000 trillion of state capital, approximately US $230 billion. Since the establishment of CMSC, SCIC has been under the management of CMSC, which further complicates the chain of state capital management agencies.

4.2.2   The Forward Agency Relationship

The motivation and autonomy issues of SCMAs in the backward agency relationship lead to their inefficient management of the state capital representatives in firms, particularly in relation to compensation.

Legally, a representative of state capital (hereafter, *rep* for short) in a firm is paid by the firm for the position he/she assumes. Of the listed firms, the compensation level is expected to be relative to competitive market rates. In practice, the actual compensation level a rep receives is only a state salary. For example, if the SCMA is the state shareholder and appoints its staff member to be a rep in an SIE, the compensation paid by the firm to the rep will not belong to the rep. Rather, the rep's compensation paid by the firm will be transferred to the SCMA. The reason is that being a staff of SCMA, the rep has already earned a state salary paid directly by the SCMA.

Consider the example of an investment officer of a SCMA who is a member of the BOD of a Vietnamese listed firm, as shown in Box 4.1. It can be seen that the level of total compensation for an experienced investment officer is modest and not comparable to the market rate. Moreover, as the payment for the board position assumed by this person is diverted to the SCMA, for the person, this compensation does not incentivise or motivate the reps to perform their role effectively.

Similarly, Vinachem, which is a large Vietnamese state-owned economic group in chemical production, also specifies that if the appointed rep assumes a full-time position in an SIE held by Vinachem, the salary of the rep is paid by the firm. However, if the rep assumes a non-executive position, the compensation paid by the firm to the rep will be transferred directly to Vinachem, and the rep will only be paid by Vinachem according to the state's payroll scale. Therefore, the compensation earned by a rep in an SIE is not competitive and is not tied to the performance of the SIE.

Box 4.1   An example of compensation for a state capital representative

SCMA investment officer: BOD member of a listed firm

Age: 36
Qualification: Master's
degree
Experience: 13 years of
experience in the finance
industry
Job title in the SCMA:
Investment officer
Portfolio under management:
5 firms
Board participation:
non-executive director of a
listed firm

Remuneration:
- From the SCMA: Fixed salary according to
  state salary levels.
- From firm: approximately VND 250m/year
  paid by the firm for the non-executive director
  position, to be transferred to the SCMA

Furthermore, the performance of a rep is assessed based on complying with the State and the Communist Party's directions, political characteristics and ethical conducts, management capability and firm performance,[10] the order of which reflects that the role of a rep in the firm is expected to be more political than economic. As a result, the reps are not well motivated to be a good principal for the firm.

The second issue relates to the potential conflicting voices representing state ownership in a firm. In many cases, there can be more than one representative of state capital in an SOE. As illustrated in Fig. 4.8, the state shareholder has various paths to be involved with the governing bodies of an investee firm. An SCMA can send its people to participate in the Supervisory Board, BOD and the sub-committees of BOD. Alternatively, it can also appoint some senior executives in the firm as reps holding the state's votes in the firm. The level of board participation depends on the level of shareholding of the SCMA. For example, as of December 2014,[11] the SCIC held 57.79% of common equity of VCG, a large construction and exporting firm listed on the HNX. The SCIC assigned state votes to the CEO and six directors on board (out of a total of nine), ranging from 5.43% to 7.51% each. Three of the five members of the Supervisory Board

---

[10] Article 9, Decree No. 66/2011/ND-CP.
[11] Data collected from BOD and BOM information available at http://www.cafef.vn

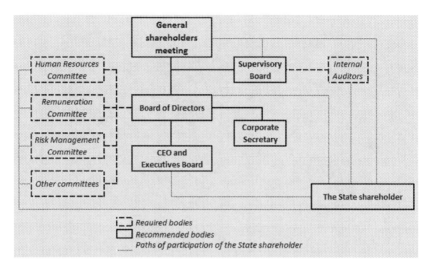

Fig. 4.8 Corporate governance structure of listed firms with State capital

were SCIC's investment officers. As illustrated in this example, in a firm with multiple state reps or proxies, state capital voting power can be allocated equally or unequally to each rep. In shareholders' meetings or board meetings, the voting power of each rep thus depends on the size of state capital represented. In cases where the reps do not agree on their votes or are uncertain about how they should vote, they will have to report the issue back to the SCMA for guidance, adding more layers of decision-making and agency costs to the firm.

These challenges in the current model of state capital management in Vietnam lead to the possibility that the proxy state shareholder in state-invested firms is not motivated to effectively exercise the rights and responsibilities of share ownership. It can be said that the SCMA is not motivated in its position of an agent in the backward agency relationship, which, in turn, results in its reps being an inefficient principal of the firm in the forward agency relationship, potentially leading to *principal costs*.

Overall, state capital is not effectively monitored in the current model. Government agencies do not have the oversight capacity, and there is no rewarding system for the performance of SOEs (Freeman & Van Lan, 2006). To improve the monitoring oversight and performance, the Prime Minister approved reform proposals from each ministry, line ministry, provincial governments and state-owned corporations and economic groups to speed up the reform process of this sector in 2015. Although the Operating Regulation for State Capital Representatives, Circular No. 21/2014/TT-BTC, was issued by the Ministry of Finance in April 2014, detailed guidance governing the compensation of the state capital reps in firms is yet available. This issue remains unresolved to date.

4.3   RESEARCH HYPOTHESES DEVELOPMENT

The review of agency theory literature and the discussion of the practical corporate governance challenges happening in the market lead us to consider a new theoretical framework for the governance of SOEs. Based on the theoretical framework, we model the impacts of state ownership and state control via regulation and on firms' M&A performance. Our model also considers typical corporate governance features of firms in the market and their impacts on M&A performance. This section explains our derivation of the research hypotheses for the empirical study undertaken on listed firms in Vietnam.

4.3.1   Hypotheses Development: State Ownership and M&As

Whether state ownership affects firms' organisational outcomes is an interesting empirical question. It can be inferred from the preceding analysis that SOEs are not independent in their decision-making since they are used as channels for the government to implement political and economic policies. Political interferences could burden firms' resources, resulting in possible principal costs manifested by the low economic efficiency of state-owned firms. This is not unique to Vietnam.

The state sectors are constrained by various social, political and economic objectives and tend to bear the burden of large labour surplus and heavy corporate debt (Bai et al., 2006). Likewise, the potential agency costs resulting from inadequate monitoring by the state shareholder could also be a contributing factor to the inefficiency of the state-owned sector. Due to these potential principal costs and agency costs, it is plausible that state-owned firms are less efficient at conducting M&As, hence, creating less value for their shareholders via M&A than other firms do. This is the *inefficiency hypothesis*.

However, the quality of governments across the world is not the same. La Porta et al. (1999) find that the heterogeneity of location, legal system and cultural background explains the difference in government performance. Additionally, state-owned firms enjoy a number of privileges, such as business networking and funding access. Allen et al. (2005) find that in China, most bank credit serves the state sector and listed sector. Chinese banks favour industrial state-owned firms (Wei & Wang, 1997), and state-owned banks tend to be less strict when they lend to firms with greater state ownership (Firth et al., 2008). State-owned firms tend to have good political connections. It has been reported that politically connected acquirers receive preferential treatment and acquire higher-quality firms during full privatisation in China (Tu et al., 2013).

If state-owned firms make good use of such privileges to get a deal approved quicker, find a trusted M&A partner or access funds for the deal, they could implement their M&A activity at a relatively lower transaction and capital costs. Therefore, an alternative hypothesis, which is the *privileges hypothesis*, could be that M&A by state-owned firms create more value for shareholders than normal firms. The efficiency hypothesis and the privileges hypothesis lead to opposite expected value created from M&A by the state-owned sector, as illustrated by Box 4.2. Adopting the agency perspective as explained in Sect. 4.1, our conjecture was the *inefficiency hypothesis*.

Box 4.2   Hypotheses regarding the impact of state ownership of acquirers on M&A results

Hypothesis	Main argument	Expected impact of the factor on M&A performance	Expected sign
Inefficiency hypothesis	State-owned firms are less efficient than non-state-owned firms in M&A due to political interference and the agency problem of having the state shareholder.	There is a *negative* relationship between the state ownership level of acquirers and firms' M&A performance.	-
Privileges hypothesis	State-owned firms receive more privileges in access to resources, funding and administrative supports in deal structuring and approval. M&A deals could be done at lower capital and transaction costs.	There is a *positive* relationship between the state ownership level of acquirers and firms' M&A performance.	+

Box 4.3 The regulatory hypothesis

Hypothesis	Main argument	Expected impact of the factor on M&A performance	Expected Sign
Regulatory hypothesis	Firms in regulated industries face more constraints in conducting M&As than firms in deregulated industries.	Firms in heavily regulated industries create *less* shareholder wealth from M&A and *less* improvement in operating performance post-M&A than firms in deregulated industries.	–

4.3.2   Hypothesis Development: State Control via Industry Regulations and M&A

In terms of state control via industry regulations, the high regulatory control level, coupled with government bureaucracy, is likely constraining rather than facilitating business activity. While government regulation affects all sectors of an economy, the regulated industries are subject to a higher level of intervention and policy risk (García-Canal & Guillén, 2008). When an industry is deregulated, M&A activity increases and the deals in deregulated industries tend to create more value than those in regulated industries. We, therefore, hypothesised that the M&A of Vietnamese firms in deregulated industries would generate more value and produce better operating performance than those in regulated industries. In other words, it could be anticipated that the level of state control via its role as an industry regulator has a negative impact on a firm's M&A performance. Hereafter, this is referred to as the *regulatory hypothesis* in this book.

4.3.3   Hypothesis Development: Corporate Governance Structure and M&A Performance

The heterogeneity of ownership motives among different firm shareholders permeates through the firm's operation and strategic decisions as each group wants their interests to be considered. Likewise, the firm's corporate governance structure is the outcome of a complex internal negotiation and interaction process between various shareholders to maximise their influence on the firm (Coase, 1937). An example is the dominance of state representatives on boards of Chinese listed firms as opposed to few board seats occupied by individual and non-state institutional shareholders (Su et al., 2008). With a duty to uphold the government's economic and political policies, it is clear that these state representatives will exercise their voting power to direct the firm's decisions towards the state's objectives. However, the performance of SIEs, especially listed ones, is not based on the success of the state's objectives. The dilemma facing managers of listed SIEs is that the capital market assesses their performance in terms of its economic efficiency and profitability and hence market value. As a result, in the firm's best interest, its corporate governance, most importantly, board structure, should be re-balanced against the excessive power of the state shareholder or any other blockholders.

It was worth noting that a relatively high number of listed firms in Vietnam had their CEO as Chairman,[12] which led us to wonder if that corporate governance structure benefits the firm. Having a powerful CEO who is also the chairman of the board, which is known as CEO duality, could arguably be a structure that helps the firm re-balance its board against the state shareholder by placing more weight on the CEO's voice on the board, which can reduce principal costs. Nevertheless, this structure is generally viewed as a double-edged sword (Firth et al., 2014) that could lead to a trade-off between agency costs and principal costs. The argument as to whether CEO duality causes substantial agency costs can run both ways.

Early leadership studies on CEO duality provided evidence of the underperformance of firms with duality (Rechner & Dalton, 1991; Pi & Timme, 1993; Baliga et al., 1996). However, the counter-argument is that the cost of separation should not be underestimated. Such costs are related to information coordination and leader succession planning. Supporters of CEO duality are Brickley et al. (1997) and Dey et al. (2011), who find low announcement returns and poor subsequent performance after US firms announce the separation of CEO and Chairman roles.

---

[12] At the time the research was undertaken from 2013 to 2015, even though the practice was not recommended by the World Bank and IFC (2010, 2012). Please note that the new Law on Enterprises (2020) does not allow SOEs to have CEO duality.

The studies that support CEO duality are in line with the stewardship theory, which argues that a CEO is a good steward of corporate assets (Donaldson & Davis, 1991). Stewardship theorists arguments are based on positive aspects of CEO duality, including empowerment for better leadership (Desai et al., 2003), better communication between management and the board, avoiding information transfer costs (Brickley et al., 1997). In the Australian context, Christensen et al. (2013) also show that small listed firms can achieve optimal governance with less sophisticated structures.

In the institutional context of the Vietnamese market, is the agency theory or stewardship theory more relevant to CEO duality? The answer to this question depends mostly on the motivations of Vietnamese CEOs. If Vietnamese CEOs are driven by personal interests, given the weak monitoring power of the large shareholder, who is often the state, agency costs will likely be high. This is the *agency hypothesis*. However, there are at least four factors that may support stewardship motivation, leading to the *stewardship hypothesis*.

Firstly, CEOs, especially those in SOEs, may view their business leadership role as a stepping stone to a political career, similar to what is observed in China (Li & Qian, 2013). A track record of being a good steward of state assets is critical for future political promotion.

Secondly, Vietnamese CEOs face a market disciplinary threat if they harm their firm value as Vietnamese firms do not have well-established anti-takeover provisions that could insulate them from the market for corporate control (Pham et al., 2015). If CEOs make self-serving acquisitions that destroy firm value, the firm will face a threat of being taken over.

Moreover, CEOs of listed Vietnamese firms are under the additional monitoring of the obligatory Supervisory Board and other recommended sub-committees under the BOD (See Fig. 4.8: Corporate governance structure of listed firms with State capital). Specifically, the Supervisory Board has a minimum of three members who are independent of the CEO. Its members are often internal inspectors, internal auditors or representatives of blockholders and institutional investors. The Supervisory Board has access to all company records and reports directly to the BOD and the GSM.

Furthermore, additional monitoring can come from local Communist Party committees or branches within the firm (Chang & Wong, 2004). It is observed in China that a large number of Chinese listed firms have a party secretary, 7% of which have the secretary as CEO, 16% as COB and

Box 4.4   Hypotheses on the possible impact of CEO duality on firms' M&A outcomes

Hypothesis	Main argument	Expected impact of the factor on M&A performance	Expected sign
Agency hypothesis	CEO duality impairs the effectiveness of the board's monitoring function and allows the CEO to pursue personal interests.	Firms with CEO duality create *less* shareholder wealth from M&A and *less* improvement in operating performance post-M&A than non-duality firms.	−
Stewardship hypothesis	A CEO is motivated to be a good steward of corporate assets, and CEO duality empowers the CEO to deliver strong, unified leadership.	Firms with CEO duality create *more* shareholder wealth from M&A and *more* improvement in operating performance post-M&A than non-duality firms.	+

25% as a board director (Yu, 2013). The various theoretical stands of CEO duality in the literature give rise to the following hypotheses about its possible impact on organisational outcomes. Our conjecture was the *stewardship hypothesis*.

4.4   The Theoretical Framework

We argue that state ownership, regulatory control and corporate governance are important institutional factors to be examined in corporate research in the context of Vietnam. Both factors of state ownership and regulatory control reflect typical features of Vietnam's past centrally planned economy in which resources ownership and control resided in the state. In this context, the corporate governance structure of a firm is also likely shaped by the institutional forces of its environment. The firm chooses the board structure that optimally helps it to overcome the institutional constraints and maximises firm value. The linkage from the current institutional setting of a market and the typical corporate structure to its prior economic structure is supported by the theory of path dependence (Bebchuk & Roe, 2000). Therefore, we propose the following theoretical framework, which consists of the three pillars of state ownership, regulatory control and corporate governance for studies on emerging market firms. We applied this framework in our research on corporate M&A performance of listed firms in Vietnam. Central to this framework is the role of the state as a shareholder (See Fig. 4.9).

Taken altogether, we designed a study to unpack the questions of whether institutional factors such as state ownership, regulatory control and the firm's corporate governance structure affect a firm's M&A decisions and outcomes. These empirical questions demand empirical evidence. Chapter 5 explains the methodology of the research. Chapters 6, 7 and 8 are devoted to findings from the qualitative and quantitative studies and discuss if our hypotheses were supported or rejected by the empirical evidence.

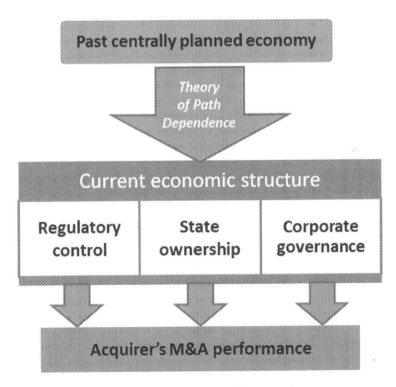

Fig. 4.9 The overall theoretical framework of the research

REFERENCES

Aharoni, Y. (1982). State-owned Enterprise: An Agent Without a Principal. In *Public Enterprise in Less-developed Countries* (pp. 67–76). Cambridge University Press. https://doi.org/10.1017/CBO9780511752988.005.

Allen, F., Qian, J., & Qian, M. (2005). Law, Finance, and Economic Growth in China. *Journal of Financial Economics, 77*(1), 57–116.

Allen, N. B., Iftekhar, H., & Mingming, Z. (2009). Bank Ownership and Efficiency in China: What will Happen in the World's Largest Nation? *Journal of Banking and Finance, 33*(1), 113–130.

Armour, J., Hannsman, H., & Kraakman, R. (2009). *Agency Problems, Legal Strategies, and Enforcement.* Discussion Paper No. 644, 7/2009, Harvard Law School, Cambridge, MA.

Bai, C.-E., Lu, J., & Tao, Z. (2006). The Multitask Theory of State Enterprise Reform: Empirical Evidence from China. *The American Economic Review, 96*(2), 353–357.

Baliga, B. R., Moyer, R. C., & Rao, R. S. (1996). CEO Duality and Firm Performance: What's the Fuss? *Strategic Management Journal, 17*(1), 41–53.

Barca, F., & Becht, M. (2001). *The Control of Corporate Europe.* Oxford University Press.

Bebchuk, L. A., & Roe, M. J. (2000). A Theory of Path Dependence in Corporate Ownership and Governance. *Stanford Law Review, 52*(1), 127.

Berle, A. A., & Means, G. C. (1932). *The Modern Corporation and Private Property.* The Macmillan Company.

Brickley, J. A., Coles, J. L., & Jarrell, G. (1997). Leadership Structure: Separating the CEO and Chairman of the Board. *Journal of Corporate Finance, 3*(3), 189–220.

Chang, E. C., & Wong, S. M. L. (2004). Political Control and Performance in China's Listed Firms. *Journal of Comparative Economics, 32*(4), 617–636.

Chen, S., Sun, Z., Tang, S., & Wu, D. (2011). Government Intervention and Investment Efficiency: Evidence from China. *Journal of Corporate Finance, 17*(2), 259–271. https://doi.org/10.1016/j.jcorpfin.2010.08.004

Chen, Y. Y., & Young, M. N. (2010). Cross-border Mergers and Acquisitions by Chinese Listed Companies: A Principal–principal Perspective. *Asia Pacific Journal of Management, 27*(3), 523–539.

Christensen, J., Kent, P., Routledge, J., & Stewart, J. (2013). Do Corporate Governance Recommendations Improve the Performance and Accountability of Small Listed Companies? *Accounting & Finance, n/a-n/a.* https://doi.org/10.1111/acfi.12055

Claessens, S., Djankov, S., Fan, J., & Lang, L. (1999). *Expropriation of Minority Shareholders: Evidence from East Asia.* Policy Research Paper 2088. World Bank, Washington DC.

Claessens, S., Djankov, S., & Lang, L. H. P. (2000). The Separation of Ownership and Control in East Asian Corporations. *Journal of Financial Economics, 58*(1–2), 81–112.

Coase, R. H. (1937). The Nature of the Firm. *Economica, 4*(16), 386–405.

Desai, A., Kroll, M., & Wright, P. (2003). CEO Duality, Board Monitoring, and Acquisition Performance: a Test of Competing Theories. *Journal of Business Strategies, 20*(2), 137–156.

Dey, A., Engel, E., & Liu, X. (2011). CEO and Board Chair Roles: To Split or Not to Split? *Journal of Corporate Finance, 17*(5), 1595–1618.

Dharwadkar, R., George, G., & Brandes, P. (2000). Privatisation in Emerging Economies: An Agency Theory Perspective. *The Academy of Management Review, 25*(3), 650–669.

Donaldson, L., & Davis, J. H. (1991). Stewardship Theory or Agency Theory: CEO Governance and Shareholder Returns. *Australian Journal of Management (University of New South Wales), 16*(1), 49.

Fan, J. P. H., Wei, K. C. J., & Xu, X. (2011). Corporate Finance and Governance in Emerging Markets: A Selective Review and an Agenda for Future Research. *Journal of Corporate Finance, 17*(2), 207–214.

Firth, M., Lin, C., & Wong, S. M. L. (2008). Leverage and Investment under a State-owned Bank Lending Environment: Evidence from China. *Journal of Corporate Finance, 14*(5), 642–653.

Firth, M., Malatesta, P. H., Xin, Q., & Xu, L. (2012). Corporate Investment, Government Control, and Financing Channels: Evidence from China's Listed Companies. *Journal of Corporate Finance, 18*(3), 433–450.

Firth, M., Wong, S. M. L., & Yang, Y. (2014). The Double-edged Sword of CEO/Chairperson Duality in Corporatised State-owned firms: Evidence from top Management Turnover in China. *Journal of Management & Governance, 18*(1), 207–244.

Freeman, N., & Van Lan, N. (2006). *Corporate Governance in Vietnam: The Beginning of a Long Journey.* Private Sector Discussions. World Bank, Washington, DC.

García-Canal, E., & Guillén, M. F. (2008). Risk and the Strategy of Foreign Location Choice in Regulated Industries. *Strategic Management Journal, 29*(10), 1097–1115.

Gedajlovic, E. R., & Shapiro, D. M. (1998). Management and Ownership Effects: Evidence from Five Countries. *Strategic Management Journal (1986–1998), 19*(6), 533.

Goergen, M., Renneboog, L., & Correia da Silva, L. (2005). When do German firms Change Their Dividends? *Journal of Corporate Finance, 11*(1–2), 375–399.

Gugler, K., & Yurtoglu, B. B. (2003). Corporate Governance and Dividend Payout Policy in Germany. *European Economic Review, 47*(4), 731–758.

Gupta, N. (2005). Partial Privatisation and Firm Performance. *The Journal of Finance, 60*(2), 987–1015.

Hill, C. W. L., & Snell, S. A. (1989). Effects of Ownership Structure and Control on Corporate Productivity. *The Academy of Management Journal, 32*(1), 25–46.

Holderness, C. G., & Sheehan, D. P. (1988). The Role of Majority Shareholders in Publicly Held Corporations: An Exploratory Analysis. *Journal of Financial Economics, 20*(0), 317–346.

Holmén, M., & Knopf, J. D. (2004). Minority Shareholder Protections and the Private Benefits of Control for Swedish Mergers. *Journal of Financial and Quantitative Analysis, 39*(01), 167–191.

IFC. (2010). *Corporate Governance Manual.* Hanoi International Finance Corporation.

IFC. (2012). *Vietnam Corporate Governance Scorecard.* International Finance Corporation.

IMF. (2020). Fiscal Monitor, April.

Jensen, M. C. (1986). Agency Costs of Free Cash Flow, Corporate Finance and Takeovers. *The American Economic Review, 76*(2), 323–329.

Jensen, M. C., & Meckling, W. H. (1976). Theory of the Firm: Managerial Behavior, Agency Costs and Ownership Structure. *Journal of Financial Economics, 3*(4), 305–360.

Jiang, Y., & Peng, M. W. (2011). Principal-principal Conflicts During Crisis. *Asia Pacific Journal of Management, 28*(4), 683–695.

Joskow, P. L., & Noll, R. G. (Eds.). (1981). *Regulation in Theory and Practice: An Overview.* The MIT Press.

La Porta, R., Lopez-de-Silanes, F., & Shleifer, A. (1999). Corporate Ownership around the World. *Journal of Finance, 54*(2), 471–517.

Li, J., & Qian, C. (2013). Principal-principal Conflicts Under Weak Institutions: A Study of Corporate Takeovers in China. *Strategic Management Journal, 34*(4), 498–508.

Lins, K. V. (2003). Equity Ownership and Firm Value in Emerging Markets. *Journal of Financial and Quantitative Analysis, 38*(1), 159–184.

Martynova, M., & Renneboog, L. (2008). A Century of Corporate Takeovers: What Have We Learned and Where Do We Stand? *Journal of Banking & Finance, 32*(10), 2148–2177.

Milhaupt, C. J., & Pargendler, M. (2017). *Governance Challenges of Listed State-Owned Enterprises around the World: National Experiences and a Framework for Reform.* Working Paper N° 352/2017, European Corporate Governance Institute (ECGI) Working Paper Series in Law, April.

Morck, R., Wolfenzon, D., & Yeung, B. (2005). Corporate Governance, Economic Entrenchment, and Growth. *Journal of Economic Literature, 43*(3), 655–720.

OECD. (2019). *Summary Record.* 12th Meeting of the Asia Network on Corporate Governance of State-Owned Enterprises Manila, Philippines

Pham, N., Oh, K. B., & Pech, R. (2015). Mergers and Acquisitions: CEO Duality, Operating Performance and Stock Returns in Vietnam. *Pacific-Basin Finance Journal, 35*, 298–316. https://doi.org/10.1016/j.pacfin.2015.01.007

Phan, P. H., & Hill, C. W. L. (1995). Organisational Restructuring and Economic Performance in Leveraged Buyouts: An Ex Post Study. *Academy of Management Journal, 38*(3), 704.

Pi, L., & Timme, S. G. (1993). Corporate Control and Bank Efficiency. *Journal of Banking and Finance, 17*(2–3), 515–530.

Rechner, P. L., & Dalton, D. R. (1991). CEO Duality and Organisational Performance: A Longitudinal Analysis. *Strategic Management Journal, 12*(2), 155–160.

SCIC. (2021). Retrieved February 15, 2021, from http://www.scic.vn/index.php/vi/hoa-t-a-ng-kinh-doanh/danh-ma-c-qua-n-la

Shleifer, A., & Vishny, R. W. (1994). Politicians and Firms. *The Quarterly Journal of Economics, 109*(4), 995–1025.

Shleifer, A., & Vishny, R. W. (1997). A Survey of Corporate Governance. *The Journal of Finance, 52*(2), 737–783.

Stan, C. V., Peng, M. W., & Bruton, G. D. (2014). Slack and the Performance of state-owned Enterprises. *Asia Pacific Journal of Management, 31*(2), 473–495.

Su, Y., Xu, D., & Phan, P. H. (2008). Principal–Principal Conflict in the Governance of the Chinese Public Corporation. *Management and Organization Review, 4*(1), 17–38.

Sun, Q., & Tong, W. H. S. (2003). China Share Issue Privatisation: The Extent of its Success. *Journal of Financial Economics, 70*(2), 183–222.

Tu, G., Lin, B., & Liu, F. (2013). Political Connections and Privatisation: Evidence from China. *Journal of Accounting and Public Policy, 32*(2), 114–135.

Vu Thanh Tu Anh. (2012). *Restructuring of SOEs in Viet Nam*, Fulbright Economics Teaching Program, Vietnam Program, Harvard Kennedy School, 14 March 2012, Hanoi.

Walsh, J. P., & Seward, J. K. (1990). On the Efficiency of Internal and External Corporate Control Mechanisms. *Academy of Management. The Academy of Management Review, 15*(3), 421.

Wang, K., & Xiao, X. (2009). Ultimate Government Control Structures and Firm Value: Evidence from Chinese Listed Companies. *China Journal of Accounting Research, 2*(1), 101–122.

Wei, S.-J., & Wang, T. (1997). The Siamese Twins: Do State-owned Banks Favour state-owned Enterprises in China? *China Economic Review, 8*(1), 19–29.

World Economic Forum (WEF). (2019). Global Competitiveness Report 2019, Switzerland.

Wu, J., Xu, D., & Phan, P. H. (2011). The Effects of Ownership Concentration and Corporate Debt on Corporate Divestitures in Chinese Listed Firms. *Asia Pacific Journal of Management, 28*(1), 95–114.

Yeh, Y.-H., & Woidtke, T. (2005). Commitment or Entrenchment?: Controlling Shareholders and Board Composition. *Journal of Banking & Finance, 29*(7), 1857–1885.

Yu, M. (2013). State ownership and Firm Performance: Empirical Evidence from Chinese Listed Companies. *China Journal of Accounting Research, 6*(2), 75–87.

CHAPTER 5

The Empirical Research: Design and Methods

The empirical analysis conducted in relation to the research questions in our study examines the underlying characteristics, motivation and rationale of strategic M&A decisions of SIEs in Vietnam. This chapter explains the design of the research and the major hypotheses in that context.

This study investigated the M&A activity in Vietnam—a nascent but growing market for corporate control. Vietnam is a rising economic power in Southeast Asia and a promising market for M&A. M&A activity, in both domestic and cross-border deals, has grown substantially in recent years as the country's economic prominence increases. According to the Ministry of Planning and Investment's FDI data from 2016 to 2019, there seemed to be a shift from greenfield investments to M&A, with the monthly average of M&A of US $285 million to US $1.16 billion per month in 2019 (World Bank, 2019).

M&A plays an important role in the economic development of Vietnam as it is an increasingly popular form of FDI. It eases the country's shortage of capital, promotes the development of local entrepreneurship and provides a supporting mechanism for the reform of the state-owned sector.

This was the first large-scale empirical research on M&A in Vietnam in the context of corporate governance. Vietnam presents a unique setting for studying M&A because in this market, rather than being purely economically driven, an M&A decision of a firm is affected by institutional factors and hence motivations. This study explained how state ownership in listed companies affects their M&A activity and identifies those

© The Author(s), under exclusive license to Springer Nature Singapore Pte Ltd. 2021
N. Pham, K.-B. Oh, *State on Board!*,
https://doi.org/10.1007/978-981-16-3525-0_5

institutional factors. The first section of the chapter introduces our methodological framework. The second and third sections discuss the qualitative and quantitative methods used in this study.

5.1   Research Methodology

The first component of this research was a qualitative study using in-depth interviews conducted with 31 M&A professionals and corporate managers of acquiring firms, including listed SIEs. The aim of the qualitative study was to unpack factors that motivate firms to undertake M&A and those that drive M&A performance for Vietnamese firms in general and SIEs in particular.

The second component addressed other research questions using a quantitative approach conducted on listed firms in Vietnam, including listed SIEs, covering all publicly reported transactions in which a minimum of 10% of equity had been acquired after the transaction. The final sample consisted of 188 cases, including 88 M&As carried out by SIEs and 100 by non-SIEs. The main quantitative analysis methods were univariate analysis and multivariate ordinary least squares regression (OLS). The variables allowed for triangulation of performance measurement methods from different perspectives, including accounting-based indicators for the firm's internal perspective and stock price reactions from the market perspective. The quantitative model also considered a diverse set of factors comprising institutional factors, firm factors and decision-makers' individual characteristics. In terms of state-related factors, included in the model were state ownership level, the impact of state control via industry regulation and CEO duality, a feature representing the heritage of a centrally planned economy.

5.1.1   The Mixed-Methods Design with a Pragmatic Worldview

This study employed the mixed-methods design, which grounds on pragmatism.[1] The belief underlying the pragmatic worldview is that knowledge

---

[1] Pragmatists could employ mixed methods to study both the external world existing out there independent of the minds, as in positivism and post-positivism, and that nested in the mind, as in constructivism (Creswell, 2014). Indeed, a practical research philosophy should guide methodological choice. The value of multiple methods is the neutralisation of the biases and weaknesses of each form of data and triangulation of data sources by systematically converging quantitative with qualitative databases. One database could be used to check the accuracy of or help explain the other database. Both subjective and objective points of view are

is created through actions and interactions, and reality is multiple and constructed. The complexity of reality calls for combining different methods to integrate different theoretical perspectives in understanding and interpreting the data. Pragmatic researchers often combine qualitative and quantitative methods (Corbin & Strauss, 2008).

The choice of a research approach depends on the research problem and questions (Morse & Niehaus, 2009). If a research study aims to explore and understand the unknown factors of a phenomenon that have not been studied substantially in the literature, it merits a qualitative approach. If a research study is to identify variables influencing an outcome or to test a theory, the best approach is the quantitative approach. A mixed-methods design is proper when neither the quantitative nor the qualitative approach in itself is sufficiently adequate to answer the research question.

The use of the mixed-methods approach benefits from the complementary strengths of both qualitative and quantitative approaches (Guba & Lincoln, 1994). The qualitative design allows for an in-depth understanding of the phenomenon and improves validity, which is often the weakness of a quantitative model (Creswell, 2008). On the other hand, the quantitative design is robust in terms of reliability and generalisability (Brewer & Hunter, 2006), which may not be the case for a qualitative study due to its potential subjectivity biases (Babbie, 2008).

This study used both qualitative and quantitative methods to investigate a new area of research that is relatively unexplored and quantify the degree of the pervasiveness of each key factor on decision-making. Two sets of qualitative and quantitative data were collected and analysed separately. Findings from the two data sets were put together in a meaningful way to develop an overall interpretation. Morse and Niehaus (2009) differentiate between a multiple research programme, a series of complete related qualitative and/or quantitative research projects and a mixed-methods design, which comprises a core component and a supplementary component(s). The supplementary component does not usually stand as a separate research project and typically employs a strategy methodologically different from the method used for the core component.

well accepted by pragmatists, and both inductive and deductive logic could serve pragmatic research (Tashakkori & Teddlie, 1998). Further advocacy for the use of the mixed-methods approach includes its advantages in addressing the complexity of the research problem and presenting a greater diversity of views and perspectives (Tashakkori & Teddlie, 1998). The mixed-methods design can also serve the purpose of methodological triangulation in which different data sources are combined to study the same social phenomenon (Denzin, 1978)

This research investigated the pervasive factors that drive M&A performance of listed SIEs and non-SIEs in Vietnam. While the literature on M&A in developed markets provides a clear direction of the variables that influence the activity, less is known about such activity in emerging markets, especially in Vietnam. According to Morse and Niehaus (2009), when the concept is immature due to a conspicuous lack of theory and previous research and the available theory may be inaccurate, inappropriate, incorrect or biased, there is a need for qualitative research. With the absence of prior research in M&A in Vietnam as an emerging market, it is useful to employ a qualitative approach to identify the locally relevant factors for Vietnamese firms in general and listed SIEs in particular.

The qualitative study consisted of a series of interviews with managers of M&A advisory firms as well as acquiring firms. The identified factors were put together with the other factors discussed in prior literature available from emerging and developed markets to form a set of variables hypothesised to affect M&A outcomes. A quantitative study was then conducted to examine how these factors drive M&A motivations and results in Vietnam's emerging market. The quantitative research was based on secondary data published by listed firms.

It is worth noting that the term "mixed" does not imply "a blending of research methods" (Morse & Niehaus, 2009: p. 10). Instead, the mixed-methods design needs to be systematically planned so that the research adheres to the inherent rules and assumptions in each paradigm. Although it can provide a broader and more significant impact than research that uses a single method only (Morse & Niehaus, 2009), it is usually a challenging one to conduct. Practical challenges include the expertise required and the time-intensive nature of collecting and analysing qualitative and quantitative data. A clear understanding of the flow of research activities in the design is essential, which will be discussed next.

5.1.2   Mixed-Methods Strategy: Exploratory Sequential Mixed Methods

This study followed an exploratory sequential mixed-methods design,[2] as depicted in Fig. 5.1.

---

[2] Other mixed-methods designs are convergent parallel mixed methods and explanatory sequential mixed methods and exploratory sequential mixed methods. (See Creswell (2014) for more details.) In a convergent parallel mixed-methods approach, the investigator typically collects both quantitative and qualitative data at the same time and integrates the analysis and

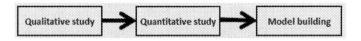

Fig. 5.1   Research design: exploratory sequential mixed methods

The first phase was a qualitative component to identify new factors relevant to emerging markets' M&A, followed by the second phase, a quantitative study. Qualitative data serve this purpose well as they are locally grounded, case-specific, rich and holistic (Miles & Huberman, 1994). As such, a qualitative study could be the best strategy to explore a new area and develop hypotheses. The initial QUAL study served to identify the driving attributes, themes and factors. The factors or characteristics identified in the initial stage were further statistically analysed using QUAN data by quantitative techniques of univariate and multivariate analysis. The purpose of the QUAN analysis was to confirm or expand the inferences resulting from the initial QUAL analysis. The overall research design is depicted in Fig. 5.2.

The following sections describe the qualitative study and quantitative study in more detail concerning the research methods, data collection procedures and data analysis techniques. A summary is provided in Table 5.4.

5.2   THE QUALITATIVE STUDY

The qualitative approach is typically employed to understand a particular activity or phenomenon, in this case, M&A transactions, with due emphasis on the meanings, experiences and views of the participants. The diversity of businesses in Vietnam in terms of ownership and governance characteristics and the dominant shareholding by the state makes it even more appealing to use the qualitative approach. The objective is to obtain an in-depth understanding of how the ownership and governance structure of a business may affect its decisions. Specifically, we wanted to identify the motivations, characteristics and performance drivers of M&A transactions by Vietnamese firms in general and listed SIEs in particular.

interpretation of findings to obtain a comprehensive understanding of the research problem. In an explanatory sequential mixed-methods approach, the quantitative data results are further explained with qualitative data, more popularly applied in fields that are more quantitatively oriented.

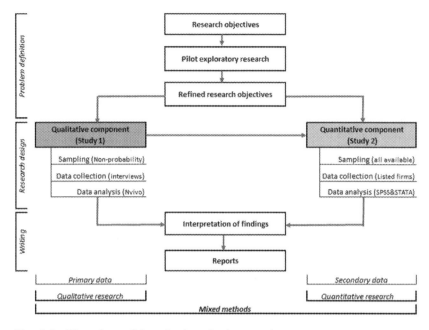

Fig. 5.2 Flow chart of the mixed-methods research process

The diversity of the participating organisations provided insights on how the diverse characteristics influence the M&A process and results.

In the qualitative component, we kept an open mind about anything deemed relevant by the respondents to better understand their experience, perspective and perceptions. The result of the first stage was a descriptive understanding of the motivations and the outcome of M&A and the impacts of institutional factors such as state ownership and state control, as in the participants' view. The focus was to understand why and how things occur.

Driven by the desire to explore new factors to modify existing M&A theories originating from the developed markets, this research utilised the grounded theory approach[3] in the qualitative study. Grounded theory is

---

[3] The approach applied in this research, however, deviates from the traditional school of grounded theory. This research relies on a set of a priori concepts including institutional factors and firm-specific factors proposed in the theoretical framework to explore new factors and form hypotheses.

advisable when there is little or no prior knowledge of an area or a need for new theoretical explanations built on previous knowledge to explain changes in the field.[4]

5.2.1   Research Questions

The research questions to be answered in the qualitative study are as follows:

RQ1.   What are the motivations of M&A conducted by listed Vietnamese firms in general and by SIEs in particular?

RQ2.   What are the important factors affecting M&A outcomes of listed Vietnamese firms in general and SIEs in particular?

This study was conducted in two major commercial cities of Vietnam, Hanoi and Ho Chi Minh City (HCMC). The participants in the interviews were M&A professionals (P) and corporate managers (M) of firms that had acquired another firm (fully or partially) in the past.

5.2.2   Qualitative Methods: In-depth Interviews

Interviewing is a popular method for data collection in qualitative research. An interview could be conducted anywhere between totally unstructured with all open-ended questions and highly structured with all closed-ended questions. The approach used in this research lies in the middle of this continuum, consisting of semi-structured interviews and a combination of closed-ended questions (respondent profile, firm and transaction information) and open-ended questions (M&A motivations and results) in each interview. M&A, in itself, is a structured process with different factors coming into play at the various stages of that process. Therefore, the interviews were structured to explore factors relevant to each step of the M&A process.[5] We encouraged the participants to elaborate on their views and opinions on these issues.

The qualitative study did not utilise the focus group interview as it would be less effective than individual interviews. As respondents were

---

[4] The grounded theory approach is widely used in organisational research (Martin & Turner, 1986).

[5] As specified in Chapter Appendix

senior business people, it would not be practically convenient to arrange a time to bring them together. Furthermore, the interviews focused on the organisational and transactional specific information, which could be sensitive if discussed publicly. Therefore, the only method conducted for the qualitative data collection was individual in-depth interviews.

5.2.3 Sampling

The investigation aimed at two groups, the acquiring firms and the M&A advisory firms. For the first group, the selection of respondents was made so that their combination represented the typical firm types available in the Vietnamese market. As the aim of the investigation was to find out how state ownership affects the M&A outcomes, the focus of the sampling was to ensure the diversity of ownership structure (i.e. SOEs and non-SOEs, publicly listed and private firms). The heterogeneity of ownership types among firms is an important feature that may influence the motivation and result of M&A. Purposive sampling for heterogeneity was, thus, the most suitable method (Tashakkori & Teddlie, 1998).

The sampling procedure was stratified, non-random sampling, which is similar to a stratified sample but in a convenient way. Firms were initially selected non-randomly from a list of M&A deals obtained from the annual Vietnam M&A forum meeting of 2010 and 2011 and a self-collected list of M&A transactions available through public sources.[6] The selection was made based on the availability of contact information about the acquiring firm and its location. Initial direct phone calls to establish a contact person at the firm resulted in a meagre success rate—only 2 out of 35 phone-contacted companies and zero out of 10 emailed companies after multiple times. The researcher had to change strategy by utilising an introduction from personal contacts to approach firms that have conducted M&A.

Not the whole sample has to be pre-specified. Qualitative sampling tends to evolve after fieldwork begins (Miles & Huberman, 1994). Indeed,

---

[6] Public sources of M&A deal information include Stoxplus' Annual M&A reports (http://www.vnexpress.net, http://www.vneconomy.vn, http://www.cafeF.vn, http://www.vietstock.vn, http://www.stockbiz.vn), Sai Gon Economic Times, NhipcauDautu (The Business Review) (http://www.nhipcaudautu.vn), (http://www.baomoi.com), Vietnam Investment Review (http://www.vir.com.vn), Thoi Bao Chung Khoan Viet Nam, (http://www.tbck.vn), Tin Nhanh Chung Khoan (http://www.tinnhanhchungkhoan.vn), Thoi Bao Tai Chinh Viet Nam (http://www.thoibaotaichinhvietnam.vn) and websites of major securities companies in Vietnam.

Table 5.1   Interview respondents' sample description

	Acquirers	M&A advisors	Total
SIE	6	0	6
Non-SIE	14	11	25
Subtotal	*20*	*11*	*31*
Listed	6	3	9
Unlisted	14	8	22
Subtotal	*20*	*11*	*31*

we were introduced to other prospective firms by several respondents after their interview. Approximately 20% of the sample was recruited in this "snowball" sampling method. In the Vietnamese culture, Vietnamese may have a poor view of *strangers*, but very high regard for *friends*; an introduction helps facilitate access to potential participants. The likelihood of sample recruitment success is higher when another informant introduces an informant. This could be either conceptually driven sequential sampling (Miles & Huberman, 1994) or a practical approach to increasing the sample size. The resulting sample consisted of 20 acquiring firms in total, including six SIEs. There were six listed firms among the 20 acquirers sampled in terms of listing status, as in the cross-tabulated Table 5.1.

For the second group, the M&A advisory firms, we sent out an invitation of participation by email to a number of contacts in securities firms, and the response was good. We managed to interview 11 managers in charge of M&A advisory services of these firms, none of which were state-owned firms.[7] The resulting sample was as follows:

5.2.4   Data Collection and Analysis

Interviewing research is a systematic process with ethical concerns embedded in all stages.[8] Data were collected from November 2012 to February

---

[7] The detailed description of the firms and the participants is in Appendix 3—*List of Participants: Group 1—M&A professionals (P)* and Appendix 4—*List of Participants: Group 2—Corporate Managers (M)*.

[8] Detailed information on the research plan, the ethical procedure by the university and plan for dissemination of the research findings was provided to each participant to create professional trust in the participants, which could reduce the probability of intentional misinformation and controlled behaviour. For the full discussion of the interviews and ethics procedures, the Research Information Sheet and Consent Form, Interview Fact Sheets and

2013, including 31 interviews, which were on average 45 minutes. One potential issue with this type of sample is that as the respondents are senior in the job, the so-called high-status interviewee (King, 2004a, p. 19), it is critical that the interviewer positions himself or herself at an appropriate level to the respondent. Both overfamiliar or over-nervous impressions will most likely lead to shallow and surface-level answers to the questions asked (King, 2004a).

Preliminary analysis of qualitative data summarises issues emerging during data collection and identifies further questions to be asked to gain holistic data. Preliminary data analysis is an ongoing process parallel with data collection by checking and tracking the data to see the emerging themes and issues to be followed up. It is a process of engagement with the text but not so much as to critique it (Grbich, 2007).

In this study, preliminary data analysis started simultaneously with data collection. This is an advisable practice as it helps researchers recognise patterns and themes from the participants' perspective earlier in the research. In subsequent interviews, we explored unanticipated issues raised by previous respondents. As a result of this step, each interview was summarised on an Interview Fact Sheet. In each sheet, we highlighted the main concepts, themes and issues obtained from the interview (Fig. 5.3).

We then displayed in a matrix format of questions by respondents to summarise hundreds of pages of field notes in a visible way that could facilitate within-case and across case/site/group analysis. The display of data was in an organised, compressed and efficient format that prepared for interpretation. To analyse data matrices, we paid particular attention to identify any relationships or patterns based on continually comparing and contrasting between rows or between columns. The matrix needed to be firmly grounded or guided by the research questions.

In a qualitative study, the researcher must develop a typology of categories or themes that summarises narrative data. Qualitative data from interviews were analysed both deductively and inductively. Deductive analysis in this research follows the template approach or also called the framework approach. Template analysis works well for studies with a sample size of 20 to 30 to compare different groups' perspectives within a specific context (King, 2004b). This research started with an initial coding template

Analysis Memos, please see Pham, N. (2015). The Impact of the State on M&A performance: an Empirical Study on Vietnam. Department of Finance. Melbourne, Australia, La Trobe University. PhD

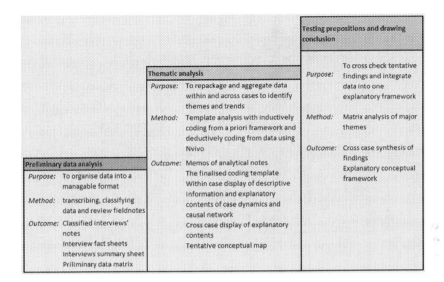

Fig. 5.3 The ladder of qualitative data analysis used in this research

consisting of a priori codes and verified or modified it with emerging themes (codes) through data collection and analysis. The research questions and the interview guideline best served as the initial template of codes. Please see Appendix 4 for the coding template.

The inductive analysis captures emerging codes. With the conceptual mapping approach, qualitative analysis allows the data to speak for themselves (Grbich, 2007). The researcher segments, categorises and reorganises the data based on repeated words and phrases to allow analytical themes to emerge.

Coding is an essential activity in both deductive and inductive analyses. A code is a label to index a section of text to a specific theme or issue. Codes could be merely descriptive or interpretative (inferential). Codes are to be organised in a hierarchical system, with higher-order codes being generated from groups of clustered codes to analyse texts at different specificity levels both within and between cases. Codes can then be added, deleted or modified in terms of scope and higher-order classification during the analysis (King, 2004b).

At a higher level of analysis, we used explanatory pattern codes to identify emergent themes or constructs. A pattern code becomes qualified

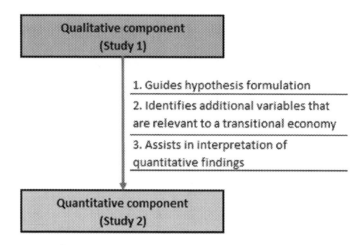

Fig. 5.4   The link between the qualitative study and the quantitative study

when the conditions under which it holds are specified. This is to verify the pattern and clarify the parameters and their relationships to add strength to the inferences. Quality codes are rigorous as they carry a lot of information, suggest thematic links and organise data into an inclusive and meaningful whole, conducted using Nvivo (Version 10).

5.2.5   *Linking the Qualitative Study (1) and Quantitative Study (2)*

The qualitative study in the first stage was followed by a quantitative study in the second stage. The findings obtained from the first stage provided critical input that guided hypothesis formulation, identified relevant variables for the quantitative research and helped us interpret quantitative results. The link between the two stages of the research is illustrated in Fig. 5.4.

5.3   THE QUANTITATIVE STUDY

The main objective of the quantitative study was to conduct an empirical analysis of performance of M&A of SIEs and non-SIEs in Vietnam, using publicly available data from listed firms.

As most of the financial data used in this quantitative component were obtained from audited annual reports of listed firms, this type of data provides an additional valuable advantage of credibility. Primary data from interviews and survey questionnaires may suffer from personal biases, which are not the real concern of secondary audited financial information.

5.3.1   Sampling

This study examined domestic acquisitions by listed firms in Vietnam since the beginning of the two Vietnamese stock markets, Ho Chi Minh City Stock Exchange (HSX) in 2000 and Hanoi Stock Exchange (HNX) in 2005. As the Vietnamese stock markets are young, this is a unique opportunity to see how the stock market facilitates the development of the market for corporate control.

The deal-specific information was obtained from *ThomsonONE.com Investment Banker* database. Our sample included all domestic M&A by listed Vietnamese firms in which at least 10% of the ordinary equity of the target was acquired, and the acquirer was not an investment fund or a brokerage firm.

Ten per cent equity holding enables the shareholder to have material influence over a business. Under the 114th Article of the *Enterprises Law 2014* of Vietnam, a shareholder holding at least 10% of the ordinary shares for a minimum period of six months can nominate board members and can request the Supervisory Board to investigate and report on issues related to the management of the company of their concern. Under section 3, Article 114, a shareholder holding at least 10% of the ordinary shares can request the company to convene an extraordinary general meeting (EGM) of shareholders to make critical decisions.

Only the first transaction was included for an acquirer that acquired the same target in multiple acquisitions in one year. We ensured that the acquisition announcement was not made on the same day as other major corporate events to avoid a contaminated sample.

The filtering criteria resulted in a sample size of 188 cases conducted from the period 2004 to 2013. The industry distribution of the sample (see Fig. 5.5 and Table 5.2) was somewhat similar to that described in the survey by Vuong et al. (2009), who studied private and listed companies. According to the caveats of data quality on private deals, we decided to examine only deals of listed acquirers whose information could be reliably verified.

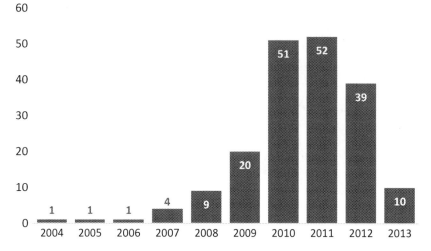

Fig. 5.5 Number of M&A deals conducted by listed acquirers in Vietnam

Table 5.2 Frequency distribution by years and industries

Sample distribution by years			Sample distribution by industries		
	Number	*%*		*Number*	*%*
2004	1	0.5	Consumer products and services	4	2.1
2005	1	0.5	Consumer staples	38	20.2
2006	1	0.5	Energy and power	27	14.4
2007	4	2.1	Financials	10	5.3
2008	9	4.8	Healthcare	4	2.1
2009	20	10.6	High-tech/telecom.	4	2.2
2010	51	27.1	Industrials	51	27.1
2011	52	27.7	Materials	19	10.1
2012	39	20.7	Media and entertainment	6	3.2
2013	10	5.3	Real estate	25	13.3
Total	**188**	**100.0**	*Total*	*188*	*100%*

We obtained financial data of listed firms from the Datastream database. We manually collected ownership and governance data from companies' annual reports and prospectus, accessed via the two official stock exchanges. For a detailed description of data sources for the specific variables, please see Appendix 6—*List of Variables and Data Sources.*

5.3.2   Research Questions and Hypotheses

The overarching research question addressed by the quantitative study was whether institutional factors affect the M&A performance of listed firms in Vietnam. Given the institutional setting of Vietnam, as discussed in Chap. 4, the institutional factors to be examined in this study include state ownership of acquirers, state control via industry regulation and corporate governance and leadership. Specifically, the quantitative research addressed the following research questions.

RQ3.   Does state ownership in an acquirer affect the performance of its M&A?

RQ4.   Does state control via industry regulation affect firms' M&A performance?

RQ5.   Does the corporate governance structure of an acquirer affect its M&A performance?

The research questions were translated into the following key research hypotheses:

1. The State ownership level of an acquiring firm is negatively associated with the performance of its M&A, measured by announcement stock returns and changes in operating performance, that is, the *inefficiency hypothesis.*
2. M&As conducted by firms in non-regulated industries create more favourable announcement stock returns and better post-M&A performance changes than do those by firms in regulated industries, that is, the *regulatory hypothesis.*
3. M&As conducted by firms with CEO duality have more favourable announcement stock returns and better post-M&A performance changes than do those by firms without CEO duality, that is, the *stewardship hypothesis.*

To operationalise the key concepts in the research questions, we transformed the institutional factors into measurable and observable characteristics, together with other controlling variables for hypothesis testing.

5.3.3   The Quantitative Study: Research Approach

Contextual variables and actors in a given environment are important determinants of corporate actions. To capture the impacts of institutional factors, we adopted the fundamental approach suggested by Fan et al. (2011) for corporate research in emerging markets. To ensure that the quantitative models reflect the typical features of an emerging market, we included a rich set of control variables that reflected the institutional factors, firm performance and governance features and individual characteristics of the decision-makers to analyse Vietnamese M&A, as illustrated by Fig. 5.6.

We focused on state-related institutional factors that could affect firms' M&A performance. Firstly, *state ownership* was measured by the presence of the state among the firm's shareholders as a dummy variable and the size of the equity held by the state in the firm, which is a continuous variable. State ownership was also examined in a number of other aspects, including if the state holds a minority or majority level in the acquiring firm and if the state is the largest shareholder of the firm. We also

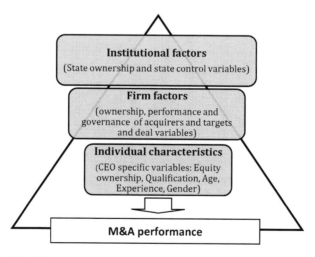

Fig. 5.6 The full model: the fundamental approach

Fig. 5.7 Empirical model of institutional factors and corporate M&A performance

considered the type of the government's agency managing state capital at the firm.

Secondly, we designed a dummy variable reflecting whether the firm was in a regulated industry.

Lastly, the state-influenced corporate governance was reflected by the board leadership structure of CEO duality, the practice rooted in the centralisation of power ideology of the past command economy and stems from the practices of state-owned enterprises. CEO duality was represented by a dummy variable which takes the value of one if the acquiring firm is led by the CEO duality structure and zero otherwise.

For the dependent variable, M&A performance (see Fig. 5.7), we used both the stock's cumulative abnormal returns (CARs) around the announcement date and post-deal changes in operating performance for two reasons.

The first reason to combine the two measurements of M&A performance was to reflect both short-term and long-term views about performance. On the one hand, short-term assessment was based on stock price reaction around announcement time as stock returns are calculated and cumulated within windows of a few days around the announcement. This was a typical event study design in which short-term stock price movements upon an announcement of a corporate event are assumed to reflect changes in the firm's intrinsic value (Brown & Warner, 1980; Fama et al., 1969). On the other hand, the long-term performance measurement was based on changes in operating performance within two years after the deal (Carline et al., 2009; Ghosh, 2001; Ismail et al., 2009).

The second reason was that the two measurements provide multiple perspectives on performance. Stock price reactions suggested how the market views the value created from the deal, whereas changes in operating performance revealed how the M&A affects the firm's internal fundamental performance. In that sense, both internal and external perspectives of performance were considered when measuring performance. Each will be discussed in turn next.

Cumulative Abnormal Returns: The Wealth Impact of M&A
This quantitative study followed the standard event study methodology for studying the impacts of specific corporate events or market events on the relevant firms. The method examines share prices' reactions to merger announcements around the announcement time, that is, calculating abnormal returns to shareholders. A merger or acquisition decision is among the most important strategic decisions made by the firm. Its announcement often conveys messages about changes in the firm's structure, business scale and scope, which causes the market to form expectations of changes in firm value. Such events, when announced, are often accompanied by an observable change in stock prices of related firms. Therefore, the wealth created for shareholders is measured by the abnormal return that the announcement brings to shareholders of merging firms.

There is a need to neutralise the change in share prices due to factors other than the specific announcement under investigation to avoid cross-sectional dependence. Abnormal return can be measured as the excess return over the expected return anticipated if the merger proposal was not announced. In this research, the market model is employed to calculate expected returns, which was introduced by Fama et al. (1969) and improved by Brown and Warner (1980). (See Fama (1998) for the advantages of the market model over other approaches.)

$$\text{In the estimation period}: R_{it} = \alpha_i + \beta_i R_{Mt} + e_{it} \qquad (5.1)$$

$$\text{In the event time window}: \overline{R}_{it} = \hat{\alpha}_i + \hat{\beta}_i R_{Mt} \qquad (5.2)$$

$$\text{In the event time window}: AR_{it} = R_{it} - \overline{R}_{it} \qquad (5.3)$$

In the event time window of $(-n; +n)$ days/weeks/months:

$$CAR_i = \sum_{t=-n}^{+n} AR_{it} \qquad (5.4)$$

This model works under the multivariate normal distribution of returns assumption. In the estimation period, we regressed the actual daily returns of a stock (i) (R_{it}) on actual daily market returns (R_{Mt}) via an OLS regression equation, as in Equation (5.1). The equation produced estimates of α and β, which reflected the normal co-variability between the stock and the market. The estimated $\hat{\alpha}_i$ and $\hat{\beta}_i$ were then used to estimate the expected return of the stock ($\overline{R}_i$) for each day in the event time window, as in Equation (5.2). To eliminate the possible impact of the merger information leakage, the estimation period should end a period before the announcement. The abnormal return, Equation (5.3) the residuals, would be the difference between the actual return and the estimated expected return using the market model. The cumulative abnormal return (CAR) for (-n, +n) days was the cumulative sum of the daily abnormal returns from the day (-n), that is, n days before the event is announced to the day (+n), that is, n days after the event date, as in Equation (5.4).

Under the abnormal return approach, a clear time window around the merger announcement should be identified, and the abnormal return to shareholders will be calculated cumulatively within that time frame to obtain the cumulative abnormal return (CAR). The event time window could be measured by days (Brown & Warner, 1985), weeks (Hawawini & Swary, 1990), months (Brown & Warner, 1980) or years (Ghosh, 2001; Gregory, 1997). The event window is normally but not necessarily placed symmetrically around the event date. For example, an eleven-day event time window includes five days before the announcement and five days after the announcement. Most popular event time windows in M&A studies are CAR(-1, +1), (-2, +2), (-3, +3), (-1, 0) and (0, +1) in days (Pham et al. 2015).

Figure 5.8 describes the measurement windows applied in this research, which were adopted from the measurement windows by Cai and Sevilir (2012) and Balachandran et al. (2008, 2012). Returns were calculated on a daily basis. Data for the estimation of Equation (5.1) was obtained from

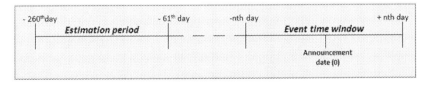

Fig. 5.8 Event study methodology measurement windows

the 200-trading day estimation window, 60 days away from the event date, ranging from the -61st to -260th trading day. Event time windows examined were CAR(0, +1), CAR(-1, +1) and CAR(-2, +2).

As the event study methodology assumes market efficiency, there is a potential problem of the market being fundamentally inefficient, from constant overreaction or under-reaction of stock price to information and not correcting itself in a timely manner (Masulis et al. 2007). Besides, insider trading can start weeks before the event announcement (Keown & Pinkerton, 1981; Meulbroek, 1992). The short-term announcement returns may not represent the true impact of the event and longer-term time windows are occasionally examined in M&A research (Agrawal et al., 2013). It is necessary, therefore, to investigate a number of other event-time windows, including *CAR (-4, +4)*, *CAR (5, +5)* and *CAR (-10, +10)* for robustness.

ΔROA and ΔEPSG: The Efficiency Impact and Growth Impact of M&A

We used the *Change in ROA (ΔROA)* and *Change in EPS growth (ΔEPSG)* to measure the impact of M&As on operating performance. The former represents the gain in efficiency for the acquirer due to the acquisition, whereas the latter reveals the growth impact. To reflect operating performance free from possible distortions of financing choice and depreciation policies, we calculated ROA as earnings before interests, tax, depreciation and amortisation (EBITDA) divided by total assets (Cai & Sevilir, 2012).

The acquirer's industry-adjusted ROA was calculated by subtracting the mean ROA in their industry from the firm's ROA, based on the two-digit SIC codes. Subsequently, *ΔROA* is obtained by taking the difference between post-M&A ROA and pre-M&A ROA of the acquiring firm.

The following set of equations explains the calculation of post-M&A ΔROA.

$$\left(Industry.Adjusted\right)ROA = ROA_{firm} - ROA_{industry\ mean} \tag{5.5}$$

$$Pre.deal\ ROA = \frac{ROA_{t-1} + ROA_{t-2}}{2} \tag{5.6}$$

$$Post.deal\ ROA = \frac{ROA_{t+1} + ROA_{t+2}}{2} \tag{5.7}$$

$$\Delta ROA = \left(post.deal\ ROA\right) - \left(pre.deal\ ROA\right) \tag{5.8}$$

We used a similar procedure to obtain $\Delta EPSG$, which measures the difference in post- and pre-deal EPS growth.

Data Analysis

We examined if the mean CARs and changes in operating performance (ΔEPSG and ΔROA) were significantly different from zero on the full sample.

Earlier findings from the US and UK markets (Alexandridis et al., 2010; Higgins, 2013; Mulherin & Boone, 2000) indicate that M&A transactions do not increase shareholders' value. However, evidence from some Asian Pacific markets shows significantly positive M&A abnormal returns (Kale, 2004; Ma et al., 2009; Shams et al., 2013). It is necessary to understand the pattern of stock returns from M&As in Vietnam.

All hypotheses were tested using both univariate and multivariate analyses. In all regression models, we controlled for relevant firm-specific and deal-specific variables. The logic is that if the impact of the main predictor on the dependent variable remains statistically significant after controlling for all other factors, the main predictor is an important driver of the dependent variable. The advantage of this study is the comprehensive set of control variables employed in the models, which enhances the reliability of the claimed findings (Table 5.3).

All regressions were checked for heteroskedasticity and multicollinearity problems and run with robust standard errors options. As M&A are observed to occur in waves and within a wave, they strongly cluster by industries (Andrade et al., 2001). Therefore, industry dummies and year dummies were included in all models to control for industry and year effects.

We conducted a two-stage least squares regression and an analysis using propensity score matching for further robustness checks to ensure that the claimed findings are not voided by endogeneity in model design.[9]

In conclusion, the research is designed with multiple triangulation of approaches, perspectives and measures. Table 5.4 summarises the main

---

[9] Endogeneity is a fundamental problem of causal inference, especially with binary treatments (Imbens & Wooldridge, 2009). The potential endogeneity issue of corporate governance—corporate performance research—should be acknowledged. If not addressed, endogeneity could result in "a serious methodological problem" (Iyengar & Zampelli, 2009). The possible solution, where applicable, is the two-stage least squares regression (Ramdani & Witteloostuijn, 2010) that includes instrumental variables (IV). Additionally, we checked to ensure that the results are not biased caused by endogeneity of the main predictor being a dummy variable. We used the propensity score matching (PSM) analysis technique (Armstrong et al., 2010; Tucker, 2010) to match the treatment group and control group so that the distribution of measured baseline covariates is similar between treated and untreated subjects.

Table 5.3 Summary of hypotheses and econometric techniques

Hypothesis	Equation	OLS regressions			Fixed effects		Other techniques	
		Dependent variable	Main predictor	Control variables	Years	Industries	2SLS	PSM
1a	1	CAR(-1, +1)	SOE dummy	Yes	Yes	Yes		Yes
	2		G ownership (%)	Yes	Yes	Yes		
1b	3	ΔEPSG	SOE dummy	Yes	Yes	Yes		Yes
	4		G ownership (%)	Yes	Yes	Yes		
	5	ΔROA	SOE dummy	Yes	Yes	Yes		Yes
	6		G ownership (%)	Yes	Yes	Yes		
2a	7	CAR(-1, +1)	RI dummy	Yes	Yes	Yes		Yes
2b	8	ΔEPSG	RI dummy	Yes	Yes	Yes		Yes
	9	ΔROA	RI dummy	Yes	Yes	Yes		Yes
3a	10	CAR(-1, +1)	SA dummy	Yes	Yes	Yes		Yes
3b	11	ΔEPSG	SA dummy	Yes	Yes	Yes		Yes
	12	ΔROA	SA dummy	Yes	Yes	Yes		Yes
4	13	CAR(-1, +1)	PL dummy	Yes	Yes	Yes		Yes
5a	14	CAR(-1, +1)	Duality dummy	Yes	Yes	Yes	Yes	Yes
5b	15	ΔEPSG	Duality dummy	Yes	Yes	Yes	Yes	Yes
	16	ΔROA	Duality dummy	Yes	Yes	Yes	Yes	Yes

features of the qualitative and quantitative studies. The findings from the qualitative study will be discussed in Chap. 6 to provide an understanding of the motivations and performance drivers of M&A of listed Vietnamese firms in general and SIEs in particular. Chapters 7 and 8 will discuss findings from the quantitative study, focusing on the performance aspect of M&A.

Table 5.4   Summary of the qualitative and quantitative study

	Qualitative component (Study 1)	Quantitative component (Study 2)
Purpose	To explore the motives and performance drivers of M&A of Vietnamese firms in general and SOEs in particular	To understand the relationship between institutional factors and M&A performance, measured by shareholders' return and firm financial performance changes due to M&A
Research questions answered	1. What are the motivations for firms to conduct M&A in Vietnam? 2. What are the factors that determine the success of an M&A in Vietnam?	3. Does state ownership in an acquirer affect the performance of its M&A? 4. Does state control via industry regulation affect firms' M&A performance? 5. Does the corporate governance structure of an acquirer affect its M&A performance?
Specific research questions or hypotheses	The M&A motives and factors affecting M&A performance of SOEs are different from those of non-SOEs	1. Inefficiency hypothesis (on state ownership) 2. Regulatory hypothesis (on industry regulation) 3. Stewardship hypothesis (corporate governance structure: CEO duality)
Type of data	Primary data (from in-depth interviews)	Secondary data (from listed firms)
Approach	Qualitative method	Quantitative method: Econometric techniques for event study methodology
Sampling method	Non-probability sampling techniques (purposive sampling, stratified for heterogeneity and snowball sampling technique to increase sample size)	All available and accessible M&A transactions of listed Vietnamese firms are examined
Data collection	Time: Nov 2012–Feb 2013 Place: Hanoi and HCMC	Time: Feb 2013–June 2013 Data sources: ThomsonONE Investment banker database for M&A deals, Datastream database for financial information and HOSE and HNX official websites for annual reports and interim corporate governance reports
Sample	31 interviews with 11 M&A advisors and 20 managers of acquiring firms, of which 6 are state owned and 14 are non-SOEs	188 deals conducted by firms listed in HOSE and HNX whose information about the acquiring firm was available
Data analysis	Coding in Nvivo10 Thematic analysis	Univariate and multivariate analysis using multiple regression techniques in SPSS21 and STATA12

APPENDIX 1: INTERVIEW GUIDELINES
(CORPORATE MANAGERS)

The interview

Interviewed company	Location
Recording method	Time

The respondent

Respondent name	Years at company
Respondent position	Direct involvement with the M&A Yes/No

Acquirer (A)	**Target (T)**
Name	Name
Year founded	Year founded
Size (total asset $)	Size (total assets $)
Employees	Employees
Location	Location
Industry	Industry
State-owned status	State-owned status
Listing status	Listing status

Items	Questions	Notes
M&A transaction	When did the acquisition happen? How many per cent of ownership of T was acquired by A? At what price? Was the acquisition in cash or in security?	
M&A motivations	What was the motivation of the M&A? From the perspective of the A and that of T? Was the motivation related to: • An asset owned by the T • The financial condition of T • The management of T • The cash flow problem/potential of T • The cash flow of the A • The fitness between T and A • Synergies between T and A • Tax motivation (Did T have tax loss credits?) • The management experience of A • The M&A experience of A • Market entry and expansion for A • Value chain backward and forward integration • Industry pressure • Regulatory pressure • Others	Tick the ones mentioned and follow up to ask the respondent to be specific

(*continued*)

(continued)

M&A process	How could A identify T? Was there any financial intermediaries/advisor involved in designing the deal? How long was the negotiation process? Did A encounter any difficulty in the negotiation process? What was the value of the deal? How was the target valued? Did A encounter any difficulties with market regulators? How did managers, employees, investors and business partners react to the M&A?	
M&A results	Did the company think that the acquisition was successful/not successful? Why? Did the M&A contribute to the long-term strategic plan of the company? How did the company measure M&A results financially? (Stock price movement? Rate of return? Operating performance?) Relatively to the industry, has the performance of the company after the M&A been good?	
Important factors	What factors caused the acquisition to be successful/unsuccessful? • Target selection • Valuation and payment • Type of deal (related or diversified) • Synergies • Governance and management, pre- and post-acquisition • Ownership structure, pre- and post-acquisition • Risk management • Factors external to A and T	Tick the ones mentioned and follow up to ask the respondent to be specific
Additional notes	Any unexpected issues?	

Appendix 2: Interview Guidelines (M&A Professionals)

The interview		
Interviewed company	Location	
Recording method	Time	
The respondent		
Respondent name	Years at company	
Respondent position	Direct involvement with M&A services	Yes/No
The firm		
Name	Year founded	
Size (total asset $)	Employees	
HO location	Listing status	
State-owned status		

Items	Questions	Notes
General M&A activity	How has the M&A activity developed in recent years in Vietnam? In terms of the following aspects: • Domestic deals, cross-border deals • Types of deal (related vs. diversified) • Deal attitudes (hostile vs. friendly) • Popular payment methods • Popular valuation methods • Deal premiums • Popular M&A industries • Market responses • The development of M&A professional services Future trend of the activity in Vietnam?	
M&A process	Please describe a typical M&A transaction: • How could A identify T? • Types of financial intermediaries/advisors involved in deal making • Due diligence process • The negotiation process • Valuation process • Dealing with market regulators • Risks to closing a deal	

(*continued*)

(continued)

M&A motivations	What are the popular M&A motivations in Vietnam? • An asset owned by the T • The financial condition of T • The management of T • The cash flow problem/potential of T • The cash flow of the A • The fitness between T and A • Synergies between T and A • Tax motivation • The management experience of A • The M&A experience of A • Market entry and expansion for A • Value chain backward and forward integration • Industry pressure • Regulatory pressure • Others	Tick the ones mentioned and follow up to ask the respondent to be specific
M&A results	Does the M&A advisory firm follow up and assess the performance of the acquisition of the client after the deal is completed? • Assessment criteria (subjective management assessment, shareholder return, improvement in operating performance?) • Any absolute measurement versus relative measurement	
Important factors	What factors determine the acquisition to be successful/unsuccessful? • Target selection • Valuation and payment • Type of deal (related or diversified) • Synergies • Governance and management, pre- and post-acquisition • Ownership structure, pre- and post-acquisition • Risk management • Factors external to A and T • The roles of M&A professionals	Tick the ones mentioned and follow up to ask the respondent to be specific
M&A of SOEs	Has the firm ever provided M&A advisory services to any SOEs? Do M&As by SOEs share the same motivations and performance drivers with those by non-SOEs?	
Additional notes	Additional comments	

Appendix: 3 List of Participants: Group 1—M&A Professionals

Short ID	Case ID	Location	Interview date	Length (mins)	SOE status	Listed status	Years founded	Job title
P1	P-HQA1	Hanoi	3/12/2012	90	Non-SIE	Unlisted	2006	Senior analyst
P2	P-NDP2	Hanoi	4/12/2012	60	Non-SIE	OTC	2007	Hanoi branch manager
P3	P-HVB3	Hanoi	6/12/2012	40	Non-SIE	Unlisted	2003	Director, Hanoi Branch
P4	P-BS4	Hanoi	10/12/2012	50	Non-SIE	Unlisted	2004	Senior reporter
P5	P-TN5	Hanoi	10/12/2012	40	Non-SIE	Unlisted	2008	CEO, founder
P6	P-NTP7	HCMC	17/12/2012	45	Non-SIE	Listed	2003	Senior advisor
P7	P-KN8	HCMC	18/12/2012	40	Non-SIE	Unlisted	2008	CEO, founder
P8	P-PNQ10	HCMC	19/12/2012	45	Non-SIE	Unlisted	2006	Deputy director, corporate finance
P9	P-NPH11	HCMC	20/12/2012	50	Non-SIE	OTC	2007	Deputy director, corporate finance
P10	P-NHL12	HCMC	21/12/2012	40	Non-SIE	Unlisted	2003	Director, HCMC branch
P11	P-NVD16	Hanoi	8/01/2013	40	Non-SIE	Unlisted	2002	Deputy director, corporate finance

APPENDIX 4: LIST OF PARTICIPANTS: GROUP 2—CORPORATE MANAGERS

	Case ID	Interview date	Time	Job title	SOE status	Listed Status	Years founded	Acquirer's Industry	Deal time	Target listing status	Target SOE status
Location: Hanoi											
M1	M-PHH6	10/12/12	60 mins	Investment director	SIE	Unlisted	2003	Finance and banking	2010	Listed	Non-SIE
M2	M-TA9	19/12/12	40 mins	CEO, founder	Non-SIE	Unlisted	2001	Manufacturing	2006	Unlisted	SIE
M3	M-NDH13	21/12/12	60 mins	CFO	SIE	Listed	1999	Cement production	2009	Listed	SIE
M4	M-TTF14	21/12/12	60 mins	CFO	Non-SIE	Listed	2000	Furniture	2010	Listed	Non-SIE
M5	M-NVD15	7/01/13	40 mins	CEO, founder	SIE	Listed	1960	Construction	2010	Unlisted	SIE
M6	M-SHB17	10/01/13	30 mins	Deputy director	Non-SIE	Listed	1993	Finance and banking	2012	Unlisted	Non-SIE
M7	M-VAM18	17/01/13	60 mins	CEO, founder	Non-SIE	Unlisted	2006	Finance and banking	2012	Unlisted	Non-SIE
M8	M-NKV19	18/01/13	45 mins	CFO	SIE	Listed	2003	Real estate	2010	Unlisted	SIE
M9	M-NHL20	22/01/12	45 mins	Compliance officer	SIE	Unlisted	1981	Finance and banking	2011	Unlisted	Non-SIE
M10	M-LAT21	23/01/13	45 mins	Deputy director	Non-SIE	Unlisted	1985	Energy	2007	Unlisted	SIE

(continued)

(continued)

Case ID	Interview date	Time	Job title	SOE status	Listed Status	Years founded	Acquirer's Industry	Deal time	Target listing status	Target SOE status
M11 M-BAN22	23/01/12	30 mins	Deputy director	SIE	Unlisted	1988	Diversified	2009	Unlisted	SIE
M12 M-MAS23	24/01/13	45 mins	CFO	Non-SIE	Listed	2004	Food and beverage	2011	Listed	Non-SIE
M13 M-DON24	25/01/13	60 mins	CEO, founder	Non-SIE	Unlisted	1994	Electrical equipment	2011	Unlisted	SIE
M14 M-HPG25	25/01/13	45 mins	CFO	Non-SIE	Listed	1992	Mining and manufacturing	2009	Unlisted	Non-SIE
M15 M-BTC26	28/01/13	45 mins	CEO	Non-SIE	Unlisted	1985	Diversified	2009	Unlisted	Non-SIE
M16 M-NHT27	29/01/13	45 mins	CEO	Non-SIE	Unlisted	2001	Real estate	2010	Unlisted	Non-SIE
M17 M-NHN28	30/01/13	40 mins	Deputy director	Non-SIE	Unlisted	2005	Accounting and auditing services	2010	Unlisted	Non-SIE
M18 M-LCG29	30/01/13	40 mins	CFO	Non-SIE	Unlisted	1996	Construction and manufacturing	2006	Listed	SIE
Location: Ho Chi Minh City										
M19 M-HMH30	31/01/13	50 mins	Deputy director	Non-SIE	Unlisted	1997	Healthcare	2011	Unlisted	Non-SIE
M20 M-MGS31	31/01/13	40 mins	Deputy director	Non-SIE	Unlisted	2004	Media	2011	Unlisted	Non-SIE

APPENDIX 5: CODING TEMPLATE

Primary code	Secondary code	Type of code	Note
Cross-border		Classification code	A priori
Domestic		Classification code	A priori
Deal valuation		Content code	A priori
Deal challenges		Content code	A priori
Deal structuring		Content code	A priori
Synergies		Content code	A priori
	Operational synergies	Classification code	Emerged
	Management synergies	Classification code	Emerged
	Marketing synergies	Classification code	Emerged
	Financial synergies	Classification code	Emerged
Direct quotes		Content code	A priori
Emerging market issues		Content code	A priori
M&A trends		Content code	A priori
Industry factors		Content code	A priori
	Industry competition	Content code	Emerged
	Legal requirements	Content code	Emerged
Professional services		Content code	A priori
Motivations		Content code	A priori
	Strategic assets	Content code	Emerged
	Land-use rights	Content code	Emerged
	Business licence	Content code	Emerged
	Business projects/contracts	Content code	Emerged
	Certificates	Content code	Emerged
	Economies of scale	Content code	A priori
	Valuation	Content code	A priori
	Political motivation	Content code	Emerged
	Distribution	Content code	Emerged
	Cost savings	Content code	Emerged
	Marketing/branding	Content code	Emerged
	Restructuring	Content code	Emerged
Publicity		Content code	A priori
M&A results		Content code	A priori
Management issues		Content code	A priori
Private targets		Classification code	A priori
Listed targets		Classification code	A priori
Regulatory environment		Content code	A priori
SOE		Classification code	A priori
Diversification		Classification code	A priori

Appendix 6: List of Variables and Definitions

Variables	Definitions⁺	Data source
Acquirer duality	An indicator variable which takes on the value of one if the CEO of the acquiring firm also served as its Chairman of the Board of Directors and zero otherwise.	Company annual reports
Acquirer SOE	An indicator variable which takes on the value of one if the acquiring firm had equity owned by the government and zero otherwise.	Company annual reports
G ownership	Percentage of equity ownership of the acquirer held by the government.	Company annual reports
Acquirer leverage	Total long-term debt as percentage of total common equity.	Datastream
Acquirer size	Natural logarithm of market value of equity of the acquiring firm (in millions of VND), calculated as the number of shares outstanding multiplied by the stock price at two months prior to deal announcement.	Datastream
Acquirer Tobin's Q	Market value of assets over book value of assets of the acquiring firm.	Datastream
Acquirer operating cash flow	Acquirer's cash flow from operating activities divided by total assets.	Datastream
Acquirer ROA	The acquiring firm's earnings before interest, tax and depreciation and amortisation (EBITDA), scaled by book value of assets.	Datastream
Acquirer board size	Total number of directors on board of the acquiring firm.	Company annual reports
Acquirer auditor	An indicator variable that takes on the value of one if the acquiring firm had one of the Big 4 firms as their auditor and zero otherwise.	Company annual reports
Non-executive	Percentage of non-executive directors on board of the acquiring firm.	Company annual reports
CEO degree	An indicator variable which takes on the value of one if the CEO of the acquiring firm had a business-related degree and zero otherwise.	Company annual reports/prospectus
CEO age	The age of the CEO of the acquiring firm at deal announcement time.	Company annual reports/prospectus
CEO ownership	Percentage of equity ownership of the acquirer held by the CEO and his/her family members.	Company annual reports/prospectus
Acquirer insiders	Percentage of equity ownership of the acquirer held by its directors, executives and other employees.	Company annual reports/prospectus

(*continued*)

(continued)

Variables	Definitions[+]	Data source
Acquirer Dom institutional	Percentage of equity ownership of the acquirer held by investors that were registered with the State Securities Commission as a Vietnamese legal entity.	Company annual reports/prospectus
Acquirer foreign institutional	Percentage of acquirer's equity held by investors that were registered with the State Securities Commission as a foreign legal entity.	Company annual reports/prospectus
Target listing status	An indicator variable that takes on the value of one if the target firm was a listed firm (on HNX or HSX) and zero otherwise.	Company annual reports/prospectus
Target SOE status	An indicator variable that takes on the value of one if the target firm had the state among its shareholders and zero otherwise.	Company annual reports/prospectus
Deal type	An indicator variable taking the value of one if the deal is related (acquirer and target sharing the same 2-digit SIC code) and zero otherwise.	ThomsonONE[++]
Equity acquired	The size of the equity of the target owned by the acquirer after the deal, measured in percentage.	ThomsonONE
Toehold	An indicator variable that takes on the value of one if the acquirer owned a non-zero percentage of target's equity prior to the announcement date and zero otherwise.	ThomsonONE
Pre-deal ROA	The average of industry-adjusted ROA in the two years prior to the deal announcement for the acquiring firm.	Datastream
Pre-deal EPS growth	The average of industry-adjusted EPS growth in the two years prior to the deal announcement for the acquiring firm.	Datastream
Pre-deal sales per share growth	The average of industry-adjusted growth of sales per share in the two years prior to the deal announcement for the acquiring firm.	Datastream
$\Delta EPSG$	The acquirer's change in industry-adjusted growth in EPS from two years before to two years after deal completion.	Datastream
ΔROA	The acquirer's change in industry-adjusted ROA from two years before to two years after deal completion.	Datastream
$CAR(-n, +n)$	Cumulative abnormal returns for the acquirer using the market model estimated based on the return data of 200 trading days ending 60 days before the announcement date.	Datastream

+Except for where indicated differently, measured values are taken for the financial year ending before the deal announcement date.
++ThomsonOne.com Investment Banker database

References

Agrawal, A., Cooper, T., Lian, Q., & Wang, Q. (2013). Common Advisers in Mergers and Acquisitions: Determinants and Consequences. *Journal of Law and Economics, 56*(3), 691–740.

Alexandridis, G., Petmezas, D., & Travlos, N. G. (2010). Gains from Mergers and Acquisitions Around the World: New Evidence. *Financial Management, 39*(4), 1671–1695.

Andrade, G., Mitchell, M., & Stafford, E. (2001). New Evidence and Perspectives on Mergers. *The Journal of Economic Perspectives, 15*(2), 103–120.

Armstrong, C. S., Jagolinzer, A. D., & Larcker, D. F. (2010). Chief Executive Officer Equity Incentives and Accounting Irregularities. *Journal of Accounting Research, 48*(2), 225–271.

Babbie, E. R. (2008). *The Basics of Social Research.* Thompson Wadsworth.

Balachandran, B., Faff, R., & Theobald, M. (2008). Rights Offerings, Takeup, Renounceability, and Underwriting Status. *Journal of Financial Economics, 89*(2), 328–346.

Balachandran, B., Faff, R., Theobald, M., & van Zijl, T. (2012). Rights Offerings, Subscription Period, Shareholder Takeup, and Liquidity. *Journal of Financial and Quantitative Analysis, 47*(1), 213–239.

Brewer, J., & Hunter, A. (2006). *Foundations of Multi-method research: Synthesising styles.* Sage.

Brown, S. J., & Warner, J. B. (1980). Measuring Security Price Performance. *Journal of Financial Economics, 8*(3), 205–258.

Brown, S. J., & Warner, J. B. (1985). Using Daily Stock Returns: The Case of Event Studies. *Journal of Financial Economics, 14*(1), 3–31.

Cai, Y., & Sevilir, M. (2012). Board Connections and M&A Transactions. *Journal of Financial Economics, 103*(2), 327–349.

Carline, N. F., Linn, S. C., & Yadav, P. K. (2009). Operating Performance Changes Associated with Corporate Mergers and the Role of Corporate Governance. *Journal of Banking & Finance, 33*(10), 1829–1841.

Corbin, J. M., & Strauss, A. (2008). *Basics of Qualitative Research: Techniques and Procedures for Developing Grounded Theory.* Sage.

Creswell, J. W. (2008). *Qualitative Inquiry and Research Design: Choosing Among five Traditions.* SAGE.

Creswell, J. W. (2014). *Research Design: Qualitative, Quantitative, and Mixed Methods Approaches.* SAGE Publications.

Denzin, N. K. (1978). *The Research Act: A Theoretical Introduction to Sociological Methods.* McGraw-Hill.

Fama, E. F. (1998). Market Efficiency, Long-term Returns, and Behavioral Finance. *Journal of Financial Economics, 49*(3), 283–306.

Fama, E. F., Fisher, L., Jensen, M. C., & Roll, R. (1969). The Adjustment of Stock Prices to New Information. *International Economic Review, 10*(1), 1–21.

Fan, J. P. H., Wei, K. C. J., & Xu, X. (2011). Corporate Finance and Governance in Emerging Markets: A Selective Review and an Agenda for Future Research. *Journal of Corporate Finance, 17*(2), 207–214.

Ghosh, A. (2001). Does Operating Performance Really Improve Following Corporate Acquisitions? *Journal of Corporate Finance, 7*, 151–178.

Grbich, C. (2007). *Qualitative Data Analysis: An Introduction.* SAGE.

Gregory, A. (1997). An examination of the Long Run Performance of UK Acquiring Firms. *Journal of Business, Finance and Accounting, 24*, 971–1002.

Guba, E. G., & Lincoln, Y. S. (Eds.). (1994). *Competing Paradigms in Qualitative Research.* Sage.

Hawawini, G., & Swary, I. (1990). *Mergers and Acquisitions in the US Banking Industry.* Elsevier Science Publishers.

Higgins, H. N. (2013). Conflicts of Interest between Banks and Firms: Evidence from Japanese Mergers. *Pacific-Basin Finance Journal, 24*(0), 156–178.

Imbens, G. W., & Wooldridge, J. M. (2009). Recent Developments in the Econometrics of Program Evaluation. *Journal of Economic Literature, 47*(1), 5–86.

Ismail, A., Davidson, I., & Frank, R. (2009). Operating Performance of European Bank Mergers. *The Service Industries Journal, 29*(3), 345–366.

Iyengar, R. J., & Zampelli, E. M. (2009). Self-selection, Endogeneity, and the Relationship between CEO Duality and Firm Performance. *Strategic Management Journal, 30*(10), 1092–1112.

Kale, P. (2004). *Acquisition Value Creation in Emerging Markets: An Empirical Study of Acquisitions in India.* Academy of Management Proceedings. 2004. H1-H6. 10.5465/AMBPP.2004.13863267.

Keown, A. J., & Pinkerton, J. M. (1981). Merger Announcements and Insider Trading Activity: An Empirical Investigation. *The Journal of Finance, 36*(4), 855–869.

King, N. (Ed.). (2004a). *Using Interviews in Qualitative Research.* Sage Publications.

King, N. (Ed.). (2004b). *Using Templates in the Thematic Analysis of Text.* SAGE Publications.

Ma, J., Pagan, J. A., & Chu, Y. (2009). Abnormal Returns to Mergers and Acquisitions in Ten Asian Stock Markets. *International Journal of Business, 14*(3), 235–250.

Martin, P. Y., & Turner, B. A. (1986). Grounded Theory and Organisational Research. *The Journal of Applied Behavioural Science, 22*(2), 141–157.

Masulis, R. W., Wang, C., & Xie, F. E. I. (2007). Corporate Governance and Acquirer Returns. *The Journal of Finance, 62*(4), 1851–1889.

Meulbroek, L. K. (1992). An Empirical Analysis of Illegal Insider Trading. *The Journal of Finance, 47*(5), 1661–1699. https://doi.org/10.2307/2328992

Miles, M. B., & Huberman, A. M. (1994). *Qualitative Data Analysis: an Expanded Sourcebook.* SAGE Publications.

Morse, J. M., & Niehaus, L. (2009). *Mixed Methods design: Principles and Procedures.* Left Coast Press.

Mulherin, J. H., & Boone, A. L. (2000). Comparing Acquisitions and Divestitures. *Journal of Corporate Finance, 6*(2), 117–139.

Pham, N. (2015). *The Impact of the State on M&A performance: an Empirical Study on Vietnam.* Thesis, Department of Finance. Melbourne, Australia, La Trobe University. PhD.

Pham, N., Oh, K. B., & Pech, R. (2015). Mergers and Acquisitions: CEO Duality, Operating Performance and Stock Returns in Vietnam. *Pacific-Basin Finance Journal, 35,* 298–316. https://doi.org/10.1016/j.pacfin.2015.01.007

Ramdani, D., & van Witteloostuijn, A. (2010). The Impact of Board Independence and CEO Duality on Firm Performance: A Quantile Regression Analysis for Indonesia, Malaysia, South Korea and Thailand. *British Journal of Management, 21*(3), 607–627.

Shams, S., Gunasekarage, A., & Colombage, S. R. N. (2013). Does the Organisational Form of the Target Influence Market Reaction to Acquisition Announcements? Australian Evidence. *Pacific-Basin Finance Journal, 24*(0), 89–108.

Tashakkori, A., & Teddlie, C. (1998). *Mixed Methodology: Combining Qualitative and Quantitative Approaches.* Sage.

The World Bank. (2019). Taking Stock December 2019 Finance in Transition: Unlocking Capital Markets for Vietnam's Future Development. http://documents1.worldbank.org/curated/en/971881576078190397/pdf/Finance-in-Transition-Unlocking-Capital-Markets-for-Vietnam-s-Future-Development.pdf

Tucker, J. W. (2010). Selection Bias and Econometric Remedies in Accounting and Finance Research. *Journal of Accounting Literature, 29,* 31–57.

Vuong, Q. H., Tran, T. D., & Nguyen, T. C. H. (2009). *Mergers and Acquisitions in Vietnam's Emerging Market Economy, 1990–2009.* CEB Working Paper. Centre Emile Berhheim, Solvay Brussels School of Economics and Management. Brussels, Belgium.

CHAPTER 6

Qualitative Findings: M&A Motivations and Performance Drivers

The strategic motivations and performance drivers of state-owned firms, especially those with mixed ownership, are arguably an underexplored area of research. Fforde, a scholar who has written extensively on Vietnamese SOEs, comments that *"Just because something is called an SOE means neither that you know what it actually is, nor whether you should like or dislike what it contributes to development"* (Fforde, 2007, p. 227).

This chapter presents the findings of the first phase of the research, the exploratory qualitative study, from the thematic analysis of the interviews' data. The study aims to understand the motivations and success factors of M&A of SIEs and non-SIEs in Vietnam.

The two groups of respondents are the M&A professionals (P) and corporate managers (M) of an acquiring firm. We asked the former group to comment on the M&A activity in Vietnam in general, the popular deal motivations and deal performance determinants. We only asked questions regarding deal motivations and performance with the latter group, as illustrated in Fig. 6.1. Among the respondent acquirers, there were six state-owned firms, three of which were listed on the stock exchange.

We conducted a review of the literature related to M&A motivations and performance to help design the semi-structured interviewing questions. The unstructured part of the interviews allows the researcher flexibility to follow up on emerging issues or concepts raised by the participants. The list of relevant prior studies reviewed that guided the interview

© The Author(s), under exclusive license to Springer Nature
Singapore Pte Ltd. 2021
N. Pham, K.-B. Oh, *State on Board!*,
https://doi.org/10.1007/978-981-16-3525-0_6

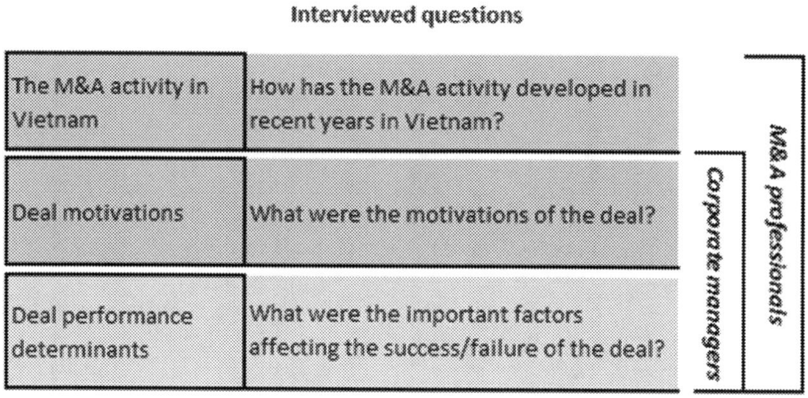

Interviewed questions

The M&A activity in Vietnam	How has the M&A activity developed in recent years in Vietnam?		
Deal motivations	What were the motivations of the deal?	Corporate managers	M&A professionals
Deal performance determinants	What were the important factors affecting the success/failure of the deal?		

Fig. 6.1   The groups of respondents and questions asked

questions is provided in Appendix 1 and the framework for codes analysis in Appendix 2.

Adopting the grounded theory methodology, we were mindful that the participant and his/her information might drive the interview rather than the pre-specified factors or parameters. Therefore, the findings reported in this chapter are organised according to themes and sub-themes that emerged during the interviews. Although we chose to discuss the common patterns of the experience among the cases, this is not, by any means, to undervalue the particular context and complexity of each M&A case.

As shown by the word frequency tag cloud[1] in Fig. 6.2, the most frequent factors respondents mentioned during their interviews were management, strategic assets, market conditions, competitive forces, legal and political environment, valuation, capital, equity, cash, the state, SOEs, land, costs, sales, banks and foreign investors.

6.1   M&A OF SIEs

It seems that the state-owned sector of Vietnam is a puzzle that needs more research attention. The SOE sector has always been an attractive but challenging M&A market. Among the 20 M&A cases interviewed, there were six cases with state-owned acquirers and eight related to state-owned targets.

[1] Using Tagxedo—an online application that allows users to create tag clouds by importing texts (http://www.tagxedo.com/app.html)

Fig. 6.2 Word frequency tag cloud

A typical feature of the M&A market in Vietnam was the participation of SOEs on both buy and sell sides. The privatisation process in Vietnam has increased the supply of fully or partially privatised firms as potential target firms in the market. Besides, SOEs are also very active acquirers in both listed and unlisted markets. As SOEs are typically perceived to be relatively less efficient than private firms (Allen et al., 2005; Firth et al., 2012, 2013) and SOEs' decisions are driven by multiple socio-economic objectives of the government (Firth et al., 2012), SOEs likely conduct M&A differently from that of non-SOEs. Thus, one crucial question that this qualitative study also addressed was whether SOEs' M&A were motivated and performed differently to those of non-SOEs.

> SOE deals usually are very large and complicated. SOEs are run in a management style that is motivated by both political and business philosophy. (Respondent P7)

6.2   M&A Motivations

Almost all motivations in the theoretical framework identified from prior literature, except for tax, were mentioned at least once in the interviews, suggesting that Vietnamese firms are no different from other firms when

Table 6.1   Deal motivations as identified by participants and ranking

What was the motivation of the deal?[a]	Ranking
The assets owned by the target	1
Restructuring and cost-cutting	2
Types of synergies	3
External factors (such as industry regulation and competition)	4
Market entry, expansion, value chain integration	5
The management, financial performance of the target	6
The valuation of the target	7
The fitness between the acquirer and target	8
The management, performance and acquisition experience of the acquirer	9
The cash flow of the acquirer and target	10
Other alternatives rather than M&A considered	11
Tax motivation	n/a

[a]For the detailed analysis of M&A motivations, performance drivers and interview quotes, please see Pham, N (2015)

it comes to M&A criteria and decision-making. Participants suggested undervalued targets, cash, connections, competition, overcoming legal barriers, economies of scale, cost management and market entry and expansion as M&A motivations.

Although each deal was unique, there seemed to be a number of common motivations that drove the M&A cases interviewed. The most frequently mentioned motivations were strategic asset acquisition and restructuring to respond to changes in the industry's competitive landscape. Synergies were also identified as important. However, since the participants mentioned synergies in the context of the deal success factors, we will discuss synergies in the next section as a driver of deal performance (Table 6.1).

6.2.1   Strategic Assets

The highest frequency count or top motivation was "an important asset" owned by the target firm. This leads our discussion to the characteristics of these assets and the available options for firms to obtain these assets.

It appears that one thing these assets had in common was their underlying legal rights to conduct business. Conditional business activities such as mining (P1 and M14), energy power plant (M15), cement production (M13) and financial services (M7) required a business to fulfil certain

Table 6.2   List of strategic assets discussed by the respondents

Respondent	Strategic assets	Acquirer	Target
P1	Mines and mining licence	Non-SIE	SIE
M3	Specialised plant with a fully approved licence	SIE	SIE
M4	An approved forestation project and land	Non-SIE	Non-SIE
M7	A fund management licence	Non-SIE	Non-SIE
M13	A product quality certificate and a sales contract	Non-SIE	SIE
M14	A mining licence	Non-SIE	Non-SIE
M15	State-approved hydropower projects with sales contracts	Non-SIE	SIE
M10, M16	The land-use right for a strategic location	Non-SIE	SIE

conditions, capabilities and resources to be able to operate in the field. These legal or regulatory barriers to entry sustain the industry's positive economic profit (non-normal profit) condition. Both groups of interviewees, corporate managers and M&A professionals, contended that the process to obtain a business licence in Vietnam was complicated, making firms with existing business licences attractive targets (Table 6.2).

In 60% of the interviewed cases, the target that had a strategic asset was an SIE. Both SIE and non-SIE targets owned strategic assets, in the form of business licences in conditional business activities and approved projects. Apart from that, SIE deals, however, were related to land-use rights and secured sales contracts (particularly with large state-owned groups).

The motive for acquiring strategic assets could be understood in light of the firm's resource-based view in which firms always have a need to generate or obtain resources and utilise them effectively (Barney & Hesterly, 2006). The valuable, rare, imperfectly imitable and non-substitutable assets of a firm determine its competitive advantage and performance (Barney, 1991). In the same line, according to Amit and Schoemaker (1993), these assets are considered "strategic" as they are difficult to trade and appropriate and specialised resource bestows the firm's competitive advantages. There are often challenging barriers to owning these assets. However, if a firm can overcome the obstacles to obtain these resources and enhance the productivity of the resources, this effort will pay off from the economic rents it creates (Makadok, 2001).

What are the barriers or obstacles, and why do firms choose business acquisition as a solution to acquire these assets?

Firstly, as an industry evolves, its regulatory environment changes and access to resources becomes more limited. In a conditional business activity, incumbent firms have access to resources, licences and approvals, which are essential assets sought by new entrants. SIEs are typically among the incumbent firms.

Over time, the regulators tend to tighten the requirements for new entrants to access such resources. The shortcut for latecomers is thus to acquire an incumbent firm that owns the needed resources. SOEs, for example, are attractive targets for M&A for having valuable land-use rights. Private firms usually find it very difficult, if not impossible, to be allocated land at great locations.

Similarly, first-comer firms find easier access to assets such as mining licences, brokerage and fund management licences and trade contracts compared to latecomers. Around the Vietnamese stock market boom in 2005–2007, the number of new financial firms increased substantially. The issue was that many of these firms were not performing well. After the financial crisis in 2008, they were just a shell with a financial licence. The State Securities Committee then decided to consolidate the industry and almost stopped granting new licences. The firm of Respondent M17 chose to acquire a financial firm with a fund management licence to enter this business rather than applying for it from SSC.

> We were profitable, and we had international fund management experience. Yet, since they (SSC) had almost stopped issuing new licences, it would be challenging for us to apply for one. We also considered the application fees, preparation expenses and the opportunity cost of not accessing the required minimum capital of VND 25 billion to be deposited with the SSC during the application processing time, which we did not know how long it would be. We decided to buy a financial firm with a licence instead. (Respondent M7, CEO, a private financial firm)

Some other managers (Respondent M4, M10 and M14) explicitly mentioned that when the regulations became stricter, they chose to acquire a licence or a restricted resource via M&A. Essentially, M&A provides firms with a solution to close their resource gaps as the acquisition of resources is much faster than internal development (Deng, 2009).

Another example of strategic assets mentioned in the interviews is the power purchasing agreement (PPA) of power plants in the electricity market. First, it is necessary to understand the competitive landscape of the power market in Vietnam. It is a highly regulated market with an average annual growth of power demand of 14.5% from 2001 to 2010 (Nguyen, 2012). Despite the government's effort to restructure the electricity sector in recent years,[2] the market is still dominated by Electricity Vietnam (EVN). While EVN is a state-owned monopsony that buys electricity from the power plants, it is also a monopoly in supplying electricity to end users across the national power grid that it owns. According to the Institute of Energy, EVN directly owned 55.3% of all power plants that sell electricity to the national grid. Power-generating companies compete to sell electricity to EVN. EVN determines if it signs a long-term PPA with a power plant and the price for the agreement. State-owned power plants have advantages in obtaining a PPA. This explains why both Respondents M10 and M13 mentioned the target firm's existing sales contract with EVN as the motivation of the deal. Both of these target firms were SIEs.

Secondly, apart from the legal barriers applied to particular restricted business activity, there might be non-legal, unofficial or unwritten barriers to obtaining these assets. Theoretically, any process should be transparent, and the outcome is based on merit. In practice, there may be unwritten rules or hurdles that require political connection to unblock. Firms with political connection enjoy more favourable regulatory conditions (Agrawal & Knoeber, 2001) and have more access to resources (Claessens et al., 2008). Agrawal and Knoeber (2001) reported that politically experienced directors benefit their firms in predicting government actions in regulated industries, public procurement and changing trade policies for US firms. For firms under weak market conditions, institutional and legal protection and political connections are even more crucial (Li et al., 2008). Firms without such links could be disadvantaged.

The resource-based view from the strategic management literature, thus, offers an exciting insight to understand the motivation of Vietnamese firms' M&A. There are always assets that, though costly, must be acquired because they are necessary resources for a firm to survive in this changing

---

[2] EVN was restructured as a holding company in 2006. In 2007, the government approved the equitisation plan to partially privatise its operating units, with EVN retaining the majority of the equity. The equitisation process, however, has been delayed since then due to the difficulty in attracting investors due to the global market. In 2006, the government passed the plan to reform the electricity market with the first phase being to establish a competitive generation market, the second phase being to build a competitive wholesale market and the last phase being a competitive retail market towards 2022 (Nguyen, 2012).

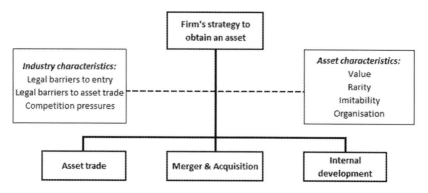

Fig. 6.3   Strategies to obtain an asset

environment (Akdoğu, 2011). The diagram below depicts the nexus between using M&A as a strategy for organisational restructuring and asset acquisition within the context of the "Value, Rarity, Imitability and Organisation" (VRIO) model and Porter's Five Forces model.

From the analysis in the preceding chapter, we develop the framework shown in Fig. 6.3, which integrates the VRIO model (Barney & Hesterly, 2006) and elements of Porter's Five Forces model (Porter, 2008) to explain a firm's decision on the alternatives to the strategy to obtain an asset. To obtain an asset, options available to a firm include, firstly, asset trade, which is to acquire the asset via its market; secondly, M&A, which is to purchase the business that owns the asset; and lastly, to generate the asset internally. The decision of a firm on the strategy to obtain an asset depends on industry characteristics (Porter, 2008) and the characteristics of the asset itself, as illustrated by the VRIO model (Barney & Hesterly, 2006). If there is a liquid market for the asset, it could be obtained via asset trade. Nevertheless, in cases where legal barriers do not allow the asset to be transferred, asset trade is not a viable option. Examples of non-transferable assets are certain land-use rights and business licences. The option to generate the asset internally is advisable when it can be done timely to ensure the relevance of the value of the asset and with reasonable costs. In other cases, obtaining the asset via M&A should be considered. From the interviews with corporate managers, it seems that M&A should be the preferred strategy under the following conditions:

- The asset is valuable to the firm because:
  - There are high entry barriers in the industry, and the asset itself can be an effective barrier to entry.
  - Competition in the industry is not perfect, and there is possibly economic rent that motivates firms to obtain the strategic asset to enter into or remain in the industry.
- The asset is rare, and there is no available market for asset trade.
- The asset is not imitable and not substitutable.
- The organisation has the required capacity to exploit its value.
- There are legal barriers to asset trade, that is, the asset is not transferable.
- There are barriers to generating the asset, including regulatory restrictions or significant transaction costs.

This analysis highlights an important issue that, when a market is imperfect with various barriers and explicit and implicit transaction costs, M&A through the market for corporate control could be more efficient than the market for resources as an effective channel for firms to access strategic assets.

The notes from the interviews on M&A motivations and a brief description of the strategic assets involved in the deals are provided in Appendix 3 and Appendix 4 at the end of the chapter.

6.2.2 Restructuring for Efficiency

Other M&A motivations drawn from the interviews were related to efficiency improvement and restructuring for both SIEs and private firms. Both corporate manager and M&A professional groups agreed that Vietnamese firms needed to restructure to improve efficiency and M&A could be a vehicle. Efficiency improvement gains were expected from better capital management of the target firm (M1), economies of scales of distribution channels (M2, M3, M4, M8, M9, M12 and M20), cost savings (M8) and refocusing on core business (P5 and M8). It is clear from the interviews that the scope of competition facing Vietnamese firms is no longer domestic. The need to restructure to be more efficient and to remain competitive is evident at all levels, from the government's macroeconomic policies to firms' development strategy.

One thing in common shared by the six state-owned acquirers in the sample is that M&A, for them, was a vehicle for restructuring. According to Respondent M2, managers of state-owned firms were not well prepared to compete in a less protected environment. So, when markets were opened up, these firms faced more competition and failed. Although other respondents did not elaborate on the problem of the low efficiency of SOEs that led to the M&A, the evidence of the poor performance of the state-owned sector in Vietnam is widely abundant. This poor performance has been blamed centrally on the problem of low productivity due to labour surplus in the state-owned sector, where compensation and employment are tied to cronyism rather than merit and performance (Fforde, 2007).

We also asked these SIEs whether they choose to merge or are directed by the state if they have the autonomy to select a partner and to decide the deal structure. In three out of six deals, the respondents directly mentioned that the M&A was conducted under direction from the government. An important example is a merger in case M3, which involved two listed SOEs, one of the largest deals on the stock exchange. The deal was directed by a large state-owned general corporation which was the majority owner of both firms. The purpose was to restructure for efficiency improvement, re-brand the group and consolidate the industry. Despite being listed firms with supposedly a number of public shareholders, the two firms engaged in a deal that was totally directed by the state-owned group via its ownership role. Therefore, it could be seen that SIEs' M&A are heavily influenced by the state, a typical reason for principal-principal conflict.

6.3   SIEs' M&A Performance

6.3.1   The Moral Hazard of Easy Capital

Considering the motivation for growth or restructuring of SIEs, M&A were seen as necessary. Regarding performance, however, SIEs' M&A were far from successful, despite the privileges they enjoy.

In several interviews, there were discussions of such privileges, including the strong political connection that could support the deal (Respondent M9), easier access to funding for restructuring (Respondent M1, M5 and M8) and business concessions in taxes and rates during the restructuring period (Respondent M1). This is similar to what is observed in China, where politically connected acquirers receive preferential treatment, and they have the choice to acquire higher-quality firms during privatisation (Tu et al., 2013).

In terms of funding, SOEs have easier access to external finance because banks tend to favour firms with state ownership.[3] However, our interviews revealed that the privileged access to capital of SOEs might increase the moral hazard issue in capital allocation, which could lead to wealth-destroying acquisitions.

An illustration was case M8, a listed firm founded in 2004 with 51% state capital,[4] held by a large state-owned corporation and 49% public holdings with an initial capital of VND 50 billion. Being a large SOE and a listed firm, it could mobilise funds from the securities market easily to raise its capital to VND 1000 billion after three equity issues within its first three years of listing. "*We were 'flooded' with so much money which we invested in poor projects via M&A*", its CFO commented. The company conducted several large acquisitions to expand across the nations. Nevertheless, it soon learned that the expansion was so rapid that it did not have the capacity to manage effectively. In 2012, it was struggling with approximately VND 1200 billion in debts.

Strikingly, it was the moral hazard of having easy access to capital, coupled with weak management competence. This problem was not unique to the SOE in this case. Prior to 2012, many SOEs in Vietnam invested capital in non-core business activities that were not well managed.

The over-diversification problem, weaknesses in corporate governance and the failure in managing complicated business models gave rise to the national bad debt crisis in Vietnam. The alarming level of bad debt within the SOE sector in the nation heightened in 2009–2010 with the instances of Vinashin and VinaLines[5] among other well-established SOEs, resulting in a call for further reform of the state-owned sector. In 2012, the government demanded SOEs to divest all investments in non-core business activities.

---

[3] Abundant evidence in the literature from China (Aivazian et al., 2005; Cull & Xu, 2003; Firth et al., 2008, Wei & Wang, 1997)

[4] As at the time of the interview in December 2012, the state capital in the firm has been reduced to approximately 36% of equity.

[5] Vinashin, the Vietnam National Shipbuilding Industry Group, is the biggest shipbuilding company in Vietnam. The group multiples inefficient investments in a diversified range of fields, resulting in a huge loss of VND 900 billion. Similarly, due to the same problem, VinaLines, the Vietnam National Shipping Lines, another large state-owned group, reported a loss of VND 1685 billion or US $81 million in the financial year of 2009–2010. (http://www.amcham-vietnam.com/5558/the-unlearned-lesson-vinashin-vinalines-and-other-soes-inefficiencies/).

Theoretically, this issue represents an agency cost to the firm and non-state shareholders of the listed SOE discussed above. Inefficient capital investment by management and weak monitoring by the state shareholder adversely affected the return on capital of minority shareholders, that is, the principal-principal problem.

6.3.2   The State as a Shareholder

The interviews with the managers of the state-owned acquiring firms revealed several issues regarding the way the state exercises its ownership rights and responsibilities, including marginalising minority shareholders in decision-making, "term-bound" thinking, rent-seeking mindset, favour-granting attitude and board participation.

Marginalising Minority Shareholders
The first issue is the possibility of expropriating minority shareholders' interest due to the heterogeneity of ownership motives inherent in SOEs, as argued in Chap. 4. In the merger of M3, despite the dissatisfaction of some institutional minority shareholders, after two rounds of voting, the merger went ahead with an equity exchange ratio that disadvantaged the shareholders of the target firm, according to Respondent M3. This was because the state shareholder controlled both the target and acquiring firm, and it insisted that these two firms would merge. The state share-holder decided the deal's structure, conducted the valuation, determined the payment method and exchange ratio and the governance of the newly merged firm. Apparently, the state shareholder's decision will serve its own interest, which could marginalise minority investors. Additionally, the minority shareholders of both acquirer and target firms were also affected when the government directed the state shareholder to change their investment strategies, such as those SOEs having to fully divest their acquired business due to over-diversification and poor performance (M5 and M9)

"Short-termism" or "term-bound" Economic Thinking and Behaviour
Second, from the interviews, we gathered evidence of "short-termism" or "term-bound" thinking among SOE managers. The exact Vietnamese term is "tư duy nhiệm kỳ". This concept refers to the phenomenon in which the economic thinking and behaviour of an individual, a business or a state organisation are shaped by the political term or the serving term of

the individual. Surprisingly, to the best of my knowledge, there has been no equivalent term in the current Western literature. We roughly translated it into English as "short-termism" or "term-bound" behaviour. This translation, however, is far from perfect as it does not have the notation of the thinking being constrained by the length of the political term.

As this concept is highly contextual, it is important to look into the root of the concept in the context of Vietnam.

Vietnam used to have a centrally planned economy until Doi Moi in 1986 (the Reform). Five-year master plans, corresponding to the five-year cycle of the National Congress of the Communist Party, guide the economy, similar to the model of the former Soviet Union and the current People's Republic of China. Although the country has moved towards a market economy, Vietnam still retains the same planning behaviour in which one national master plan maps strategies for development with growth targets and development guidelines for all provinces. Political leaders, at both central and local levels, therefore, are under a lot of pressure to meet the growth target of their term.

Like China, their political advancement in the party hierarchy partly depends on their performance, measured by the regional economic growth achieved within their term. Political leaders, in many cases, are promoted from CEOs and directors of SOEs. Therefore, while running an SOE or sitting on its board, these managers or directors may be driven by their political aspirations rather than just maximising firm value. Respondent M8 used the term "term-bound" thinking when mentioning the directors representing state capital on the board:

> Their view is limited by the five-year term. They do not share the same long-term view of the business. (Respondent M8)

Respondent M2 and M5 also pointed to "short-termism" as an essential issue in SOE leadership in a broader context or, in other words, a systematic problem. According to these two experienced managers, as SOEs were explicitly regarded as tools for the government to control the macroeconomy,[6] they were vulnerable to economic policy changes every time a new five-year national economic plan was introduced. Specifically, the five-year plan introduced in 2001 of the 9th National Party Congress upheld the role of SOEs as the primary force of economic development

[6] In the Party Documents of the 9th National Party Congress.

and encouraged the large state-owned corporations to develop into economic groups by investing in a diversified range of business activities. This led to a boom of M&A by the state-owned sector in the period of 2005–2008.

The evaluation of the two consecutive five-year plans from 2001 to 2010, however, concluded that most large SOEs over-diversified and were not capable of management, resulting in loss of state capital in many cases. To rectify the problem, in the 2011–2016 plan, the 11th National Party Congress asked SOEs to refocus on their core business. SOEs were then given three years until 2015 to divest capital from investments unrelated to the core business, many of which were investments in listed companies.[7] The pressure for SOEs to divest or exit a firm, in turn, would lead to significant changes in the ownership structure and board composition of the divested firm.

As a result, in 2012, the pressure of selling from SOEs selling shares of companies not related to its core business activity drove the stock market down, representing a critical risk of having an SOE as a shareholder. This is how "term-bound" thinking and behaviour at the macro level could affect firms at the micro level.

Business Mindset of SOEs: Rent-Seeking or Value-Creating
Another fascinating insight gained from the interview with Respondent M8 was concerning the need to change the mindset of business leaders when SOEs, especially those with mixed ownership, have to cope with the changing environment.

This was the case of a firm that started as an SOE in the property development and construction sector. After a few years of being listed on the stock exchange, the state reduced the company's ownership from a majority to a significant minority holding.

In the very early years, the company earned a superior profit from its rent-seeking[8] business model. According to the CFO of the company, their business model was simple. Good political connections facilitated access to lands, most of which were classified as rural lands for farming, at

---

[7] Government Resolution No. 26/NQ-CP, dated 9 July 2012 requiring large state-owned groups to divest all non-core business investments by 2015.

[8] In economics, the term "rent-seeking" refers to obtaining control of land or natural resources and profiteering by manipulating the social and political environment, rather than by creating new wealth.

low to almost no costs. The company then applied to convert the land to a commercial or residential purpose—the market value of the land rocketed by multiple times. In the past, this firm's superior profitability came from obtaining land-use rights and transferring the mere title to property developers.

This is a typical example of rent-seeking behaviour. A business builds political connections and lobbies to gain access to resources at the disadvantages of those not having the same status (Claessens et al., 2008). The situation, however, changed when land-use rights were revalued at market price when initially allocated to businesses. The company, in this case, could no longer earn superior profit by subsequently transferring the land-use rights to other parties. The firm acquired a number of companies as a way to move down the value chain into infrastructure development, property development and construction and asset management. As the firm did not have the expertise in these areas, they struggled to manage these acquisitions. From a cash-rich firm, they morphed into a financially distressed firm within less than five years. The critical issue for this firm was its inability to transit from a rent-seeking business to a true value-creating model.

Another issue with the rent-seeking business model is ethical and legal risks. SOEs may benefit from the strong political connection of the state shareholder in winning contracts and obtaining project approvals. However, due to the corruptive practices of the system and the lack of transparency, the boundary between legal rent-seeking behaviour and corruptive lobbying for economic privileges is vague. This puts the firm and other non-state shareholders at risk.

According to Respondent M2, the CEO of a company that had partially acquired an SOE in manufacturing, after the acquisition, his primary focus was to ensure that the firm could transform itself from a political to a business mindset in leadership. This leadership was even more critical when the country itself was struggling to transition from a planned to a more market-oriented economy. Firms had to formulate appropriate strategies for themselves to adapt to these market changes. In his view, firms had to be proactive and use M&A as a vehicle for change, but it should be well planned to suit the business's capacity and strategy.

Favour-Granting Attitude
The fourth issue identified from the interviews was the "favour-granting attitude" of representatives of the state capital. In the case of M8, the state

shareholder was an SOE group, represented by two directors (out of five) on the firm's board. The two directors were managers of the shareholder SOE. As commented by the CFO (M8), there were particular costs involved.

> They [the state capital representatives] are SOE employees. They think that they are in a position to favour our company rather than being an owner. We have to pay for their travels and accommodation, dine them and wine them every time they come for a board meeting. (Respondent M8, CFO, a listed SOE)

He seemed to suggest that there were costs involved with the firm having to please the state capital representatives. The state capital representatives still maintain the favour-granting mindset of a typical SOE employee, and the firm needed to incentivise them to do their job. This is the explicit part of principal costs, the tip of an iceberg. The question is, however, whether these costs were spent to encourage more effective ownership responsibility of the state shareholder or for managers to "lobby" or "bribe" for favourable decisions from the state shareholder. The boundary is not clear.

The principal problem of the state as the shareholder could be severe for the firm if managers can manipulate the votes of the state to obtain a favourable outcome for themselves. In cases of significant state ownership, the vote of the state capital representative is essential to the firm. Managers tend to seek in-principle agreement from the state capital representatives before the matter is discussed in board meetings with all directors or put to the vote in shareholders' meetings. Lobbying, and even bribery, could involve extravagant dinners or expensive gifts, which increases the agency costs of the firm. Such practices are inequitable to other shareholders. The principal cost of the state shareholders, coupled with the agency cost of managerial behaviour, disadvantages minority shareholders.

The State Representation on the Board of Directors: Tokenism or Political Dominance

According to Respondent M5, the CFO of a listed firm with state capital held by a state-owned group, there were cases of "board sitters" who basically agreed with most small proposals of management. They took a long time to obtain direction from their superior for important management proposals such as M&A. Case M3, however, was on the other end of the

Fig. 6.4 Role of the
state on the board

inactive   political
tokenism   dominance

The state on BOD

spectrum where the representatives of state capital dominated the boards
of both the acquirer and target firms.

As discussed in Chap. 4, the remuneration of state capital representatives is typically unrelated to the performance of the firm in their charge.
State capital representatives have a weak incentive to devote time and
effort to board activities, and their board role can thus be relatively passive
(Fig. 6.4).

The channel through which the state shareholder controls an investee
firm is board participation, which could range from inactive tokenism to
political dominance. The voting power of the state is vested in representatives of the state capital, who largely determine how the ownership rights
and responsibilities of the state are exercised.

6.3.3 Putting the Term "Principal cost" into Perspective

If the term "agency cost" in agency theory refers to the costs of aligning
the behaviour of management—the agent employed by shareholders—
with shareholder wealth maximisation, then we propose that the costs
incurred by the firm in getting the shareholders to exercise their ownership
rights and responsibilities should be termed "principal costs".

We argue that although the principal-principal conflict is a type of
agency problem, "principal cost" is not, and should not be viewed as, a
subset of agency cost. The agency cost is generally understood to mean
the cost caused by managers, whereas principal cost is incurred because of
the principal.

This is, indeed, not the first time the term has been mentioned.
"Principal cost" was discussed by Dalziel et al. (2011) in the context of
initial public offerings of US firms. As the ownership structure of US firms
is widely dispersed, the principal-principal problem and its resulting principal costs are not a concern in the US market as they might be in other
markets where concentrated holding style is more evident (Claessens
et al., 2000; La Porta et al., 1999). Therefore, the relevance of the concept to the context in which it was introduced could be limited. However,

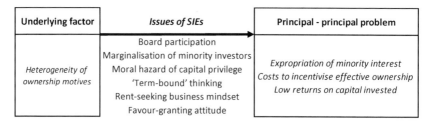

Underlying factor	*Issues of SIEs*	Principal - principal problem
Heterogeneity of ownership motives	Board participation Marginalisation of minority investors Moral hazard of capital privilege 'Term-bound' thinking Rent-seeking business mindset Favour-granting attitude	*Expropriation of minority interest* *Costs to incentivise effective ownership* *Low returns on capital invested*

Fig. 6.5   Elements of principal costs

for partially privatised SOEs in emerging markets, the issue becomes relevant and thus deserves attention.

Our study identified the underlying reason for the existence of principal costs within firms with state capital and the types of behaviour of the state shareholder that cause them. Figure 6.5 depicts the analysis process for the concept. Firstly, principal costs exist due to principal-principal conflict between the state shareholder and other shareholders in which the state tends to follow its political interest. Secondly, the types of behaviour of the state shareholder that could lead to principal costs borne by the firm include moral hazard of capital use, term-bound thinking, rent-seeking mindset and favour-granting attitude of the state capital representative.

The channel through which the state shareholder can exert its influence is board participation, ranging from very inactive or political dominance.

In summary, principal costs manifest the principal-principal conflict between the state and other private shareholders in mixed-ownership SOEs. We, therefore, have developed the theoretical concept of principal costs. We now define "principal costs" as (1) the negative impacts of the state, as a principal, deviating from the shareholder wealth maximisation objective and (2) the costs incurred by the firm in incentivising the principal (as the shareholder) to exercise their ownership rights and responsibilities effectively. We also provide quantitative empirical evidence that justifies this theorisation in the following chapters.

Although our analysis focuses on the principal costs of the state shareholder, the issue could also be relevant for other types of shareholders, potentially opening a new avenue for future research on the broader implications of principal costs for corporate governance in an institutionally transitioning market.

6.4 Chapter Conclusion: Links to the Quantitative Study

The qualitative analysis highlights some significant findings on the motivation and performance drivers of M&A in Vietnam. It appears that Vietnamese firms use M&A as a way to obtain strategic resources to sustain their competitive advantages and to restructure for efficiency improvement when coping with the changing competitive landscape. The resource-seeking motive of Vietnamese M&A is quite understandable given the fact that the Vietnamese economy is still in the factor-driven stage of development. Factors that contribute to the success of a merger or an acquisition include a long-term commitment from both sides of the deal, the strategic fit between the two firms, synergies, managing the risks involving with private target firms, market risks and legal risks and management and leadership for post-deal integration. Concerning SOEs, the in-depth interviews revealed that M&A transactions related to SOEs could be motivated by non-economic factors. The deal structure could be affected or directed by the state via its ownership in the firm. There were also principal costs associating with having the state as a shareholder. In summary, SOEs are under pressure to improve efficiency to survive in a more competitive environment and transform from a rent-seeking mindset to creating a value-added business model. M&A could be a solution, but if it is not well planned or deviates away from the principle of shareholder wealth maximisation, it could be a double-edged sword.

The findings from the exploratory qualitative study highlight the need to further examine the state ownership factor in the M&A context. While the in-depth interviews allow us to gain insights and valuable concepts, there are bound to be biased as much of this discussion is from the point of view of the respondents and perceived through the lens of the researcher. Furthermore, because the issues of state ownership are not limited to only the economic discipline but also social development and politics, a study on a large scale and free from personal bias will enhance the confidence of the findings. Therefore, we conducted a further investigation in the second phase of this research using secondary data collected from 188 mergers and acquisitions of listed firms in Vietnam.

The qualitative stage of this research provided a solid contextual foundation for model building and hypothesis development and testing in the quantitative investigation. While state ownership was central to the study, it was the complementarities involving aspects of financial performance, corporate governance, ownership and leadership that were interesting. This was reflected by the full set of control variables employed in the various multivariate models and the following chapters' findings.

APPENDIX 1: ACADEMIC LITERATURE GUIDING THE INTERVIEW QUESTIONS

M&A Deal Motivations

The assets owned by the target (Barney, 1991; Deng, 2009)
The management and financial performance of the target (Hannan & Rhoades, 1987; Kusewitt, 1985)
The valuation of the target (Akdoğu, 2011; Fu et al., 2013)
The valuation of the target (Akdoğu, 2011; Fu et al., 2013)
Cash flow of the acquirer and target (Jensen, 1986)
The fitness between the acquirer and target (Gammeltoft et al., 2012)
Types of synergies (Bradley et al., 1988)
Tax motivation (Auerbach & Reishus, 1986; Hulle et al., 1991)
The management, performance and acquisition experience of the acquirer (Haleblian & Finkelstein, 1999)
Market entry, expansion and value chain integration (Hankir et al., 2011)
External factors (such as industry regulation and competition) (Ahern, 2012; Akdoğu, 2009; Walker & Chi-Sheng, 2007)
Other alternatives rather than M&A considered (Brouthers & Dikova, 2010; Dyer et al., 2004)

Important Factors Affecting the Success/Failure of the Deal

Valuation (premium, methods, payment) (Fuller et al., 2002)
Diversification versus relatedness (Lubatkin, 1987)
Synergies (Bradley et al., 1988)
Governance, management and leadership (Marks et al., 2001; Masulis et al., 2007)
Ownership structure (Fuller et al., 2002; Goranova et al., 2010; Kam et al., 2008)
External factors to the acquirer and target (Agrawal et al., 2013; Walker & Chi-Sheng, 2007)

APPENDIX 2: CODING ANALYSIS USING THE COGNITIVE MAPPING TECHNIQUE

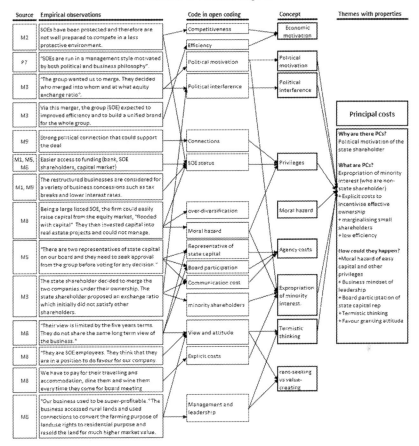

APPENDIX 3: DEAL MOTIVATIONS DISCUSSED
BY RESPONDENTS

M&A professionals		Corporate managers	
#	Deal motivations discussed	#	Deal motivations discussed
1	Personally motivated Political reasons Undervalued strategic assets Short-term investment gains Short-term capital funding	6	Valuation of the target company Directed acquisition for restructuring of SOEs
2	Backdoor listing Financially distressed targets Distribution channel Reduced costs (transaction costs for obtaining licences)	9	Distribution channel Restructuring for efficiency
3	Market access Cost saving	13	Restructuring of SOEs Distribution network and supply chain Economies of scale (cost saving) Brand value Good human resources A specialised plant to ensure inputs
4	Capital adequacy Economies of scale Improve brand awareness	14	Restructuring for efficiency Weak management Economies of scale (cost saving) Competitive environment Political connection
5	Market access	15	Restructuring of SOEs after over-diversifying Weak management (target)
7	Strategic locations of the target Distribution channels Local brand	17	Good human resources Weak management (target) Brand value and customer base, market share
8	Overall market trend Market access Distribution	18	Business licence in restricted business Market access (restricted business) Undervalued target (in distress) Connection of the target owners
10	Supply chain Restructuring after over-diversification Clear synergies Undervalued targets	19	Restructuring of SOEs and cost saving Improve core business Distribution network

(continued)

(continued)

M&A professionals		*Corporate managers*	
#	*Deal motivations discussed*	#	*Deal motivations discussed*
11	Horizontal expansion Restructuring of the SOEs Undervalued targets	20	Directed M&A for restructuring Capital adequacy Market share Distribution/customer base
12	Brand Distribution network	21	Strategic fit Land-use right at a strategic location Approved project
16	Backdoor listing Efficiency improvement (cut costs) Customer based Undervalued targets	22	Restructuring for capital adequacy and efficiency Target management
		23	Market expansion into related business Distribution network and brand value
		24	Quality certificate possessed by target Sales contract with Electricity Vietnam Strategic fit (complementary strengths) To diversify into new business activity
		25	Vertical integration to ensure supply Mining licence (fully approved)
		26	Fully approved power plant Power purchasing agreement with EVN Strategic fit with the acquirer's direction Strong independent cash flows
		27	Land-use right at a strategic location
		28	Business licence for a restricted activity Good staff with good relationship with clients Good customer base
		29	Good products Undervalued listed target Want to take over the shares of the state
		30	Market access and existing customer base
		31	Market access with existing distribution channels Business licence (approved by the Ministry of Culture and Communication)

APPENDIX 4: STRATEGIC ASSETS IN M&A

Case	Strategic asset	Explanatory notes
1	A mining licence	The acquirer was a private firm in the financial industry, whereas the target was a mining firm preparing for its IPO at the time of the deal. The acquirer paid VND 25 billion to obtain 50% of equity, knowing that the asset of the target was undervalued. After the acquisition, the acquiring firm re-evaluated the mines under the licence of the target. Six months later, the target was valued at VND 120 billion at the time of its IPO.
13	Specialised plant with licence	Both the acquirer and the target firms were publicly listed firms with state capital, in the cement manufacturing industry. The target owned and operated a clinker producing plant. As the government restricted the establishment of new cement manufacturing plants, the acquisition was the way to acquire the clinker facility, which could help the acquiring firm to reduce its dependence on imported inputs.
14	An approved forestation project and land	Both the acquirer and target firms were in the private sector. The acquirer was a foreign-invested conglomerate, and the target was in the furniture-making industry. The acquirer was looking for a supplier of pulp for paper making. Being a foreign-invested enterprise, the acquirer was not allowed to operate in certain forestation-related area. The plan was to partially acquire a subsidiary of the firm that had an approved forestation project. The firm had also secured the land for the project.
18	A fund management licence	The acquirer was a foreign-invested financial firm, and the target was a Vietnamese securities firm in financial distress. The target firm was fully licenced in stock brokerage and fund management. Due to the mushroom booming of the number of non-performing securities and fund management companies and prior to 2007–2008, the government had since restricted the establishment of new securities/investment firms. It was very difficult to obtain a new licence. The acquirer chose to acquire a shell firm with an existing/valid licence.
21	Land-use right for a strategic location	This was an experienced acquirer focusing on those targets that were privatised SOEs with good potential but poor management. The acquirer was in construction and development and asset management industry. The acquirer acquired 30% of the target in its IPO and later increased the holding to 90%. The target firm had the land-use right for a strategic position at the centre of Hanoi.

(*continued*)

(continued)

Case	Strategic asset	Explanatory notes
24	A product quality certificate and sales contract	The acquirer was a private construction firm wanting to expand into a new business activity. The target was a private company in manufacturing electrical equipment. The target had a number of product quality certificates, ISO certificates and existing sales contracts with Electricity Vietnam (EVN).
25	A mining licence	The acquirer was a large listed firm in multiple industries, one of which was steel production. The target was a private firm in the mining industry. As mining projects and exploration licences are not transferrable, and it was difficult to obtain State approval for new mining projects, the solution for the acquiring firm was to buy a firm that owned such projects. The reserves of the mines belonging to the target firm were estimated to last for 15–20 years, with 100% of output to be used to serve the acquiring firm.
26	State-approved hydropower projects with sales contracts	The acquirer was a large private group in property development and energy production. The target was a private hydropower plant that had secured a power purchasing agreement with Electricity Vietnam.
27	Land-use right for a strategic location	The acquiring firm was in construction and property development, whereas the target was in warehouse services. The target had the land-use right for a large area in a strategic location. The total value of the deal was VND 300 billion. The acquirer paid for 85% of equity by equity exchange first, and the remaining 15% of equity would be paid after the target had successfully converted the purpose of the land-use rights from an industrial warehouse to residential.

REFERENCES

Agrawal, A., Cooper, T., Lian, Q., & Wang, Q. (2013). Common Advisers in Mergers and Acquisitions: Determinants and Consequences. *Journal of Law and Economics, 56*(3), 691–740.

Agrawal, A., & Knoeber, C. R. (2001). Do Some Outside Directors Play a Political Role? *Journal of Law and Economics, 44*(1), 179–198.

Ahern, K. R. (2012). Bargaining Power and Industry Dependence in Mergers. *Journal of Financial Economics, 103*(3), 530–550.

Aivazian, V. A., Ge, Y., & Qiu, J. (2005). Can Corporatization improve the Performance of State-Qwned Enterprises even without Privatization? *Journal of Corporate Finance, 11*(5), 791–808.

Akdoğu, E. (2009). Gaining a Competitive Edge through Acquisitions: Evidence from the Telecommunications Industry. *Journal of Corporate Finance, 15*(1), 99–112.

Akdoğu, E. (2011). Value-Maximising Managers, Value-increasing Mergers, and Overbidding. *Journal of Financial and Quantitative Analysis, 46*(1), 83–110.

Allen, F., Qian, J., & Qian, M. (2005). Law, Finance, and Economic Growth in China. *Journal of Financial Economics, 77*(1), 57–116.

Amit, R., & Schoemaker, P. J. H. (1993). Strategic Assets and Organisational Rent. *Strategic Management Journal, 14*(1), 33–46.

Auerbach, A. J., & Reishus, D. (1986). *Taxes and the Merger Decision: An Empirical Analysis*. NBER Working Paper Series. NBER.

Barney, J. B., & Hesterly, W. S. (2006). *Strategic Management and Competitive Advantage: Concepts*. Pearson/Prentice Hall.

Barney, J. (1991). Firm Resources and Sustained Competitive Advantage. *Journal of Management, 17*(1), 99–120.

Bradley, M., Desai, A., & Kim, E. H. (1988). Synergistic Gains from Corporate Acquisitions and Their Division between Target and Acquiring Firms. *Journal of Financial Economics, 21*, 3–40.

Brouthers, K. D., & Dikova, D. (2010). Acquisitions and Real Options: The Greenfield Alternative. *Journal of Management Studies, 47*(6), 1048–1071.

Claessens, S., Djankov, S., & Lang, L. H. P. (2000). The Separation of Ownership and Control in East Asian Corporations. *Journal of Financial Economics, 58*(1–2), 81–112.

Claessens, S., Feijen, E., & Laeven, L. (2008). Political Connections and Preferential Access to Finance: The Role of Campaign Contributions. *Journal of Financial Economics, 88*(3), 554–580.

Cull, R., & Xu, L. C. (2003). Who Gets Credit? The Behavior of Bureaucrats and State Banks in Allocating Credit to Chinese State-owned Enterprises. *Journal of Development Economics, 71*(2), 533–559.

Dalziel, T., White, R. E., & Arthurs, J. D. (2011). Principal Costs in Initial Public Offerings. *Journal of Management Studies, 48*(6), 1346–1364. https://doi.org/10.1111/j.1467-6486.2010.01005

Deng, P. (2009). Why do Chinese Firms Tend to Acquire Strategic Assets in International Expansion? *Journal of World Business, 44*(1), 74–84.

Dyer, J. H., Kale, P., & Singh, H. (2004). When to Ally & When to Acquire. (cover story). *Harvard Business Review, 82*(7/8), 108–115.

Fforde, A. (2007). *Vietnamese State Industry and the Political Economy of Commercial Renaissance: Dragon's Tooth or Curate's Egg*. Chandos.

Firth, M., Gong, S. X., & Shan, L. (2013). Cost of Government and Firm Value. *Journal of Corporate Finance, 21*(0), 136–152.

Firth, M., Lin, C., & Wong, S. M. L. (2008). Leverage and Investment under a State-owned bank Lending Environment: Evidence from China. *Journal of Corporate Finance, 14*(5), 642–653.

Firth, M., Malatesta, P. H., Xin, Q., & Xu, L. (2012). Corporate Investment, Government Control, and Financing Channels: Evidence from China's Listed Companies. *Journal of Corporate Finance, 18*(3), 433–450.

Fu, F., Lin, L., & Officer, M. S. (2013). Acquisitions Driven by Stock Overvaluation: Are They Good Deals? *Journal of Financial Economics, 109*(1), 24–39.

Fuller, K., Netter, J., & Stegemoller, M. (2002). What Do Returns to Acquiring Firms Tell Us? Evidence from Firms That Make Many Acquisitions. *The Journal of Finance, 57*(4), 1763–1793.

Gammeltoft, P., Filatotchev, I., & Hobdari, B. (2012). Emerging Multinational Companies and Strategic Fit: A Contingency Framework and Future Research Agenda. *European Management Journal, 30*(3), 175–188.

Goranova, M., Dharwadkar, R., & Brandes, P. (2010). Owners on Both Sides of the Deal: Mergers and Acquisitions and Overlapping Institutional Ownership. *Strategic Management Journal, 31*(10), 1114–1135. https://doi.org/10.1002/smj.849

Haleblian, J., & Finkelstein, S. (1999). The Influence of Organizational Acquisition Experience on Acquisition Performance: A Behavioral Learning Perspective. *Administrative Science Quarterly, 44*(1), 29–56.

Hankir, Y., Rauch, C., & Umber, M. P. (2011). Bank M&A: A Market Power Story? *Journal of Banking & Finance, 35*(9), 2341–2354.

Hannan, T. H., & Rhoades, S. A. (1987). Acquisition Targets and Motives: The Case of the Banking Industry. *The Review of Economics and Statistics, 69*(1), 67–74.

Jensen, M. C. (1986). Agency Costs of Free Cash Flow, Corporate Finance and Takeovers. *The American Economic Review, 76*(2), 323–329.

Kam, A., Citron, D., & Muradoglu, G. (2008). Distress and Restructuring in China: Does Ownership Matter? *China Economic Review, 19*(4), 567–579.

Kusewitt, J. B. (1985). An Exploratory Study of Strategic Acquisition Factors Relating to Performance. *Strategic Management Journal, 6*(2), 151–169.

La Porta, R., Lopez-de-Silanes, F., & Shleifer, A. (1999). Corporate Ownership around the world. *Journal of Finance, 54*(2), 471–517.

Li, H., Meng, L., Wang, Q., & Zhou, L.-A. (2008). Political Connections, Financing and Firm Performance: Evidence from Chinese Private Firms. *Journal of Development Economics, 87*(2), 283–299.

Lubatkin, M. H. (1987). Merger Strategies and Stockholder Value. *Strategic Management Journal, 8*, 9–53.

Makadok, R. (2001). Toward a Synthesis of the Resource-based and Dynamic-Capability Views of Rent Creation. *Strategic Management Journal, 22*(5), 387–401.

Marks, M. L., Mirvis, P. H., & Brajkovich, L. F. (2001). Making Mergers and Acquisitions Work: Strategic and Psychological Preparation [and Executive Commentary]. *The Academy of Management Executive (1993–2005), 15*(2), 80–94.

Masulis, R. W., Wang, C., & Xie, F. E. I. (2007). Corporate Governance and Acquirer Returns. *The Journal of Finance, 62*(4), 1851–1889.

Nguyen, T. A. (2012). *A Case Study on Power Sector Restructuring in Vietnam.* Paper presented at the Pacific Energy Summit: Innovative Generation: Powering a Prosperous Asia, Hanoi. http://www.nbr.org/downloads/pdfs/eta/PES_2012_summitpaper_Nguyen.pdf

Pham, N. (2015). *The Impact of the State on M&A performance: an Empirical Study on Vietnam.* Thesis, Department of Finance. Melbourne, Australia, La Trobe University. PhD.

Porter, M. E. (2008). The Five Competitive Forces that Shape Strategy. *Harvard Business Review, 86*(1), 78–93.

Tu, G., Lin, B., & Liu, F. (2013). Political Connections and Privatisation: Evidence from China. *Journal of Accounting and Public Policy, 32*(2), 114–135.

Van Hulle, C., Vermaelen, T., & De Wouters, P. (1991). Regulation, Taxes and the Market for Corporate Control in Belgium. *Journal of Banking & Finance, 15,* 1143–1170.

Walker, M. M., & Chi-Sheng, H. (2007). Strategic Objectives, Industry Structure and the Long-term Stock Price Performance of Acquiring and Rival Firms. *Applied Financial Economics, 17*(15), 1233–1244.

Wei, S.-J., & Wang, T. (1997). The Siamese Twins: Do State-owned Banks Favor state-owned Enterprises in China? *China Economic Review, 8*(1), 19–29.

CHAPTER 7

Quantitative Findings on the Impacts of State Ownership on M&A Performance

This chapter examines state ownership on M&A performance for a better understanding of how the state influences the SOE's strategic direction and decisions. The quantitative component was based on 188 M&A deals of listed Vietnamese firms from 2004 to 2013 of both SIEs and non-SIEs. Findings from the quantitative study were organised into three main blocks addressing state ownership, regulatory control and corporate governance in the research's overall theoretical framework.

This study aimed to answer whether state ownership in an acquirer affects the performance of its M&A. We examined state ownership in various aspects and measured its presence in the firm on different scales to gauge performance. Findings from this study suggested that the short-term return performance of M&A was sensitive to State ownership. M&A announcement return was negatively linked to the size of state equity in the acquiring firm. Firms with the state as the largest shareholder generated lower returns than other firms. In terms of operating performance, state ownership was negatively related to the post-deal improvement of returns on the acquiring firm's assets and earnings growth.

© The Author(s), under exclusive license to Springer Nature
Singapore Pte Ltd. 2021
N. Pham, K.-B. Oh, *State on Board!*,
https://doi.org/10.1007/978-981-16-3525-0_7

7.1   FINDINGS ON STATE OWNERSHIP AND M&A PERFORMANCE

The findings from the in-depth interviews suggested that State ownership is an essential factor in M&A. As argued earlier in Chap. 4, the impact of state ownership on M&A performance could arguably run both ways. While the arguments of political costs of interference (Qian, 1996; Shleifer, 1998; Shleifer & Vishny, 1994; Su, 2005) and the problem of low efficiency of SOEs (Allen et al., 2005) suggest a negative impact of state ownership on a firm's M&A *(the efficiency hypothesis)*, it could be possible that the privileges enjoyed by SOEs lead to better deal outcomes (Cull & Xu, 2003; Tu et al., 2013; Wei & Wang, 1997) *(the privileges hypothesis)*. Our conjecture was the *efficiency hypothesis*.

We analysed the impact of state ownership on firms' M&A performance measured by cumulative announcement abnormal returns *(CARs)* (the wealth impact); change in return on assets, ΔROA (the efficiency impact); and in earning growth, $\Delta EPSG$ (the growth impact) using secondary financial data from listed firms.

Due to its complexity and significance, we examined state ownership with various dimensions, including the level of equity holding (minority and majority), the exact percentage of equity held by the state, whether the state was the largest shareholder of the firm and whether the state capital in the firm was managed by the State Capital Management Agency or by another state-owned corporation. The use of the multiple dimensions allowed state ownership to be measured with different scales, either as an indicator variable or as a continuous variable, with the analysis to be in both univariate and multivariate econometric settings.

The investigated relationships between state ownership of the acquiring firm and its M&A performance, measured in different aspects, are illustrated by Fig. 7.1. All models controlled for deal- and firm-specific characteristics.

7.2   LEVEL OF STATE OWNERSHIP

7.2.1   Univariate Analysis of State Ownership

We used the standard event study method developed by Brown and Warner (1985) to measure cumulative abnormal returns to acquirer shareholders—the wealth effect of an acquisition. Abnormal returns were

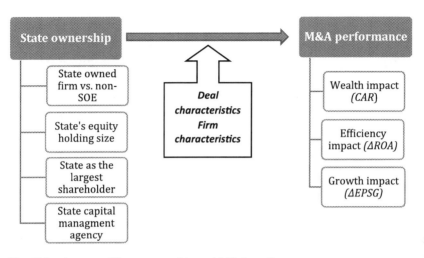

Fig. 7.1 Aspects of State ownership and M&A performance

calculated on the announcement date ($CAR(-1, 0)$), accumulated over short-term window ($CAR(-1, +1)$) and longer-term window ($CAR(-30, +30)$) around the announcement date.

We examined three levels of state ownership, including no state ownership (when the state's shareholding of the firm was zero), minority level (when the state's shareholding of the firm was larger than zero but less than 50%) and majority level (when the state's shareholding was at least 50% of the firm's equity). This sample consists of 31 firms classified as SOEs (having the state as the controlling shareholder), 57 with minority shareholding by the state and 100 with no state capital.

As shown in Table 7.1, the mean announcement return, $CAR(-1, 0)$, of the full sample was *insignificantly* negative at -0.206%, suggesting that, on average, acquirer shareholders earned a positive abnormal return on the announcement date. This finding is consistent with Iqbal and Dheeriya (1991), who find an insignificant return of -0.02% for US M&A with publicly traded targets. The mean announcement returns for acquirers were not statistically different from zero across all three sample subgroups. However, one should interpret the stock returns behaviour in an emerging market context with caution. Insignificant abnormal returns could mean no significant changes in the wealth level of the acquirers.

Nevertheless, insignificant abnormal returns could also be due to the possibility that the selected event window is not sufficiently long enough

Table 7.1 Univariate analysis of different state ownership levels

Event window	Full sample		(0) Non-SIE		(1) State ownership Level 1 (minority)		(2) State ownership Level 2 (majority)	
	Mean	Median	Mean	Median	Mean	Median	Mean	Median
CAR(−1, 0)	−0.206% (−0.886)	0.005%	−0.37% (−1.498)	0.034%	0.14% (0.149)	−0.092%	−0.29% (−0.46)	0.057%
CAR(−1, +1)	−0.28% (−1.314)	−0.17%	−0.24% (−0.92)	−0.09%	0.16% (0.17)	0.09%	−1.21%** (−2.36)	−1.12%
CAR(−30, +30)	−2.69%*** (−6.7001)	−3.29%	−1.96%*** (−5.28)	−0.96%	−3.11%*** (−4.72)	−2.78%	−4.26%*** (−9.658)	−11.73%

This table presents the mean and median cumulative abnormal return (CAR) gained by the acquiring firm over a 2-day, 3-day and 61-day event window around the announcement date for the full sample and each of the three subsamples. ***, ** and * stand for statistical significance at the 1%, 5% and 10% level, respectively to capture stock price changes (Pham et al., 2015). This could signal the problem of low market efficiency in emerging economies where information needs more time to be reflected in market prices or insider trading has moved the stock price ahead of the event announcement (Masulis et al., 2007). Therefore, several longer event windows, including a three-day window and a two-month window around the announcement date, were examined.

There was a small negative $CAR(-1, +1)$ of -0.28% experienced by the full sample, similar to the findings of -0.37% (insignificant) abnormal return to the bidders by Mulherin and Boone (2000) for the US market. However, $CAR(-1, +1)$ was statistically negative for Group 2 (-1.21%), suggesting that firms with the state as the controlling shareholder experienced significant wealth reduction during that window (Table 7.1). This is different from what is observed for the listed SOEs in China as Chinese state-owned acquirers earned a significantly positive $CAR(-1, +1)$ of 1.42%, as reported by Bhabra and Huang (2013). The difference is not surprising as Bhabra and Huang (2013) only examined cases of unlisted targets. The literature on privately held targets from developed markets does agree on the positive wealth generated for the acquirer (Chang, 1998; Iqbal & Dheeriya, 1991; John et al., 2010).

We also examined acquirer returns within +/-30 days around the announcement date because emerging stock markets may be relatively inefficient in the sense that prices react more slowly to information. One could hypothesise that due to the low level of efficiency in emerging markets, short-term event windows, normally examined in developed market literature, may not capture the event's full price impact. We found statistically significant $CAR(-30, +30)$ for the entire sample and each of the subsamples, supporting the argument of low informational efficiency in emerging markets. On the full sample, acquirers lost 2.69% of their wealth in +/-30 days around the event announcement. Wealth reduction was smallest for the group with no state ownership (Group 0) (abnormal return of -1.96%) and was more severe for firms with a higher level of state ownership in Group 1 (-3.11%) and Group 2 (-4.26%) (Fig. 7.2 and Table 7.1).

We conducted a further analysis using more indicator variables to capture the impact of different levels of state ownership on M&A performance.

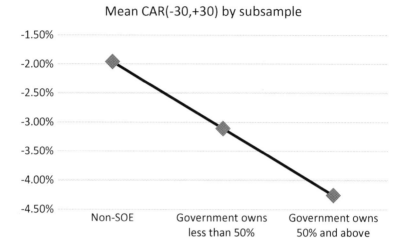

Fig. 7.2   Mean CAR(-30, +30) by subsamples

SOE:	An indicator variable taking the value of one (1) if the state held at least 50% of the equity of the firm (SOE) and zero (0) otherwise.
MINOR:	An indicator variable taking the value of one (1) if the state held more than zero but less than 50% equity of the firm and the value of zero (0) otherwise.
STATECAP:	An indicator variable taking the value of one (1) if the state held equity either at a minority level or at a majority level and the value of zero (0) otherwise.

Further univariate findings on *CAR (-1, 1), ΔROA, ΔEPSG included:*[1]

- No statistically significant difference among these two groups firms with (*STATECAP(1))* and without state capital (*STATECAP(0)*),
- Lower *CAR (-1, 1)* and *ΔEPSG (not ΔROA)* for firms that are SOEs with at least 50% state ownership compared to all other firms.
- Lower *CAR (-1, 1)* and *ΔEPSG (not ΔROA)* for firms with state capital at majority level compared to those at the minority level.

---

[1] For brevity, we do not report the univariate mean difference test results here. Results are available upon request.

These findings suggested that M&A conducted by non-SOEs resulted in better returns to shareholders and firm growth compared to those by SOEs.

7.2.2 Multivariate Analysis of State Ownership

From the univariate findings, it appeared that firms with different levels of state ownership experience different performance patterns with regard to their M&A transactions. As such, it was necessary to investigate the impacts of state ownership on M&A performance in a multivariate setting. The aim of the multivariate analysis was to verify if the investigated relationship would exist and remain significant after we control for other relevant factors. We ran the following regressions with $CAR(-1, 1)$, ΔROA and $\Delta EPSG$ as the dependent variables, each of which were regressed on the main predictors including (1) *state ownership*, measured by $STATE\%$, percentage of equity of the acquiring firm held by the state at the time of the acquisition[2]; (2) the *SOE dummy*, receiving a value of one if the state ownership was at least 50%; and (3) the *MINOR* dummy, receiving a value of one if the state ownership was present at a minority level.

Specifically, the following equations were examined in the basic models:

$$CAR(-1,1)_i = \alpha_i + \beta_{1i}MINOR + \beta_{2i}SOE + \beta_{3i}STATE\%$$
$$+\gamma_i DEAL\ CONTROLS + \theta_i FIRM\ CONTROLS + \varepsilon_i \quad (7.1)$$

$$\Delta ROA_i = \alpha_i + \beta_{1i}MINOR + \beta_{2i}SOE + \beta_{3i}STATE\%$$
$$+\gamma_i DEAL\ CONTROLS + \theta_i FIRM\ CONTROLS + \varepsilon_i \quad (7.2)$$

$$\Delta EPSG_i = \alpha_i + \beta_{1i}MINOR + \beta_{2i}SOE + \beta_{3i}STATE\%$$
$$+\gamma_i DEAL\ CONTROLS + \theta_i FIRM\ CONTROLS + \varepsilon_i \quad (7.3)$$

The following sections report the regression results of the basic models and extended ones on the total sample of 188 deals. In the basic models, the relationship between State ownership variables and M&A performance variables was tested with the presence of relevant deal characteristics and

---

[2] State ownership percentage was collected from the annual report for the financial year completed before the M&A announcement date.

firm's financial characteristics. To address the potential endogeneity of the omitted variables, we extended the model with a full set of deal variables, firm's financial variables, governance and ownership variables. All models included industry and year fixed effects and heteroskedasticity robust standard errors and were free from the multicollinearity problem.

Basic Models
Basic Models (1), (4) and (7) reported in Table 7.2 examined the relationship between State ownership and firm's M&A performance, measured by *CAR(-1, 1)*, ΔROA and $\Delta EPSG$ respectively.

State ownership was represented by three variables, including *MINOR*, *SOE* and *STATE%*. The baseline regression models employ a number of firm- and deal-related variables to control for factors that have been shown to affect acquirer returns in the existing M&A literature. The first control variable is *SIZE*, measured by the natural logarithm of the acquirer's market value two months before the announcement date. Moeller et al. (2004) reported significantly better announcement returns for smaller acquirers. Other variables specifically related to the acquiring firm are *LEVERAGE* and *TOBINSQ* (measured by the ratio of the firm's market value to its replacement value) (Lang et al., 1989). Also, we controlled for *OCF* and *ROA* for the endogeneity of performance. *OCF* is the operating cash flow scaled by total asset and *ROA* the acquirer's EBITDA divided by total assets. These metrics are consistent with Cai and Sevilir (2012).

With regard to deal-specific characteristics, in addition to *deal size*, other deal-specific characteristics such as *deal premium* (Alexandridis et al., 2013), *payment method* (Travlos, 1987), relatedness versus diversification (Morck et al., 1990), *deal attitude* (Schwert, 2000) and *toehold* (whether the acquirer holds existing equity in the target) (Henry, 2004; Walkling & Edmister, 1985) have all been examined in the literature. Due to the data availability of these variables, only *DEALTYPE* and *TOEHOLD* were included in these models. *DEALTYPE* is a dummy variable that receives a value of 1 if the deal was classified as *related* where the acquirer and the target had the same two-digit SIC code and 0 otherwise. Similarly, *TOEHOLD* is the variable indicating if the acquirer had already held equity of the target before the acquisition.

In Model (1), *SOE* exhibited a significantly negative coefficient, suggesting that SOEs generated lower announcement returns for acquirer shareholders than non-SOEs did. Interestingly, the coefficient of *STATE%* was significantly positive (at a 10% level). Taken together, state ownership

Table 7.2 Extended models with state ownership

Dependent variable	(1) CAR(-1, 1)	(2) CAR(-1, 1)	(3) CAR(-1, 1)	(4) ΔROA	(5) ΔROA	(6) ΔROA	(7) $\Delta EPSG$	(8) $\Delta EPSG$	(9) $\Delta EPSG$
MINOR	-0.0101 (-0.91)	-0.0098 (-0.82)	-0.0103 (-0.89)	0.0265 (0.85)			0.7168 (1.28)	1.0240 (1.63)	0.8680 (1.46)
SOE	-0.0446* (-1.87)	-0.0466** (-2.07)	-0.0415* (-1.74)	0.0833 (1.52)	0.0415 (0.91)	0.0401 (0.91)			
STATE%	0.0007* (1.70)	0.0009** (2.26)	0.0007* (1.71)	-0.0021*** (-2.66)	-0.0014* (-1.69)	-0.0015* (-1.97)	-0.0265** (-2.03)	-0.035** (-2.48)	-0.0316** (-2.44)
DEALTYPE	-0.0007 (-0.09)	0.0025 (0.31)	-0.0032 (-0.36)	-0.0029 (-0.13)	-0.0088 (-0.36)	0.0008 (0.03)	0.0555 (0.21)	0.0933 (0.35)	-0.0145 (-0.06)
ACQUIRED	-0.0002 (-1.34)	-0.0001 (-1.12)	-0.0001 (-1.00)	-0.0003 (-1.04)	-0.0001 (-0.41)	-0.0001 (-0.45)	-0.0061 (-1.53)	-0.0049 (-1.21)	-0.0021 (-0.48)
TOEHOLD	-0.0057 (-0.85)	-0.0098 (-1.47)	-0.0075 (-1.02)	-0.0029 (-0.15)	0.0002 (0.01)	-0.0040 (-0.21)	0.4550* (1.70)	0.4104* (1.67)	0.5319** (2.05)
OCF	0.0008 (0.03)	0.0074 (0.31)	-0.0014 (-0.04)	0.0932 (0.93)	0.0317 (0.34)	0.0744 (0.78)	-1.6176 (-1.12)	-2.2534 (-1.64)	-1.3827 (-0.96)
ROA	-0.0167 (-0.28)	-0.0233 (-0.37)	-0.0357 (-0.56)	-0.1140 (-0.68)			-3.0957 (-1.17)	-5.568** (-2.11)	-4.644* (-1.79)
LEVERAGE	-0.0000 (-0.44)	-0.0000 (-0.43)	-0.0000 (-0.82)	-0.0001* (-1.89)	-0.0001* (-1.82)	-0.0002** (-2.21)	-0.0007 (-0.58)	0.0019 (1.03)	0.0019 (0.96)
SIZE	0.0028 (0.99)	0.0014 (0.42)	0.0033 (0.86)	-0.0125* (-1.98)	-0.0195** (-2.42)	-0.0057 (-0.58)	-0.2206 (-1.45)	-0.351* (-1.82)	-0.1674 (-1.01)
TOBINSQ	-0.0060 (-1.50)	-0.0044 (-0.59)	-0.0032 (-0.69)	0.0119 (0.73)	0.0066 (0.35)	0.0013 (0.08)	0.2177 (1.20)	0.6650 (1.60)	0.5725** (2.43)
INSIDER		0.0006* (1.91)			0.0007 (0.67)			-0.0130 (-1.04)	

(continued)

Table 7.2 (continued)

Dependent variable	(1)	(2)	(3)	(4)	(5)	(6)	(7)	(8)	(9)
	CAR(-1, 1)	CAR(-1, 1)	CAR(-1, 1)	ΔROA	ΔROA	ΔROA	ΔEPSG	ΔEPSG	ΔEPSG
DOMESTIC		-0.0001			0.0005			0.0047	
		(-0.68)			(0.80)			(0.73)	
FOREIGN		0.0001			0.0017**			0.0188	
		(0.34)			(2.18)			(1.52)	
NON-EXECUTIVE			0.0026			-0.0112			2.1352***
			(0.17)			(-0.22)			(3.27)
BOARDSIZE			0.0005			-0.0066			-0.1186
			(0.18)			(-0.79)			(-0.90)
AUDITOR			-0.0062			-0.0135			-1.363***
			(-0.66)			(-0.58)			(-3.57)
Constant	-0.0350	-0.0220	-0.0471	-0.0363	0.0792	0.0173	1.4285	3.1993	-0.6013
	(-0.76)	(-0.40)	(-0.82)	(-0.21)	(0.47)	(0.12)	(0.81)	(1.57)	(-0.36)
Year fixed effects	Yes	Yes	Yes	Yes	Yes	Yes	Yes	Yes	Yes
Industry fixed effects	Yes	Yes	Yes	Yes	Yes	Yes	Yes	Yes	Yes
Observations	188	175	178	115	108	111	121	113	117
R-squared	0.093	0.153	0.094	0.295	0.362	0.306	0.280	0.365	0.401

This table presents heteroskedasticity consistent regression results for the sample of 188 mergers and acquisitions between 2004 and 2013 in Vietnam. The dependent variable is CAR(-1, 1), the cumulative abnormal returns of the acquirers from 1 day before to 1 day after the deal announcement, ΔROA and ΔEPSG. T-statistics are in parentheses. ***, ** and * stand for statistical significance at the 1%, 5% and 10% respectively in the acquiring firm was positively linked (though weakly) to M&A abnormal returns for shareholders, but beyond the controlling level, state ownership negatively impacted shareholders' wealth.

In Models (4) and (7), *STATE%* was inversely related to both ΔROA and $\Delta EPSG$ while the coefficients of *SOE* were not significant in any model. This means that firms with higher state capital generated lower efficiency improvement post-M&A. As the higher the level of state capital in the firm, the more likely it is that the firm is politically influenced (Shleifer, 1998), hence, politically directed in conducting their M&A. Therefore, it is less likely that their M&A will result in improvement of economic efficiency.

Extended Models
We extended the models to verify if the influence of state ownership on M&A performance would remain significant after controlling for the possible impacts of ownership and governance characteristics of the acquiring firm. The equations for these models were therefore specified as follow. The same equations were used for ΔROA and $\Delta EPSG$.

$$CAR\left(-1,1\right)_{i} = \alpha_{i} + \beta_{1i}MINOR + \beta_{2i}SOE + \beta_{3i}STATE\%$$
$$+ \gamma_{i}DEAL\ CONTROLS + \theta_{i}FIRM\ CONTROLS$$
$$+ \omega_{i}OWNERSHIP\ CONTROLS$$
$$+ \varphi_{i}GOVERNANCE\ CONTROLS + \varepsilon_{i} \qquad (7.4)$$

The ownership structure of a firm and its concentration determines its M&A performance (Bhaumik & Selarka, 2012; Caprio et al., 2011). Therefore, we included *INSIDER* (the percentage of equity held by insiders of the acquiring firm) *and DOMESTIC* (the ratio of equity held by domestic institutional investors of the acquiring firm) as additional control variables. In emerging markets, foreign institutional investors have a good monitoring impact on the invested companies (Garner & Kim, 2013). Thus, we also controlled for the equity held by foreign institutional investors by the variable *FOREIGN* (Fig. 7.3).

In terms of the governance characteristics, we added *BOARDSIZE* (the number of directors on board of the acquiring company) and *NON-EXECUTIVE*[3] (the proportion of non-executive directors of the total

---

[3] There were cases in which a director is reported as *independent* if he/she was not an executive director. Consequently, in this research, we used the term "non-executive" to refer to those directors that reported as *independent* in companies' annual reports.

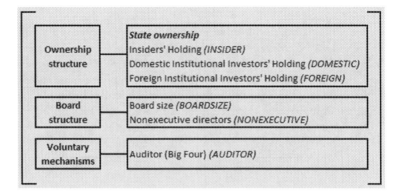

Fig. 7.3 State ownership and other variables in the extended model

board members) (Fig. 7.3). The relevance of these variables in M&A studies has been well documented in the literature. The quality of M&A decisions could be affected by board quality, which is negatively related to board size (Chatterjee & Kuenzi, 2001) and positively associated with the number of independent directors on the board (Desai et al., 2003). The challenge, however, in introducing this variable into the analysis is that while Vietnamese companies were encouraged to have more independent directors on board, according to the review of corporate governance in Vietnam by the World Bank (2013), the true level of independence of a director could always be questionable.

Furthermore, we included *AUDITOR* (an indicator variable that takes the value of one if the firm has a Big Four accounting firm as its auditor and zero otherwise) as another controlling variable reflecting firms' adoption of adequate voluntary governance mechanisms (Fig. 7.3). According to the review by Claessens and Yurtoglu (2013), emerging market firms tend to adapt to a weak institutional environment by adopting best practice voluntary corporate governance measures. Firms audited by the big accounting firms (currently, the Big Four) are perceived to have higher disclosure quality (Mitton, 2002). The decision to have a quality auditing firm as their auditor may signal the firm's commitment to improving information quality and transparency to shareholders.

Overall, it can be seen from Table 7.2 that the extended models ((2), (3) for *CAR(-1, 1)*; (5), (6) for *ΔROA*, (8) and (9) for *ΔEPSG*) confirm the impact of State ownership identified from the basic models. Similar to the findings of the basic models, *STATE%* had a weakly positive relationship with *CAR(-1, 1)* while being negatively correlated to ΔROA and $\Delta EPSG$. *SOE*, however, had a negative coefficient on *CAR(-1, 1)*, suggesting that state ownership hurts shareholders' wealth if the state holding is beyond the controlling level.

7.3   THE STATE AS THE LARGEST SHAREHOLDER

It could be argued that a firm in which the state is the largest shareholder behaves like an SOE. Seminal studies on corporate ownership report that the state holds substantial equity of publicly listed firms in many countries (La Porta et al., 1999). Even for firms in which state ownership does not exceed the controlling level, if the state is the firm's largest shareholders, it could still exert significant influence over the corporate strategy. If the same arguments of agency and political behaviour of state firms apply, it is plausible that the state's presence as the largest shareholder of the firm may negatively impact firm performance and value (Bai et al., 2004). Acquisitions made by companies under the direction of the state may serve a wide variety of motives that may not be in alignment with shareholder wealth maximisation (Vernon, 1979).

7.3.1   *Univariate Analysis*

We analysed if the impact of state ownership on a firm's M&A performance would differ based on whether the state is the largest shareholder in the firm or not. Recall that as La Porta et al. (1999) report, the two most popular types of firms in the world are family-controlled firms and state-controlled firms. Even if the state or families are not the controlling shareholders in a firm, they are typically the significant shareholder due to ownership concentration (Claessens et al., 2000). Additionally, these shareholders typically exercise their control power significantly beyond their cash flow rights, which is possible via a pyramid holding structure. Large blockholders, especially the largest shareholder, likely influence the company's decisions and performance (Truong & Heaney, 2007). The presence of other blockholders in the firm helps reduce the power of the significant shareholders. Large non-management blockholdings, for example, are positively related to firm value due to their monitoring over management (Lins, 2003). In other words, if the state is the largest shareholder of a firm, the firm may be directed towards the state's economic

Table 7.3   The State as the largest shareholder

STATE%	Observations	Mean (%)	Std. dev. (%)	Min (%)	Max (%)
LARGEST(0)	18	9.96	6.16	5.81	29.14
LARGEST(1)	70	42.77	21.58	8.10	87.87

and political interest. If other shareholders, such as families or institutional investors, are larger shareholders than the state, they can neutralise the power of the state. Consequently, it can be argued that the influence of the state on the held firm depends on whether the state is the largest shareholder of the firm.

To capture such an effect, the variable *LARGEST* was introduced to the models. *LARGEST* is an indicator variable taking a value of one (1) if the state was the largest shareholder of the acquiring firm and zero (0) otherwise. Of the 88 firms with state capital, 70 firms in which the state was the largest shareholder, ranging from 8.1% to 87.87% of equity. The state, on average, held 42.77% equity of these firms. It is probable that the state is able to exercise influence and control over the firm even when its equity holding is far less than the controlling level. At the remaining 18 firms with state capital, the state's equity stake, on average, was 9.96% (Table. 7.3).

The univariate analysis showed that having the state as the largest shareholder was associated with lower returns and growth performance. We divided the total sample of 188 firms into two groups, *LARGEST(1)* consisting of all firms with the state being the largest shareholder and *LARGEST(0)* for the remaining firms. The t-test statistics, reported in Table 7.4, lent support to the hypothesised impact of *LARGEST* on *CAR(-1, 1)* and *ΔEPSG*. However, there was no significant association between *LARGEST* and *ΔROA*. So far, the findings on the impact of *LARGEST* on a firm's M&A performance are consistent with those previously reported on the effect of state ownership, measured by *SOE* and *STATE%*. M&A of firms with the state as the largest shareholders delivered lower wealth and growth impact.

7.3.2   Multivariate Analysis with LARGEST

To confirm the state's impact as the largest shareholder, we also introduced *LARGEST* into the multivariate models, controlling for all deal- and firm-specific variables and ownership and corporate governance characteristics. The generic equation for this analysis is:

Table 7.4 The State as the largest shareholder: univariate analysis

LARGEST Group	CAR(-1, 1)			ΔROA			ΔEPSG		
	Obs.	Mean	Std. err.	Obs.	Mean	Std. err.	Obs.	Mean	Std. err.
LARGEST(0)	118	0.05%	0.4058	63	0.42%	1.40664	67	0.71%	0.2621
LARGEST(1)	70	-0.84%	0.5105	52	-1.43%	1.05878	54	0.13%	0.0941
Combined	188	-0.28%	0.3185	115	-0.42%	0.90757	121	0.45%	0.1528
Mean diff		0.89%	0.6574		0.0185%	1.82331		0.58%	0.3041

$diff = mean(0) - mean(1)$

Hypothesis	t-Test statistics	t-Test statistics	t-Test statistics
Ho: diff = 0	t = 1.3552	t = 1.01122	t = 1.9009
Ha: diff < 0	Pr (T < t) = 0.9115	Pr (T < t) = 0.8432	Pr (T < t) = 0.9701
Ha: diff ≠ 0	Pr (|T| > |t|) = 0.1770	Pr(|T| > |t|) = 0.3136	Pr (|T| > |t|) = 0.0597
Ha: diff > 0	**Pr (T > t) = 0.0885**	Pr (T > t) = 0.1568	**Pr (T > t) = 0.0299**

$$CAR(-1,1), \Delta ROA \, or \Delta EPSG_i =$$
$$f\left(LARGEST, STATE\%, and \, all \, CONTROLS\right) + \varepsilon_i \qquad (7.5)$$

As can be seen from Table 7.5, $LARGEST$ was strongly negatively related to $CAR(-1, 1)$ but not related to ΔROA and $\Delta EPSG$ at all. Furthermore, when $LARGEST$ was used instead of SOE, the coefficients of $STATE\%$ in $CAR(-1, 1)$ and ΔROA models had the same sign and significance level as previously identified. However, it should be noted that in Models (7), (8) and (9), the introduction of $LARGEST$ has weakened the relationship between $STATE\%$ and $\Delta EPSG$ as the coefficient of $STATE\%$ has become insignificant.

Overall, similar to the negative impact on firm value of the state being the largest shareholder observed in Chinese firms (Bai et al., 2004), having the state as the largest shareholder among Vietnamese listed firms was also negatively associated with firm's abnormal returns upon M&A announcement. This finding implies that the market is sceptical about the value of the M&A conducted by firms controlled or heavily influenced by the state. Investors in the market react negatively to such announcements as they expect that these M&A could be driven by the social and political interests of the state rather than the principle of shareholder's wealth maximisation. We did not document any evidence of the relationship between the state's presence as the largest shareholder of the firm and the long-term efficiency and growth performance of M&A.

7.4   State Capital Management Agency (SCMA)

In emerging markets, as discussed in Chap. 4, state capital management is the function that the State delegates to various authority levels representing local and central governments, ministries and agencies. As these state capital management agencies (SCMA) have different interests and capabilities, the effectiveness of state capital in a publicly listed firm may also depend on the competence of the managing agency.

There has been a body of literature from China that focuses on the diversity of SOEs. At the core of this stream of literature is the argument that not all SOEs are the same. It is argued that different types of SOEs, namely those affiliated with the central government or local governments, have different resources, capabilities and priorities due to multiple institutional reform processes (Li et al., 2014). The evidence from China suggests that

Table 7.5 The state as the largest shareholder and firms' M&A performance

Dependent variable	(1) CAR(-1,1)	(2) CAR(-1,1)	(3) CAR(-1,1)	(4) ΔROA	(5) ΔROA	(6) ΔROA	(7) ΔEPSG	(8) ΔEPSG	(9) ΔEPSG
LARGEST	-0.0286***	-0.0320***	-0.032***	0.0025	0.0030	0.0054	-0.6667	-0.3901	-0.3235
	(-2.62)	(-2.84)	(-2.80)	(0.10)	(0.11)	(0.20)	(-1.35)	(-0.94)	(-0.76)
STATE%	0.0006*	0.0008**	0.0007**	-0.0011*	-0.0009	-0.0011*	-0.0103	-0.0154	-0.0160
	(1.85)	(2.37)	(2.13)	(-1.88)	(-1.41)	(-1.94)	(-0.99)	(-1.61)	(-1.55)
DEALTYPE	-0.0019	0.0021	-0.0045	-0.0018	-0.0084	0.0027	0.0018	0.1036	0.0582
	(-0.24)	(0.27)	(-0.52)	(-0.08)	(-0.33)	(0.12)	(0.01)	(0.38)	(0.22)
ACQUIRED	-0.0001	-0.0001	-0.0001	-0.0003	-0.0002	-0.0002	-0.0025	-0.0055	-0.0067*
	(-1.15)	(-0.92)	(-0.87)	(-1.18)	(-0.59)	(-0.56)	(-0.59)	(-1.34)	(-1.71)
TOEHOLD	-0.0079	-0.0109	-0.0099	-0.0011	-0.0012	-0.0023	0.5027**	0.3887	0.3341
	(-1.16)	(-1.64)	(-1.33)	(-0.06)	(-0.06)	(-0.12)	(2.06)	(1.60)	(1.21)
OCF	-0.0043	0.0011	-0.0084	0.1082	0.0594	0.0836	-1.2478	-2.1768	
	(-0.14)	(0.05)	(-0.26)	(1.12)	(0.58)	(0.86)	(-0.82)	(-1.50)	
ROA	-0.0082	-0.0168	-0.0302	-0.1273	-0.1166		-4.4995*	-5.3669**	
	(-0.14)	(-0.28)	(-0.50)	(-0.76)	(-0.71)		(-1.84)	(-2.08)	
LEVERAGE	-0.0000	-0.0000	-0.0001	-0.0001*	-0.0001	-0.0002*	0.0024	0.0016	
	(-0.93)	(-0.75)	(-1.22)	(-1.91)	(-1.66)	(-1.88)	(1.16)	(1.09)	
SIZE	0.0017	-0.0001	0.0006	-0.0107*	-0.0180**	-0.0028	-0.1842	-0.3320*	
	(0.59)	(-0.04)	(0.15)	(-1.71)	(-2.33)	(-0.30)	(-1.10)	(-1.80)	
TOBINSQ	-0.0045	-0.0020	0.0002	0.0067	0.0064	-0.0033	0.5962***	0.6089	
	(-1.05)	(-0.28)	(0.03)	(0.41)	(0.33)	(-0.22)	(2.69)	(1.58)	
INSIDER	0.0004				0.0008			-0.0113	
	(1.46)				(0.78)			(-0.88)	
DOMESTIC	-0.0003				0.0006			0.0068	
	(-1.25)				(0.94)			(1.10)	

(continued)

Table 7.5 (continued)

Dependent variable	(1) CAR(-1, 1)	(2) CAR(-1, 1)	(3) CAR(-1, 1)	(4) ΔROA	(5) ΔROA	(6) ΔROA	(7) ΔEPSG	(8) ΔEPSG	(9) ΔEPSG
FOREIGN		0.0001			0.0017**			0.0191	
		(0.39)			(2.11)			(1.53)	
NON-EXECUTIVE			0.0095			-0.0180	2.1996***		
			(0.65)			(-0.36)	(3.18)		
AUDITOR			-0.0021			-0.0155	-1.2553***		
			(-0.22)			(-0.66)	(-3.18)		
BOARDSIZE			0.0014			-0.0075	-0.1455		
			(0.50)			(-0.86)	(-1.13)		
CONSTANT	-0.0214	-0.0001	-0.0196	-0.0222	0.0634	-0.0128	-0.1807	2.9213	-1.1567*
	(-0.48)	(-0.00)	(-0.35)	(-0.13)	(0.37)	(-0.08)	(-0.11)	(1.47)	(-1.73)
Year fixed effects	Yes	Yes	Yes	Yes	Yes	Yes	Yes	Yes	Yes
Industry fixed effects	Yes	Yes	Yes	Yes	Yes	Yes	Yes	Yes	Yes
N	188	175	178	115	108	111	117	113	121
R-sq	0.100	0.163	0.109	0.282	0.36	0.299	0.401	0.353	0.221

This table presents heteroskedasticity consistent regression results for the sample of 188 mergers and acquisitions between 2004 and 2013 in Vietnam. The dependent variable is $CAR(-1, 1)$, the cumulative abnormal returns of the acquirers from 1 day before to 1 day after the deal announcement, ΔROA and $\Delta EPSG$. T statistics are in parentheses. ***, **, and * stand for statistical significance at the 1%, 5% and 10% respectively

Table 7.6 Sample distribution by type of state capital management agency

		State capital management agency (SCMA)		
		SOE	SCIC	Total
State capital level	MINOR	22	35	57
	SOE	02	29	31
	Total	*24*	*64*	*88*

when the control right is decentralised from the government to an SOE, firm performance improves. The impact is more profound for firms controlled by local governments than those held by the central government (Wang & Xiao, 2009). Chen et al. (2009) also find that the operating efficiency of listed firms in China varies across types of controlling shareholders. The best performers are firms controlled by the central government. This indicates that the level of efficiency of the agencies that manage state capital may differ and thus may impact the invested firms differently.

In Vietnam, as discussed in Chap. 3, the state capital in SIEs could be managed by a local (provincial) government, the central government (normally delegated to relevant ministries) or by another SOE such as a state general corporation or economic group. The management of state capital in publicly listed firms has to be delegated to either SCIC (for both central and local government-managed firms) or an SOE. Of the 88 acquiring firms with state ownership in this sample, there were 24 firms in which SCIC-managed state capital, the professional management agency of the state. In the remaining 64 firms, the firm's state capital was represented by a state-owned economic group, typically but not necessarily in the same business area (Table 7.6). Does the type of state capital management agencies affect the M&A performance of SIEs? To answer this question, we analysed the 88 firms with state capital in the sample.

7.4.1 Univariate Analysis with SCMA

We designed the variable *SCMA* to capture the impact, if any, of the different types of state capital management agency. *SCMA* is a dummy variable that takes the value of one (1) if the state capital in the firm was managed by an SOE or zero (0) by the SCIC.[4] An SOE as a shareholder

---

[4] In several cases in this sample, state ownership representation could be traced to both an SOE and SCIC. In such cases, the firm will be classified as a SOE/SCIC (1) or (0) depending on who holds more equity in the firm.

may exercise its shareholding rights and responsibilities differently from SCIC. An SOE shareholder, especially if in the same industry with the held company, can contribute to the latter in terms of business expertise, resources, network and connections, whereas the SCIC is expected to exercise professional ownership and investment. Due to these differences, it is plausible that these two agencies of state capital contribute differently to firm's M&A decision and performance.

The following univariate analysis examined whether it matters if state capital is managed by an industry SOE or by the SCIC, a professional SCMA. As it can be seen from Table 7.7, there was no significant difference between the two groups observed for $CAR(-1, 1)$ and ΔROA. However, the result for $\Delta EPSG$ suggested that the M&A growth performance of the (0) group (SCIC-managed firms) was higher than that of the (1) group (SOE-managed firms). It could, therefore, be concluded that the professional management of state capital by SCIC in the acquiring firm was associated with better post-M&A growth.

7.4.2   Multivariate Analysis with SCMA

We also included the dummy variable *SCMA* in the multivariate models. It could be expected that the influence that the representative of state capital may have on the firm is subject to the level of equity holding of the state in the firm. Therefore, the interaction terms between SCMA and MINOR (MINOR*SCMA) and MAJOR (MAJOR*SCMA) were also included.

$$CAR\left(-1,1\right), \Delta ROA \, or \Delta EPSG_i = f$$
$$\begin{pmatrix} SCMA, MINOR, SOE, SCMA * MINOR, SCMA \\ *SOE, STATE\%, all\, CONTROLS \end{pmatrix} + \varepsilon_i \qquad (7.6)$$

Despite the initial evidence of the relationship between *SCMA* and $\Delta EPSG$ obtained from the univariate analysis, we did not find such evidence in the multiple regression models reported in Table 7.8. There was no significant association between *SCMA* and $CAR(-1, 1)$ and ΔROA either. The coefficients of *SCMA* and the interaction terms *MINOR*SCMA* and *SOE*SCMA* were all insignificant, confirming that having an SOE or SCIC manage the state capital in the acquiring firm does not impact the firm's M&A performance. This is consistent with Chen et al. (2008), who

Table 7.7 Univariate analysis: firms managed by the SCIC versus by an SOE

SCMA Group	CAR(-1, 1)			ΔROA			ΔEPSG		
	Obs.	Mean	Std. err.	Obs.	Mean	Std. err.	Obs.	Mean	Std. err.
(0)-SCIC	24	0.18%	0.4477	17	0.18%	1.6511	17	1.08%	0.4566
(1)-SOE	64	-0.51%	0.5622	45	-1.27%	1.1999	47	0.25%	0.1917
Combined	88	-0.32%	0.4266	62	-0.87%	0.9781	64	0.47%	0.1895
Mean diff		0.69%	0.9606		1.45%	2.2028		0.83%	0.4194

$diff = mean(0) - mean(1)$

Hypothesis	t-Test statistics		
	$t = 0.7160$	$t = 0.6572$	$t = 1.9829$
Ho: diff = 0			
Ha: diff < 0	$\Pr(T < t) = 0.7620$	$\Pr(T < t) = 0.7432$	$\Pr(T < t) = 0.9741$
Ha: diff ≠ 0	$\Pr(|T| > |t|) = 0.4759$	$\Pr(|T| > |t|) = 0.5136$	$\Pr(|T| > |t|) = 0.0518$
Ha: diff > 0	$\Pr(T > t) = 0.2380$	$\Pr(T > t) = 0.2568$	$\Pr(T > t) = 0.0259$

Table 7.8 The impact of the type of SCMA on firms' M&A performance

	(1) CAR(-1,1)	(2) CAR(-1,1)	(3) CAR(-1,1)	(4) ΔROA	(5) ΔROA	(6) ΔROA	(7) ΔEPSG	(8) ΔEPSG	(9) ΔEPSG
MINOR		-0.0114 (-0.85)	-0.0088 (-0.73)						
SOE	-0.0332* (-1.87)	-0.0429 (-1.61)	-0.0502** (-2.16)	0.0503 (1.16)	0.0493 (1.12)	0.0469 (1.08)	0.7556 (1.33)	1.0348 (1.65)	3.6891 (1.18)
SCMA	-0.0016 (-0.11)	0.0025 (0.17)	0.0117 (0.21)	0.0508 (1.26)	0.0566 (1.31)	0.0633 (1.45)	0.4875 (0.70)	0.0874 (0.18)	-4.7487 (-1.33)
MINOR*SCMA			-0.0122 (-0.22)						
SOE*SCMA			-0.0069 (-0.12)						
STATE (%)	0.0007* (1.78)	0.0006 (1.63)	0.0009** (2.17)	-0.0025*** (-2.92)	-0.002** (-2.51)	-0.0026*** (-2.89)	-0.035** (-2.17)	-0.0360** (-2.61)	-0.0977 (-1.39)
DEALTYPE	0.0028 (0.34)	-0.0031 (-0.35)	0.0027 (0.33)	-0.0032 (-0.14)	-0.0077 (-0.31)	0.0017 (0.07)	0.0644 (0.25)	0.0958 (0.36)	-0.4096 (-0.38)
ACQUIRED	-0.0001 (-1.13)	-0.0001 (-1.02)	-0.0001 (-1.16)	-0.0003 (-1.16)	-0.0002 (-0.68)	-0.0002 (-0.69)	-0.0066 (-1.57)	-0.0051 (-1.21)	-0.0048 (-0.26)
TOEHOLD	-0.0096 (-1.43)	-0.0074 (-1.01)	-0.0100 (-1.49)	-0.0027 (-0.15)	-0.0010 (-0.06)	-0.0062 (-0.32)	0.4318* (1.66)	0.4083 (1.65)	0.3795 (0.41)
OCF	0.0069 (0.29)	-0.0008 (-0.02)	0.0075 (0.31)	0.1041 (1.15)	0.0643 (0.62)	0.1062 (1.10)	-1.3159 (-0.85)	-2.1999 (-1.56)	-7.0180 (-1.03)
ROA	-0.0160 (-0.26)	-0.0378 (-0.62)	-0.0287 (-0.49)				-3.2515 (-1.22)	-5.6205** (-2.11)	-2.2250 (-0.20)
LEVERAGE	-0.0000 (-0.31)	-0.0000 (-0.81)	-0.0000 (-0.43)	-0.0001 (-1.57)	-0.0001 (-1.27)	-0.0002* (-1.99)	-0.0006 (-0.52)	0.0015 (1.08)	0.0127 (1.25)
SIZE	0.0015 (0.45)	0.0035 (0.84)	0.0014 (0.42)	-0.0094 (-1.40)	-0.018** (-2.15)	-0.0005 (-0.05)	-0.1805 (-1.06)	-0.3478* (-1.72)	-2.0831 (-1.42)

	(1)	(2)	(3)	(4)	(5)	(6)	(7)	(8)	(9)
TOBINSQ	-0.0039	-0.0031	-0.0042	0.0141	0.0137	0.0087	0.2136	0.6727	2.8016*
	(-0.52)	(-0.69)	(-0.55)	(0.85)	(0.69)	(0.51)	(1.14)	(1.64)	(1.69)
INSIDER	0.0006**		0.0006*		0.0007			-0.0130	
	(2.03)		(1.90)		(0.72)			(-1.03)	
DOMESTIC	-0.0001		-0.0001		0.0004			0.0044	
	(-0.67)		(-0.68)		(0.61)			(0.67)	
FOREIGN	0.0000		0.0001		0.0018**			0.0191	
	(0.13)		(0.28)		(2.37)			(1.52)	
NON-EXECUTIVE		0.0025				-0.0209			8.4581*
		(0.16)				(-0.39)			(1.85)
BOARDSIZE		0.0005				-0.0067			0.0892
		(0.17)				(-0.87)			(0.17)
AUDITOR		-0.0062				-0.0203			-4.8739**
		(-0.66)				(-0.90)			(-2.04)
CONSTANT	-0.0248	-0.0501	-0.0244	-0.1478	0.0300	-0.0831	0.6365	3.1200	10.2605
	(-0.44)	(-0.78)	(-0.42)	(-0.69)	(0.17)	(-0.47)	(0.29)	(1.39)	(0.85)
Industry FE	Yes	Yes	Yes	Yes	Yes	Yes	Yes	Yes	Yes
Year FE	Yes	Yes	Yes	Yes	Yes	Yes	Yes	Yes	Yes
Observations	175	178	175	115	108	111	121	113	117
R-squared	0.149	0.094	0.154	0.300	0.377	0.327	0.285	0.365	0.318

This table presents heteroskedasticity consistent regression results for the sample of 188 mergers and acquisitions between 2004 and 2013 in Vietnam. The dependent variables are $CAR(-1, 1)$, ΔROA and $\Delta EPSG$. T-statistics are in parentheses. ***, **, and * stand for statistical significance at 1%, 5% and 10% respectively find no impact on the firm when its control is transferred from one state entity to another state entity in China.

In conclusion, this chapter has presented the findings on the relationship between state ownership in the acquiring firm and its M&A results. We examined state ownership in the firm using different scales and reflected its presence in various aspects. Our findings suggested that the M&A short-term return performance was sensitive to state ownership in that M&A announcement return was positively linked to the size of the equity held by the state in the acquiring firm. However, M&A conducted by firms controlled by the state or firms in which the state was the largest shareholder generated lower abnormal returns to their shareholders. The market perceived these M&As to create less value for the firms. State ownership could be good for the firm, such as in accessing good targets for firms with political connections (Tu et al., 2013) and easier access to funding (Firth et al., 2008), but if the state was the largest shareholder, state ownership could harm firms' M&A value, possibly due to the political costs of interference (Firth et al., 2012; Su, 2005). In terms of the operating performance of M&A, state ownership was negatively related to the post-deal improvement of returns on assets and earnings growth of the acquiring firm.

The findings support the theoretical framework proposed in Chap. 4 that integrates the agency theory and political theory to understand the behaviour of SOEs. If the state is the most influential shareholder of a firm, it is more likely that its M&A could be driven by the non-economic interest of the state. The negative impact of the state shareholder is profound when the state is the controlling shareholder or the largest shareholder, indicating the principal-principal conflict between the state and other shareholders. The negative impact of state ownership on organisational outcomes contributes to the principal costs of the state shareholder.

The evidence regarding the association between *STATE%*—the percentage of equity held by the state—and *ΔROA* and *ΔEPSG* is consistent. However, for other dimensions of state ownership, including *SOE*, *LARGEST* and *SCMA*, there is insufficient evidence to say that they impact M&A operating performance of the acquiring firm. Table 7.9 summarises all findings in this chapter.

Apparently, these findings are better understood in connection with the findings from the qualitative study reported in Chap. 6. The presence of the state as a shareholder may pose certain constraints that can hinder the performance of a firm's M&A. As the interviews showed, supported by

Table 7.9 Summary of findings on state ownership

State ownership	Variable	Analysis	CAR(-1, 1)	ΔROA	ΔEPSG
State ownership at minority level	MINOR	Univariate	None	None	None
		Multivariate—basic models	None	None	None
		Multivariate—extended models	None	None	None
State ownership at majority level	SOE	Univariate	(-)	None	(-)
		Multivariate—basic models	(-)	None	None
		Multivariate—extended models	(-)	None	(-)
Size of equity held by the state	STATE%	Multivariate—basic models	(+)	(-)	(-)
		Multivariate—extended models	(+)	(-)	(-)
G as the largest shareholder	LARGEST	Univariate	(-)	None	(-)
		Multivariate—basic models	(-)	None	None
		Multivariate—extended models	(-)	None	None
State capital management	SCMA	Univariate	None	None	(-)
		Multivariate—basic models	None	None	None
		Multivariate—extended models	None	None	None

the literature from similar markets such as China (Chen et al., 2013), SOEs were used as tools to implement economic policies and their M&A were the vehicles. If the interest of the state is in industry consolidation, general employment stability or any other social and political goals, with substantial equity holding, it could drive the firm's M&A decisions towards non-economic objectives. This could offer an explanation for why state ownership at a minority level did not show a negative impact on firms' M&A results, whereas at a controlling level and when the state was the largest shareholder, it did. Consistent with the finding from Chap. 6 that board participation was the channel for the state to influence the firm, the higher level of equity holding would give the state more representatives on BOD, leading to more principal-principal conflict. Other insights from Chap. 6 on the rent-seeking business mindset of SOEs, "term-bound" behaviour of SOE managers and directors and the state's role on boards could be possible factors that impede effective decision-making in SOEs, resulting in the problem of low efficiency.

In addition to the direct impact of the state on businesses via state ownership of equity, the state also exerts influence on firms via its role as an industry regulator, as hypothesised in Chap. 4. The next chapter will report the impact of regulatory control on M&A performance for a more thorough understanding of how institutional forces affect corporate development in Vietnam.

REFERENCES

Alexandridis, G., Fuller, K. P., Terhaar, L., & Travlos, N. G. (2013). Deal size, Acquisition Premia and Shareholder Gains. *Journal of Corporate Finance, 20*(0), 1–13.

Allen, F., Qian, J., & Qian, M. (2005). Law, Finance, and Economic Growth in China. *Journal of Financial Economics, 77*(1), 57–116.

Bai, C.-E., Liu, Q., Lu, J., Song, F. M., & Zhang, J. (2004). Corporate Governance and Market Valuation in China. *Journal of Comparative Economics, 32*(4), 599–616.

Bhabra, H. S., & Huang, J. (2013). An Empirical Investigation of Mergers and Acquisitions by Chinese listed companies, 1997–2007. *Journal of Multinational Financial Management, 23*, 186–207.

Bhaumik, S. K., & Selarka, E. (2012). Does Ownership Concentration improve M&A Outcomes in Emerging Markets?: Evidence from India. *Journal of Corporate Finance, 18*(4), 717–726.

Brown, S. J., & Warner, J. B. (1985). Using Daily Stock Returns: The case of Event Studies. *Journal of Financial Economics, 14*(1), 3–31.

Cai, Y., & Sevilir, M. (2012). Board Connections and M&A Transactions. *Journal of Financial Economics, 103*(2), 327–349.

Caprio, L., Croci, E., & Del Giudice, A. (2011). Ownership Structure, Family Control, and Acquisition Decisions. *Journal of Corporate Finance, 17*(5), 1636–1657.

Chang, S. (1998). Takeovers of Privately Held Targets, Methods of Payment, and Bidder Returns. *The Journal of Finance, 53*(2), 773–784.

Chatterjee, R., & Kuenzi, A. (2001). *Mergers and Acquisitions: The Influence of Methods of Payments on Bidder's Share Price.* Research Papers in Management Studies. The Judge Institute of Management Studies, University of Cambridge, UK.

Chen, D., Khan, S., Yu, X., & Zhang, Z. (2013). Government Intervention and Investment Comovement: Chinese Evidence. *Journal of Business Finance & Accounting, 40*(3–4), 564–587.

Chen, G., Firth, M., Xin, Y., & Xu, L. (2008). Control Transfers, Privatisation, and Corporate Performance: Efficiency Gains in China's Listed Companies. *Journal of Financial and Quantitative Analysis, 43*(1), 161–190.

Chen, G., Firth, M., & Xu, L. (2009). Does the Type of Ownership Control Matter? Evidence from China's Listed Companies. *Journal of Banking & Finance, 33*(1), 171–181.

Claessens, S., Djankov, S., & Lang, L. H. P. (2000). The Separation of Ownership and Control in East Asian Corporations. *Journal of Financial Economics, 58*(1–2), 81–112.

Claessens, S., & Yurtoglu, B. B. (2013). Corporate Governance in emerging Markets: A Survey. *Emerging Markets Review, 15*(0), 1–33.

Cull, R., & Xu, L. C. (2003). Who Gets Credit? The Behavior of Bureaucrats and State Banks in Allocating Credit to Chinese State-owned Enterprises. *Journal of Development Economics, 71*(2), 533–559.

Desai, A., Kroll, M., & Wright, P. (2003). CEO Duality, Board Monitoring, and Acquisition Performance: a Test of Competing Theories. *Journal of Business Strategies, 20*(2), 137–156.

Firth, M., Lin, C., & Wong, S. M. L. (2008). Leverage and Investment under a State-owned bank Lending Environment: Evidence from China. *Journal of Corporate Finance, 14*(5), 642–653.

Firth, M., Malatesta, P. H., Xin, Q., & Xu, L. (2012). Corporate Investment, Government Control, and Financing Channels: Evidence from China's Listed Companies. *Journal of Corporate Finance, 18*(3), 433–450.

Garner, J. L., & Kim, W. Y. (2013). Are Foreign Investors Really Beneficial? Evidence from South Korea. *Pacific-Basin Finance Journal, 25*(0), 62–84.

Henry, D. (2004). Corporate Governance and Ownership Structure of Target Companies and the Outcome of Takeovers. *Pacific-Basin Finance Journal, 12*(4), 419–444.

Iqbal, Z., & Dheeriya, P. L. (1991). A comparison of the Market Model and Random Coefficient Model Using Mergers as an Event. *Journal of Economics and Business, 43*(1), 87–93.

John, K., Freund, S., Nguyen, D., & Vasudevan, G. K. (2010). Investor Protection and Cross-border Acquisitions of Private and Public Targets. *Journal of Corporate Finance, 16*(3), 259–275.

La Porta, R., Lopez-de-Silanes, F., & Shleifer, A. (1999). Corporate Ownership around the World. *Journal of Finance, 54*(2), 471–517.

Lang, L. H. P., Stulz, R. M., & Walkling, R. A. (1989). Managerial Performance, Tobin's Q, and the Gains from Successful Tender Offers. *Journal of Financial Economics, 24*(1), 137–154.

Li, M. H., Cui, L., & Lu, J. (2014). Varieties in State Capitalism: Outward FDI Strategies of Central and Local State-owned Enterprises from Emerging Economy Countries. *Journal of International Business Studies, 45*(8), 980–1004.

Lins, K. V. (2003). Equity Ownership and Firm Value in Emerging Markets. *Journal of Financial and Quantitative Analysis, 38*(1), 159–184.

Masulis, R. W., Wang, C., & Xie, F. E. I. (2007). Corporate Governance and Acquirer Returns. *The Journal of Finance, 62*(4), 1851–1889.

Mitton, T. (2002). A cross-firm Analysis of the Impact of Corporate Governance on the East Asian Financial Crisis. *Journal of Financial Economics, 64*(2), 215–241.

Moeller, S., Schlingeman, F. P., & Stulz, R. M. (2004). Firm Size and the Gains from Acquisitions. *Journal of Financial Economics, 73*(2), 201–228.

Morck, R., Shleifer, A., & Vishny, R. W. (1990). Do Managerial Objectives Drive Bad Acquisitions? *The Journal of Finance, 45*(1), 31–48.

Mulherin, J. H., & Boone, A. L. (2000). Comparing Acquisitions and Divestitures. *Journal of Corporate Finance, 6*(2), 117–139.

Pham, N., Oh, K. B., & Pech, R. (2015). Mergers and Acquisitions: CEO Duality, Operating Performance and Stock Returns in Vietnam. *Pacific-Basin Finance Journal, 35*, 298–316. https://doi.org/10.1016/j.pacfin.2015.01.007

Qian, Y. (1996). Enterprise reform in China: Agency Problems and Political Control. *Economics of Transition, 4*(2), 427–447.

Schwert, G. W. (2000). Hostility in Takeovers: In the Eyes of the Beholder? *The Journal of Finance, 55*(6), 2599–2640.

Shleifer, A. (1998). State versus Private Ownership. *Journal of Economic Perspectives, 12*(4), 133–150.

Shleifer, A., & Vishny, R. W. (1994). Politicians and Firms. *The Quarterly Journal of Economics, 109*(4), 995–1025.

Su, D. (2005). Corporate Finance and State enterprise Reform in China. *China Economic Review, 16*(2), 118–148.

Travlos, N. G. (1987). Corporate Takeover Bids, Methods of Payment, and Bidding Firms' Stock Returns. *Journal of Finance, 42*(4), 943–963.

Truong, T., & Heaney, R. (2007). Largest Shareholder and Dividend Policy Around the World. *The Quarterly Review of Economics and Finance, 47*(5), 667–687.

Tu, G., Lin, B., & Liu, F. (2013). Political Connections and Privatisation: Evidence from China. *Journal of Accounting and Public Policy, 32*(2), 114–135.

Vernon, R. (1979). The International Aspects of State-Owned Enterprises. *Journal of International Business Studies, 10*(3), 7–15.

Walkling, R. A., & Edmister, R. O. (1985). Determinants of Tender Offer Premiums. *Financial Analysts Journal, 41*(1), 27–37.

Wang, K., & Xiao, X. (2009). Ultimate Government Control Structures and Firm Value: Evidence from Chinese Listed Companies. *China Journal of Accounting Research, 2*(1), 109–122.

Wei, S.-J., & Wang, T. (1997). The Siamese Twins: Do State-owned Banks Favor state-owned Enterprises in China? *China Economic Review, 8*(1), 19–29.

World Bank. (2013). *Corporate Governance Country Assessment.*

CHAPTER 8

State Control, Corporate Governance and M&A Performance

This chapter completes the theoretical framework we propose in Chap. 4, which integrates corporate governance, agency and political-economic theories to evaluate SOEs and SOEs' behaviour.

This chapter consists of two sections. Section 8.1 presents how firms in regulated industries performed in M&A compared to firms in other industries. The special focus will be on whether SOEs would differ from non-SOEs regarding the impact of regulations. Section 8.2 discusses the possible impact of corporate governance, that is, board structure with CEO duality on firms' M&A performance. CEO duality is a structure in which the CEO also serves as the chairman of the board, a typical phenomenon observed at firms with a state-owned heritage of a centrally planned economy.

The empirical evidence presented in this chapter provides us with further insights into how firms' M&A performance could be affected by state-related institutional factors of emerging markets.

8.1 State Control via Industry Regulation

The first section of this chapter focuses on the impact of state control via industry regulation on firms' M&A performance. The definition of regulation in this study pertains to the power of the state to enforce an "antitrust policy and the regulation of a few industries with natural monopoly characteristics" as well as "to set prices, restrict entry, and control what products are produced" (Joskow & Noll, 1981). Therefore, a *regulated industry* refers to an industry in which economic regulations, including direct legislation and administrative regulations of price and market entries, are applied. Economic regulations do not include social regulations such as environmental, health and safety regulations (Joskow & Rose, 1989).

If being a shareholder gives the State power to influence a firm's strategy formulation and actions directly, then being a regulator, the state indirectly shapes firms' behaviour—regulations guide firms as to what is legitimate.

Although the Vietnamese economy has been actively integrating into the world economy after joining ASEAN and WTO, the Vietnamese regulatory environment remains relatively restrictive compared to other countries in the same region.

The literature on regulatory economics points to more negative than positive impacts of regulations on firms. On the one hand, firms in regulated industries have higher costs of capital (Elton & Gruber, 1971) and spend more organisational and financial resources for regulatory compliance and lobbying activities (Holburn & Vanden Bergh, 2008). On the other hand, regulated firms are not efficient because regulated industries are indeed the place where firms tend to collude (Singal, 1996) or where regulations are barriers to entry that weaken competition (Helm & Jenkinson, 1997).

There are various reasons for a firm in a regulated industry to conduct an acquisition. As our interviews in Chap. 6 revealed, firms in regulated industries may need to acquire strategic assets such as business licences, permits or access to natural resources due to restrictive barriers to entry or ownership conditions. Alternatively, M&As by firms in regulated industries can also be motivated, like any other firms, by the need to seek growth opportunities or improve efficiency.

As explained in Chap. 4, in the *regulatory hypothesis*, we expected that regulated firms might face more regulatory constraints and, therefore, deliver less value from their M&As than do other firms.

We will first portrait some profile characteristics of acquiring firms in regulated industries in terms of their acquisitions, firm performance, corporate governance and ownership structure. The section follows with a comparative analysis of M&A performance of regulated firms versus unregulated firms. The analysis presented in this chapter uncovers interesting interactions between state ownership and regulation and between regulation and firms' M&A strategy.

8.1.1 Description

The sample of 188 acquiring firms included 45 firms in regulated industries, namely Energy, Power and Utilities, Financials, Healthcare and Telecommunications,[1] which was approximately 24% of the total sample (Table 8.1). While these industries are classified as regulated, it does not mean that other industries are not regulated. Instead, it means that firms in the "regulated industries" are subject to more intense scrutiny and control. Hereafter, we use "other industries" or "unregulated industries" when referring to the less regulated industries.

Based on this classification, we created a dummy variable named *REG*. *REG* takes a value of one if the acquirer was in a regulated industry and zero otherwise. Table 8.2 provides the descriptive statistics for the two groups, regulated firms (*REG* = 1) and other firms (*REG* = 0).

Overall, acquirers in regulated industries were vastly different from acquirers in other industries in the sample in various aspects. Firstly, in terms of deal characteristics, regulated firms were more likely to acquire a target firm than an SOE. Acquisitions made by regulated firms were more diversified than those of firms in other industries.

Secondly, regarding the firms' financial performance before the deal, regulated firms had lower ROA (9.93% vs. 14.32%) and lower Tobin's Q (0.54 vs. 0.96) than their counterparts, suggesting that these firms were

Table 8.1 Sample distribution by regulated versus less regulated industries

Acquirer macro industry	Regulated industry		Full sample	
	NO	YES	Total	%
Consumer products and services	4	0	4	2.1
Consumer staples	38	0	38	20.2
Energy, power and utilities	0	27	27	14.4
Financials	0	10	10	5.3
Healthcare	0	4	4	2.1
High-technology/telecommunications	0	4	4	2.2
Industrials	51	0	51	27.1
Materials	19	0	19	10.1
Media and entertainment	6	0	6	3.2
Real estate	25	0	25	13.3
Total	143 (76%)	45 (24%)	188	100%

[1] The classification of these industries as regulated industries is based on the Government's Document No. 929/QD-TTg, as explained in Chap. 4.

Table 8.2 Descriptive statistics between firms in regulated versus other industries

Variable	REG = 0			REG = 1			Mean dif.	SE	t-test	p-value
	Obs.	Mean	SD	Obs.	Mean	SD				
TOEHOLD	143	0.4266	0.4963	45	0.4444	0.5025	-0.0179	0.0851	-0.21	0.8339
ACQUIRED	143	52.9518	35.0201	45	45.5644	32.1642	7.3874	5.8740	1.26	0.2101
TARGETG	142	0.5845	0.8358	45	0.8444	0.8779	-0.2599	0.1447	-1.80	0.0741
TARGETLIST	143	0.3776	0.4865	45	0.3556	0.4841	0.0221	0.0831	0.27	0.7908
DEALTYPE	143	0.4406	0.4982	45	0.2444	0.4346	0.1961	0.0827	2.37	0.0188
OCF	143	0.0390	0.1282	45	0.0736	0.2928	-0.0345	0.0310	-1.12	0.2662
SIZE (LnMV)	143	13.8723	1.9480	45	14.1113	1.6053	-0.2390	0.3201	-0.75	0.4561
ROA (%)	143	14.3154	8.4696	45	9.9251	7.0064	4.3903	1.3926	3.15	0.0019
LEVERAGE (%)	143	86.70	92.29	45	101.93	133.99	-15.224	17.721	-0.86	0.3914
TOBINSQ	143	0.9645	1.3870	45	0.5478	0.6061	0.4167	0.2132	1.95	0.0521
ROE (%)	143	21.7224	14.6371	45	17.32	11.65	4.4046	2.3909	1.84	0.0670
AUDITOR	143	0.5245	0.5012	45	0.6889	0.4682	-0.1644	0.0844	-1.95	0.0528
BOARDSIZE	139	6.3094	1.8488	45	6.2444	1.4795	0.0649	0.3030	0.21	0.8306
NON-EXECUTIVE	139	0.2997	0.2534	43	0.2200	0.2192	0.0797	0.0429	1.86	0.0648
CEOAGE	143	48.5734	7.9855	45	45.2889	6.7911	3.2845	1.3195	2.49	0.0137
CEOGENDER	143	0.8182	0.3871	45	0.8222	0.3866	-0.0040	0.0661	-0.06	0.9514
CEOTEARS	143	16.4126	10.3858	45	14.9111	8.7978	1.5015	1.7149	0.88	0.3824
CEODEGREE	143	0.5315	0.5008	45	0.7333	0.4472	-0.2019	0.0835	-2.42	0.0166
CEO2DEGREE	143	0.2657	0.4433	45	0.5111	0.5055	-0.2454	0.0784	-3.13	0.0020
CEOOWN	143	8.2829	13.1317	45	2.7422	6.2103	5.5406	2.0280	2.73	0.0069
CEOVOTE	143	13.5666	19.2412	45	6.8827	11.6232	6.6839	3.0317	2.20	0.0287
DUALITY	143	0.4406	0.4982	45	0.1778	0.3866	0.2628	0.0811	3.24	0.0014
G	143	11.8440	20.1399	45	32.8736	28.7337	-21.029	3.8410	-5.48	0.0000
INSIDERS	143	19.6173	17.9989	45	11.3222	15.1862	8.2951	2.9698	2.79	0.0058
DOMESTIC	136	24.6537	20.9019	44	28.1741	22.9204	-3.5204	3.7127	-0.95	0.3443
FOREIGN	134	13.6775	15.5262	44	12.1814	13.5629	1.4961	2.6185	0.57	0.5685

less efficient and less profitable than other firms, which is consistent with the usual perception of regulated firms (Singal, 1996).

With regard to corporate governance, while regulated acquirers were more likely to use a Big Four firm for their auditing service, on average, they had a smaller number of non-executive directors on board than other firms.

Next, in terms of CEO characteristics, CEOs of regulated firms owned less equity in their firm and had lower voting power than their counterparts in other firms. Interestingly, CEOs of firms in regulated industries seemed to have a specialised academic qualification other than business. The majority had at least two academic degrees, a technical degree, together with a business degree. This makes sense as firms in regulated industries operate in highly specialised and technical industries such as energy, utilities, defence and manufacturing. These businesses usually require managers with specialised qualifications possessed by their CEOs in many cases. Moreover, fewer firms in regulated industries had their CEO as the Chairman of BOD than those in unregulated industries.

Lastly, regarding ownership structure, we also documented a substantial difference in the level of state ownership among the two groups. On average, the size of state shareholding was 32.87% for regulated firms and 11.84% for other firms, suggesting that although these regulated firms have been equitised and listed, the government has not fully relaxed its ownership. Equitisation encourages competition and efficiency, but the dilemma seems to be that state control remains necessary via state ownership (even though at a lower percentage) and regulation. This is also why the level of insiders' holding was relatively higher for firms in unregulated industries than those in regulated industries. Interestingly, one would suspect that the level of equity held by foreigners would be lower for regulated firms because of restrictive government policies. Foreign ownership was capped at 49% for restrictive industries and 30% for commercial banks, according to Decree 60/2015/ND-CP. Yet, the difference between the two groups was statistically insignificant.

8.1.2 Univariate Analysis

From the univariate analysis, we did not find any clear evidence about the possible impact of *REG* on M&A performance, measured in wealth ($CAR(-1, 1)$), efficiency (ΔROA) and growth ($\Delta EPSG$). All mean differences, as reported in Table 8.3, are not statistically different from zero.

Table 8.3   Mean differences between regulated firms and other firms

Variable	REG = 0			REG = 1			Mean difference	t-test	p-value
	Obs	Mean	SD.	Obs	Mean	SD.			
CAR(-1, 1)	143	-0.21%	4.38	45	-0.51%	4.38	0.30%	0.41	0.6833
ΔROA	83	-0.39%	9.31	32	-0.48%	10.92	0.09%	0.04	0.9664
ΔEPSG	89	0.46%	1.63	32	0.41%	1.84	0.05%	0.14	0.8883

This table describes the M&A performance of the two subsamples, including firms in regulated industries (REG = 1) and firms in unregulated industries (REG = 0)

Both groups of acquirers generated negative abnormal returns to their shareholders upon announcement. While both groups of firms showed positive changes in earnings growth, neither of them had a positive post-acquisitions improvement in ROA.

Based on this result, one may think that industry regulation did not have any impact at all on firms' M&A performance. Indeed, the findings obtained from the multivariate analysis offered some opposite evidence, in line with the prior literature (Becker-Blease et al., 2007; Campa & Hernando, 2004), which we will discuss next.

8.1.3   *Multivariate Analysis: Shareholder Wealth Impact of M&As*

As regulatory control and state ownership are the two visible hands of the state in an economy, it would be difficult, if not impossible, to separate the two when studying corporate behaviour in a regulated environment. Prior studies have shown that ownership, competition and regulation have mixed effects on firms' post-privatisation economic performance (Parker, 2003). In this part of the analysis, we paid special attention to the potential interactions between different state ownership levels and state control. We cross-tabulated firms by regulated industries and the level of state ownership in Table 8.4.

In Panel A, it can be seen that the majority of the sample belonged to the category of non-SOE in unregulated industries, with SOE referring to a firm in which the state held at least 50% of equity. There were 31 SOEs, half of which were in regulated industries. Next, in Panel B, for the 70 firms in which the state was the largest shareholder, there were 28 firms in regulated industries.

Table 8.4   Cross-tabulated distribution of firms by REG and ownership

Panel A	SOE			Panel B	GLARGEST		
REG	0	1	Total	REG	0	1	Total
0	127	16	143	0	101	42	143
1	30	15	45	1	17	28	45
Total	157	31	188	Total	118	70	188

The Interaction Between REG and SOE

The following equations were used to test the regulatory hypothesis.

$$CAR(-1,1)_i = \alpha_i + \beta_{1i}REG + \beta_{2i}SOE + \beta_{3i}SOE \times REG + \beta_{4i}STATE\%$$
$$+\gamma_i DEAL\ CONTROLS + \theta_i FIRM\ CONTROLS + \varepsilon_i \qquad (8.1)$$

$$CAR(-1,1)_i = \alpha_i + \beta_{1i}REG + \beta_{2i}GLARGEST + \beta_{3i}GLARGEST \times REG$$
$$+\beta_{4i}STATE\% + \gamma_i DEAL\ CONTROLS$$
$$+\theta_i FIRM\ CONTROLS + \varepsilon_i \qquad (8.2)$$

We used a set of models to test the impact of *REG*, the main predictor under investigation, on *CAR(-1, 1)*—the wealth impact of M&As. Controlling variables in the models included all deal and firm characteristics. In Equation 8.1, state ownership was reflected by the dummy variable *SOE* and its interaction term *SOE* × *REG*. It can be seen from Model 1 of Table 8.5, on the full sample of 188 firms, that *SOE* had a robust negative coefficient, similar to the findings reported in Chap. 7. However, neither *REG* nor its interaction term with *SOE* was significant. Therefore, this model did not include any impact of *REG* on acquirers' announcement returns.

In Model 2, instead of using *SOE* to represent state-owned firms, we used *GLARGEST* and its interaction term *GLARGEST* × *REG* to examine if there was any association between regulatory control, state ownership and firm performance. *GLARGEST* reflected the fact that the state was their largest shareholder in the firm. These firms may operate like an SOE despite not being classified as an SOE. The negative coefficient of *REG* suggested that firms in regulated industries exhibited lower announcement returns than those in other industries. *GLARGEST* also had a negative coefficient due to the state's negative impact as the largest shareholder, as argued in Chap. 7.

Table 8.5 The interaction between industry regulation level and state ownership

CAR(-1, 1)	Full sample		STATE% = 0	STATE% > 0	GLARGEST = 0	GLARGEST = 1
	Model 1	Model 2	Model 3	Model 4	Model 5	Model 6
REG	-0.0134	-0.0209*	-0.0291*	-0.0445**	-0.0265**	0.0124
	(-1.31)	(-1.73)	(-1.94)	(-2.28)	(-2.08)	(0.99)
DEALTYPE	0.0026	0.0010	-0.0008	0.0039	0.0002	0.0024
	(0.36)	(0.15)	(-0.07)	(0.31)	(0.02)	(0.15)
ACQUIRED	-0.0002	-0.0002	-0.0004**	0.0000	-0.0003**	-0.0000
	(-1.58)	(-1.64)	(-2.44)	(0.14)	(-2.18)	(-0.14)
TOEHOLD	-0.0054	-0.0055	0.0032	-0.0112	0.0020	-0.0148
	(-0.83)	(-0.84)	(0.32)	(-1.13)	(0.24)	(-1.19)
OCF	-0.0012	0.0029	-0.1183***	0.0260*	-0.0987**	0.0236
	(-0.04)	(0.11)	(-2.71)	(1.96)	(-2.41)	(1.63)
ROA	0.0095	0.0065	0.0504	0.0230	0.0362	0.0489
	(0.18)	(0.13)	(0.67)	(0.41)	(0.52)	(0.61)
LEVERAGE	0.0000	-0.0000	-0.0000	-0.0001*	-0.0000	-0.0001
	(0.06)	(-0.32)	(-0.23)	(-1.89)	(-0.48)	(-1.39)
SIZE	0.0018	0.0010	0.0035	-0.0009	0.0034	-0.0006
	(0.83)	(0.44)	(1.10)	(-0.22)	(1.22)	(-0.13)
TOBINSQ	-0.0043	-0.0026	-0.0054	-0.0091	-0.0056	-0.0108
	(-1.15)	(-0.66)	(-0.97)	(-1.15)	(-1.14)	(-1.23)
SOE	-0.044**					
	(-2.25)					
STATE%	0.0005					
	(1.62)					

SOE × REG	0.0252				
	(1.30)				
GLARGEST		-0.0174*		-0.0362***	
		(-1.86)		(-3.95)	
GLARGEST × REG		0.0333**		0.0573**	
		(1.97)		(2.47)	
CONSTANT	-0.0229	-0.0146	-0.0364	0.1150**	-0.0337	0.0835
	(-0.74)	(-0.46)	(-0.85)	(2.13)	(-0.85)	(1.26)
Year fixed effects	Yes	Yes	Yes	Yes	Yes	Yes
N	188	188	100	88	118	70
R-sq	0.071	0.069	0.204	0.195	0.171	0.139

T-values are reported in parentheses. ***, **, and * stand for statistical significance at the 1%, 5% and 10% level, respectively

Another interesting finding is a positive coefficient reported for their interaction term *GLARGEST* × *REG*, which implies that firms with the state as the largest shareholder may bear less negative impact of being in a regulated industry than other firms in the same industry.

The full sample was further separated into two groups of firms with and without state ownership. We ran Model 4 on firms with state ownership. Again, the same interaction between regulation and state ownership held as in other models.

To further check whether *REG*'s impact depends on the value of *GLARGEST*, the full sample was split into firms that had the state as the largest shareholder and those that did not. According to Model 5 and Model 6, of those firms in which the state was not the largest shareholder, regulated firms had lower M&A announcement returns than unregulated firms. Such an effect was not found for firms with the state as the largest shareholder. This confirms that having significant state ownership indeed helped firms better cope with regulated industries' constraints.

These findings raise important questions as to why firms in regulated industries generated lower returns from their M&A than those in unregulated industries and how significant state ownership in a firm seemed to mitigate the negative impacts of being in a regulated industry. We will examine each in turn.

The finding that M&As by firms in regulated industries earned lower returns than those in unregulated industries is consistent with prior literature on M&As in regulated industries (Becker-Blease et al., 2007; Campa & Hernando, 2004; Srivastava & Prakash, 2014). Prior studies also show that the level of regulation impedes the development of M&A activity (Coeurdacier et al., 2009) and that deregulation reduces costs and improves investment opportunities in an industry and thus increases M&A (Boudier & Lochard, 2013). This is because government policies in these industries can have an enormous impact on firms' profitability and investment projects (García-Canal & Guillén, 2008). This is also due to the disadvantages regulated firms face in terms of costs of capital (Jorgenson & Handel, 1971). Regulated firms have to spend resources to ensure compliance with regulations. As Crain and Hopkins (2001) point out, the direct compliance costs of US firms totalled up to $295 billion in 2000. In addition to direct costs, regulated firms also spend resources to engage in political lobbying activities (Holburn & Bergh, 2008). In addition to the compliance issue, firms in regulated industries are subject to a high regulatory risk concerning the consistency of regulations and the predictability of changes in regulations. Regulatory risk also depends on the level of discretion the regulator has. If the regulator has considerable scope to interpret or implement a policy, such as deciding when to enforce a price cap, apply an entrance barrier or subsidise input costs, predicting regulatory actions becomes more challenging (Parker, 2003). The regulatory risk arises from the uncertainty of future changes when a firm makes investment decisions such as M&As.

If it is true that firms in regulated industries face limited investment opportunities and disadvantaged costs of capital, then an interesting question is why and how firms with significant state shareholding seemed to mitigate these constraints. SOEs are sometimes granted regulatory exemptions and tax concessions (OECD, 2016) and have access to cheaper finance, which would offset the higher regulatory costs. Also, firms that have stronger links to the government are in a better position to manage regulatory risks, and state ownership can provide such a link. The literature on the political actions of firms can shed light on this issue.

SOEs can manage regulatory risk better for the following reasons. Having the state as the largest shareholder, it is likely that these firms have people with good political or regulatory experience among their management and directors. In Vietnam, SOE shareholders and senior managers are likely to be Communist Party members with direct connections to the political hierarchy. Evidence from the US has highlighted the benefits of having people with a political and legal background on the board of directors in regulated industries (Hillman, 2005). When a regulated firm brings former government officials or regulators on to its board, it will understand current regulations and better anticipate possible changes in regulations (Agrawal & Knoeber, 2001). It is even more relevant to firms in transitioning markets where regulatory changes are frequent. Firms with political connections enjoy more favourable regulatory conditions (Agrawal & Knoeber, 2001) and have more access to resources (Claessens et al., 2008). This strategy may work for firms in substitute for direct political lobbying activity. In the context of Vietnam, as a single-party state where the National Assembly elects the Prime Minister along party lines, firms cannot spend financial resources for election campaigns as a way to lobby for a favourable policy outcome.

8.1.4 Efficiency and Growth Impact of M&As in Regulated Industries

We now move to examine whether REG has any impact on firms' M&A performance as measured by ΔROA and $\Delta EPSG$. Specifically, the equations are as follows:

$$\Delta ROA_i, \Delta EPSG = \alpha_i + \beta_{1i} REG + \beta_{2i} SOE + \beta_{3i} STATE\%$$
$$+\gamma_i DEAL\ CONTROLS + \theta_i FIRM\ CONTROLS + \varepsilon_i \qquad (8.3)$$

$$\Delta ROA_i, \Delta EPSG = \alpha_i + \beta_{1i} REG + \beta_{2i} GLARGEST$$
$$+\beta_{3i} GLARGEST \times REG + \gamma_i DEAL\ CONTROLS$$
$$+\theta_i FIRM\ CONTROLS + \varepsilon_i \qquad (8.4)$$

According to Table 8.7, we documented no association between firms being in a regulated industry and ΔROA and $\Delta EPSG$ as the coefficient of *REG* were consistently insignificant across all models. This finding suggested that firms in regulated industries neither outperformed nor underperformed firms in other industries in terms of operating performance impact of M&A (Table 8.6).

8.2   Corporate Governance and M&A Performance

This section sheds light on the relationship between corporate governance and firms' M&A performance.

Individuals, firms and governments interact within an institutional environment to generate wealth for the economy. Vietnamese firms are bound by a weak institutional environment characterised by high state ownership among businesses and heavy regulatory control over industries. According to the analysis in Chaps. 6 and 7, both of these institutional features have a negative bearing on firms' M&A performance. This is because an institutional environment influences firms' organisational and governance structures and their corporate investment decisions. The review of Claessens and Yurtoglu (2013) shows that emerging market firms domiciling in a weak legal and institutional environment have to adapt by adopting voluntary corporate governance measures that could serve to maximise their wealth. Therefore, this section of the chapter is devoted to examining how Vietnamese firms develop their corporate governance structure to adapt to their institutional environment, considering their state ownership heritage. We particularly focus on the board structure and executive leadership and their impacts on firms' M&A.[2]

---

[2] A part of this research was presented in Pham et al. (2015).

Table 8.6   Regulated industries and efficiency impact and growth impact of M&As

	(1)	(2)	(3)	(4)	(5)	(6)
	ΔROA	ΔROA	ΔROA	ΔEPSG	ΔEPSG	ΔEPSG
REG	-0.0410	0.0087	0.0342	0.2252	-0.1472	0.2643
	(-0.70)	(0.33)	(0.89)	(0.21)	(-0.31)	(0.44)
SOE			0.0353			0.5463
			(0.74)			(1.07)
STATE				-0.0014		-0.0212*
				(-1.40)		(-1.75)
GLARGEST	-0.0639***			-0.7297**		
	(-3.04)			(-2.05)		
GLARGEST × REG	0.1076			-0.0957		
	(1.63)			(-0.09)		
DEALTYPE	0.0124	0.0063	0.0120	0.0591	0.0203	0.0780
	(0.60)	(0.29)	(0.56)	(0.22)	(0.08)	(0.29)
ACQUIRED	-0.0004	-0.0002	-0.0002	-0.0073*	-0.0083**	-0.0073*
	(-1.25)	(-0.75)	(-0.63)	(-1.68)	(-2.12)	(-1.83)
TOEHOLD	-0.0133	-0.0141	-0.0155	0.2882	0.3688	0.3307
	(-0.67)	(-0.65)	(-0.73)	(0.99)	(1.32)	(1.16)
OCF	0.1366	0.1061	0.1496*	-0.9495	-1.3579	-0.7967
	(1.62)	(1.21)	(1.68)	(-0.66)	(-0.90)	(-0.56)
ROA	-0.1015	-0.0934	-0.0851	-2.6776	-2.9577	-2.8454
	(-0.66)	(-0.57)	(-0.55)	(-1.05)	(-1.15)	(-1.10)
LEVERAGE	-0.0001	-0.0001	-0.0001	-0.0007	-0.0004	-0.0006
	(-0.67)	(-1.23)	(-1.58)	(-0.62)	(-0.32)	(-0.48)
SIZE	-0.0160**	-0.0107*	-0.0124*	-0.2963**	-0.2564*	-0.2886**
	(-2.56)	(-1.88)	(-1.97)	(-2.39)	(-1.98)	(-2.14)
TOBINSQ	0.0177	0.0120	0.0115	0.2882*	0.2593	0.2806
	(0.99)	(0.67)	(0.62)	(1.67)	(1.47)	(1.52)
CONSTANT	0.1166	0.0838	0.1048	3.7082***	3.3006**	3.5608**
	(0.90)	(0.68)	(0.83)	(2.65)	(2.35)	(2.43)
Years fixed effects	Yes	Yes	Yes	Yes	Yes	Yes
N	115	115	115	121	121	121
R-sq	0.160	0.087	0.133	0.187	0.146	0.183

T-values are reported in parentheses. ***, ** and * stand for statistical significance at the 1%, 5% and 10% respectively

8.2.1   Descriptive Statistics

This section of the chapter completes the overall research framework by introducing board structure and corporate leadership factors into the model.

Table 8.7   Distribution of firms with CEO duality in the sample

Acquirer industry	Separated CEO and COB	Combined CEO/COB roles	Total
Consumer products and services	4	0	4
Consumer staples	18	20	38
Energy and power	22	5	27
Financials	10	0	10
Healthcare	2	2	4
High-tech/telecom.	3	1	2
Industrials	25	26	51
Materials	11	8	19
Media and entertainment	3	3	6
Real estate	19	6	25
Total	117	71	188

We observed that male CEOs dominated the sample (154 male vs. 34 female CEOs). In 61% of cases, the CEO had more substantial voting power than the COB. It was noticeable that CEO duality, the structure in which the CEO is also the Chairman of the Board (COB), was very popular among Vietnamese acquirers in the sample. Indeed, as reported in Table 8.8, CEO duality was present in 71 cases (approximately 38% of the total 188 deals). The industries that saw more CEO duality in acquirers were consumer staples, materials and industrials.

This observation raised a series of questions as to why a number of Vietnamese firms did not separate the CEO and COB roles[3] as recommended by various corporate governance guidance documents such as the IFC (2010, 2012), OECD (2015) and SSC & IFC (2019) and whether keeping the CEO duality structure benefited the firm. For Vietnamese firms, does CEO duality associate more with the agency or stewardship theory, as discussed earlier in Chap. 4? If a CEO is driven more by personal interests and conducts an acquisition for opportunistic reasons, the acquisition will not create wealth for shareholders, and CEO duality will facilitate even more self-serving decisions. Vice versa, if the CEO's motivation is to provide good stewardship to corporate assets and, in cases of SOEs, state's assets, then CEO duality should be associated with wealth-generating M&A decisions.

---

[3] Please note that our data period was from 2004 to 2013 during which CEO duality was still a popular structure, prior to OECD (2015) and SSC & IFC (2019).

Table 8.8 Descriptive statistics on firms with and without CEO duality

	Duality group (1)		Non-duality group (0)		Difference (1)–(0)	t-value
	Mean	STDEV	Mean	STDEV	Mean dif.	
Panel A: Deal characteristics						
Deal type	0.38	0.49	0.40	0.49	−0.021	(−0.290)
Equity acquired	44.33	35.05	55.35	33.50	−11.02	(−2.148)**
Panel B: Target characteristics						
Target listing status	0.41	0.495	0.35	0.48	0.0580	(0.795)
Target government ownership	0.69	0.89	0.62	0.83	0.0618	(0.479)
Panel C: Acquirer characteristics—firm descriptive information						
Age at acquisition	20.57	12.60	18.15	12.37	2.4261	(1.289)
SIZE (Ln(AMV))	13.45	1.58	14.22	1.98	−0.7747	(−2.959)***
Acquirer auditor	0.42	0.50	0.65	0.479	−0.2270	(−3.104)***
Acquirer board Size	5.70	1.07	6.63	1.98	−0.9310	(−4.133)***
Ln (boardsize)	1.72	0.18	1.85	0.29	−0.1248	(−3.643)***
Non-executive	0.29	0.23	0.27	0.26	0.0227	(0.601)
Operating cash flow (OCF/TA)	0.05	0.26	0.05	0.11	0.0023	(0.070)
EBITDA (million, VND[a])	276,591	520,270	755,799	1,115,964	−479,208	(−3.986)***
Net income (million, VND)	191,033	409,117	427,315	652,120	−236,282,422	(−3.052)***
ROA1 (EBITDA/total asset)	0.13	0.08	0.14	0.09	−0.0075	(−0.598)
ROA2 (Net income/total asset)	0.08	0.07	0.08	0.07	−0.0016	(−0.161)
Debt as % of equity (%)	69.91	80.78	102.75	113.83	−32.83	(−2.126)**
Tobin's Q	0.77	0.72	0.92	1.49	−0.1503	(−0.794)
ROE	0.18	0.13	0.22	0.15	−0.0469	(−2.240)**
Panel D: Acquirer characteristics—ownership information						
Government equity holding (%)	10.88	19.03	20.52	26.20	−9.6336	(−2.909)***
Ownership by insiders (%)	22.72	16.45	14.54	17.76	8.1837	(3.148)***

(continued)

Table 8.8 (continued)

	Duality group (1)		Non-duality group (0)		Difference (1)−(0)	
	Mean	STDEV	Mean	STDEV	Mean dif.	t-value
Total holding by domestic institutional investors (%)	19.42	16.95	29.22	22.99	−9.7981	(−3.276)***
Total holding by foreign institutional investors (%)	16.14	16.30	11.56	14.00	4.5861	(1.923)**
Panel E: Acquirer characteristics—CEO/COB information						
CEO gender	0.76	0.43	0.86	0.35	−0.0941	(−1.553)
CEO age	52.30	7.47	45.05	6.71	7.2445	(6.872)***
CEO years with the company	21.47	9.49	12.77	8.88	8.6956	(6.340)***
CEO degree	0.49	0.50	0.63	0.48	−0.140	(−1.869)*
CEO double degree	0.17	0.38	0.42	0.50	−0.250	(−3.899)***
CEO ownership	15.83	15.46	1.57	3.62	14.25	(7.640)***
CEO votes	25.71	21.86	3.63	6.60	22.08	(8.287)***

This table presents the descriptive statistics for the two groups, duality firms and non-duality firms. The mean value, standard deviation for each group and the mean difference between them are reported. T-values are in parentheses. ***, ** and * stand for statistical significance at the 1%, 5% and 10% respectively.
[a]VND is Vietnamese Dong, for which the exchange rate was approximately VND20,000/USD at the time the data was collected in 2013

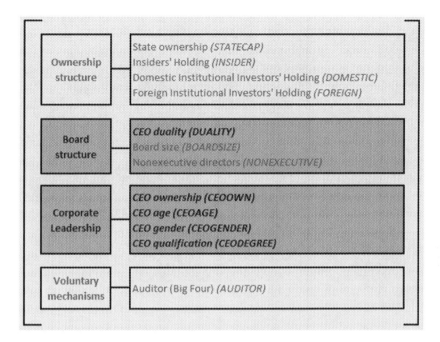

Fig. 8.1   Corporate governance variables in the model

As a result, we examined CEO duality as a critical feature of the board structure. Together with CEO duality were CEO characteristics, including CEO equity ownership, CEO age, gender and qualification representing corporate leadership information, as highlighted in Fig. 8.1.

Table 8.8 profiles the two groups of firms with and without CEO duality. The overall observation is that firms led by CEO duality were more mature at the acquisition time (aged 20.57 years vs. 18.15 years of non-duality firms), acquired more equity in their transactions (55.35% of equity vs. 44.33%), had smaller board sizes and were less likely to hire a Big Four auditing firm. While acquiring firms led by CEO duality were significantly smaller in market value, they had higher returns on assets, lower leverage ratio and higher Tobin's Q ratio. The ROE for non-duality firms was relatively high, which could possibly be affected by their substantial leverage of 102.75% compared to 69.91% for duality firms.

The two groups of acquirers differed significantly in all aspects of ownership, see Panel D. Firms with CEO duality had lower state ownership and ownership by domestic institutional investors than non-duality firms. On average, the state owned 10.88% of the former, whereas, in the latter group, the state capital was up to 20.52%. This was expected as, according to the Law of Enterprises (2014), CEO duality was only allowed at non-SOEs.[4] For SOEs, CEO and chairman functions must be separated. However, many of these duality firms used to be wholly state-owned firms prior to listing.

To understand CEO duality, we sketched the profile of these CEO/COBs (see Panel E). CEO/COBs were significantly different from other CEOs in age, experience, education, backgrounds and equity ownership. A CEO/COB was older, had worked for the firm for a substantially longer time and owned more equity of the firm. On average, the CEO/COB had worked for their company for 21.47 years and held 15.85% equity of the firm, whereas the non-dual CEO had worked for 12.77 years and owned only 1.57%. Longer employment and larger ownership stake imply significant accumulation of both the human capital and financial capital of the CC in the firm. Greater commitment and loyalty of the CEO/COB group helps reduce agency problems and the costs of monitoring (Lambert, 1983).

8.2.2   Univariate Analysis

Wealth Impact

Table 8.9 presents the cumulative abnormal returns for the acquirer shareholders around the M&A announcement, with both t-statistics for mean and Wilcoxon signed-rank test statistic for median abnormal returns. Non-parametric tests are preferred for judging the significance for event studies on small stock exchanges (Bartholdy et al., 2007; Corrado & Truong, 2008). In terms of *CAR(-1, +1)*, we found that the mean (median) abnormal return for the non-duality firms was -0.73% (-0.68%), significantly different from zero, suggesting that acquisitions made by these firms reduced value for acquirer shareholders. Economically, the positive mean (median) difference of 1.19% (1.78%) for *CAR(-1, +1)* suggested that M&As by duality firms created more value for their shareholders. We also calculated cumulative abnormal returns for longer windows,

---

[4] The new Law of Enterprise (2020), to be effective from 1 January 2021, will no longer allow listed companies and public companies to have CEO duality (see Article 156 on Chairman of the Board of Directors).

Table 8.9 Univariate test of cumulative abnormal return

	Full sample		Non-duality group (0)		Duality group (1)		Difference (1)−(0)	
	Mean	Median	Mean	Median	Mean	Median	Mean dif.	Median dif.
CAR(−1,1)	−0.2785	−0.179	−0.7262*	−0.6845**	0.4592	1.094	1.1854*	1.7785**
	(−0.875)	(0.913)	(−1.882)	(2.301)	(0.841)	(1.309)	(1.815)	(2.458)

This table reports mean and median cumulative abnormal return (in percentage) employing the market model for the 3-day window around the M&A announcement. Significance levels of mean and median abnormal returns are reported in parentheses using the t-test statistic and Wilcoxon signed-rank test statistic, respectively. This table also provides t-test statistics for the mean difference and Mann-Whitney test statistics for the median difference across the different groups. ***, ** and * stand for statistical significance at the 1%, 5% and 10% respectively including those from 1 to 10 days before and after the event. All results pointed to a higher level of wealth created from M&A for firms with CEO duality structure.[5]

Efficiency and Growth Impact
We examined whether M&A improved firm's operating performance and whether a change in an acquirer's operating performance (if any) was different among the two groups of firms. If the market is rational, the positive abnormal returns to shareholders of the acquiring firms with CEO duality should reflect fundamental improvements in their ΔROA and $\Delta EPSG$.

From Table 8.10, the pre-deal performance information indicates that prior to the deal, duality acquirers were more efficient (with higher ROA) but had limited growth opportunities than non-duality firms. So, the motivation for duality firms to conduct M&A possibly was to pursue

Table 8.10 ΔROA and $\Delta EPSG$ of duality versus non-duality firms

Industry-adjusted performance indicators (%)	Non-duality firms (0)		Duality firms (1)		Mean difference	
	Mean	STDEV	Mean	STDEV	(1)–(0)	
Pre-deal ROA	-1.0106	9.1223	2.7037	9.8346	3.7143	(2.450)**
Pre-deal EPS growth	5.4656	24.520	-2.0469	6.5218	-7.5125	(-2.894)***
Pre-deal sales per share growth	0.3388	1.7266	-0.4304	2.7318	-0.7692	(-2.163)**
Change in ROA (ΔROA)	-2.2176	8.6922	2.9664	10.749	5.1840	(2.801)***
Change in EPS growth ($\Delta EPSG$)	-0.0413	0.7771	1.3645	2.4080	1.4057	(3.682)***
Change in sales (per share) growth ($\Delta SPSG$)	-0.0431	2.4350	0.2383	0.8668	0.2814	(0.671)

This table presents the descriptive statistics for the two groups, duality firms and non-duality firms. The duality group includes firms that had the CEO as the chairman of the board of directors. Non-duality firms are those that separated the CEO and Chairman roles. The mean value for each group and the mean difference between the two groups are reported. T-values are reported in parentheses. ***, ** and * stand for statistical significance at the 1%, 5% and 10% respectively

[5] For results of other windows, please see Pham et al. (2015)

growth rather than improve efficiency. The positive values for both ΔROA and $\Delta EPSG$ after M&A for the duality group showed that these firms had improved growth and efficiency relative to their industry, whereas the non-duality firms failed to do so post-M&A.

8.2.3   Multivariate Analysis

In a multivariate setting, CEO duality leadership structure is reflected by DUALITY—a dummy variable receiving a value of one if the acquiring firm was led by CEO duality and zero otherwise.

For the wealth impact of M&As, we regressed acquirer's abnormal returns, CAR(-1, +1), on DUALITY, the primary independent variable, controlling for factors known to affect M&A announcement returns in the literature. The full set of control variables included those used earlier models in Chap. 7 and acquirer CEO's characteristics, namely equity ownership, age, gender and qualification, following Cai and Sevilir (2012). CEO equity ownership helps mitigate agency problem due to conflicts of interest between management and shareholders (Kim & Lu, 2011). However, CEO ownership could lead to entrenchment in M&A in cases of weak boards (Chan & Emanuel, 2011). CEO gender is a relevant control variable as it is known to affect firms' risk aversion in M&A (Martin et al. 2009).

DUALITY consistently had a significantly positive coefficient across all CAR(-1, 1) models, as reported in columns (1) to (4) of Table 8.12.[6] The magnitude of the coefficients suggested a strong positive economic impact of the variable on abnormal returns to shareholders, supporting steward-ship theory. The result is inconsistent with Masulis et al. (2007) and Desai et al. (2003), which could be explained by the difference in institutional settings between Vietnamese and US markets. It seems that in the Vietnamese market, CEO duality bears strategic benefits that outweigh the agency costs of such a structure, fully supporting the stewardship view.

Across all regressions in columns (5) to (8), DUALITY had a significant positive impact on $\Delta EPSG$, suggesting that deals associated with CEO

---

[6]The equations are tested and are found to be free from multicollinearity problem. For heteroskedasticity, we employed the Breusch-Pagan test and Koenker test (which is rigorous for small sample size) to check the data. Both tests identified significant existence of hetero-skedasticity in our data. Therefore, our regression coefficients are estimated based on hetero-skedasticity adjusted standard errors (HCREG).

Table 8.11 Drivers of M&A returns for firms with and without state capital

	FOR G = 0 GROUP			FOR G > 0 GROUP		
	(1)	(2)	(3)	(1)	(2)	(3)
DUALITY	0.1643	0.3002	0.1926	0.5035**	0.5853**	0.3676*
	(0.95)	(1.25)	(1.17)	(2.48)	(2.45)	(1.71)
ACQUIRED	-0.2602	-0.3071**	-0.2294	-0.1416	-0.1294	-0.1395
	(-1.58)	(-2.03)	(-1.46)	(-1.22)	(-1.12)	(-0.96)
BOARDSIZE	-0.0664			0.2946**		
	(-0.37)			(2.54)		
AUDITOR	0.0974			0.0422		
	(0.66)			(0.28)		
NON-EXECUTIVE	0.0492			-0.1489		
	(0.42)			(-1.36)		
CEOOWN		0.0669			-0.2931***	
		(0.63)			(-2.80)	
CEOAGE		-0.2509			0.0222	
		(-1.46)			(0.17)	
CEOGENDER		0.1728*			0.0919	
		(1.71)			(0.77)	
CEODEGREE		-0.1893			-0.0187	
		(-1.63)			(-0.13)	
INSIDERS			0.3625***			-0.1146
			(2.91)			(-0.74)
DOMESTIC			0.1939			-0.406***
			(1.38)			(-2.71)

FOREIGN			0.1371			-0.1286
			(0.91)			(-0.76)
Deal controls	Yes	Yes	Yes	Yes	Yes	Yes
Firm controls	Yes	Yes	Yes	Yes	Yes	Yes
Industry fixed effects	Yes	Yes	Yes	Yes	Yes	Yes
Year fixed effects	Yes	Yes	Yes	Yes	Yes	Yes
N	90	100	91	88	88	84
Adj. R-sq	0.018	0.107	0.049	0.099	0.070	0.186

This table presents heteroskedasticity consistent regression results for the sample of 188 mergers and acquisitions between 2004 and 2013 in Vietnam. The dependent variable is CAR(−1, 1), the cumulative abnormal returns of the acquirers from 1 day before to 1 day after the deal announcement. Standardised coefficients are reported. T-statistics are in parentheses. ***, ** and * stand for statistical significance at the 1%, 5% and 10% respectively duality delivered more improvements in post-M&A growth performance than those with non-duality leadership. This finding implies that positive market reactions to M&A deals by CEO duality-led firms were fundamentally grounded, in line with the stewardship view of CEO duality for delivering better M&A results, supporting Hypothesis 2. Other drivers of growth performance of M&A included *TOEHOLD, ROA, SIZE, TOBINSQ, AUDITOR, NON-EXECUTIVE, CEOAGE* and *DOMESTIC*.

The same analysis was conducted with the dependent variable being *ΔROA*. The results are presented in columns (9) to (12) of Table 8.12. These models had low explanatory power, and the coefficient of *DUALITY* failed to retain its statistical significance after variables related to CEO and ownership structure were introduced. The difference in the results with *ΔEPSG* versus *ΔROA* agreed with the prior speculation of this research that M&A by CEO duality firms tended to be driven by the need for growth rather than efficiency improvement.

8.2.4   Linking CEO Duality and State Ownership

In this section, we take one further step to examine the link between CEO duality and state ownership, both of which have been proven to impact firms' M&A as shown in Chap. 7 and previous sections of this chapter.

When we split the full sample into two subgroups, including firms with state capital (SIEs) and those without (non-SIEs), an exciting observation arisen. It appears that the impact of *DUALITY* on firms' M&A performance was actually more profound for firms with state capital than those without. It can be seen from Table 8.11 that while the coefficients of *DUALITY* were significant across the three models for firms with state capital, those for private firms were not. This finding is puzzling as to why CEO duality resulted in better acquirer returns for SIEs than non-SIEs. As we have argued that when the market has a positive perception of CEO duality, it could be interpreted that the market believes in the stewardship theory of leadership. The question now becomes why stewardship theory is more relevant to SIEs than non-SIEs and whether agency theory is not a concern for Vietnamese SIEs.

It is not a coincidence that this finding is consistent with how CEO duality is viewed in China (Peng et al., 2007). Vietnam and China are similar in terms of the current political structure under the ruling of a Communist Party and the strong link between the political and economic systems.

Table 8.12 DUALITY and CAR, post-M&A changes in earnings growth and ROA

	(1)	(2)	(3)	(4)	(5)	(6)	(7)	(8)	(9)	(10)	(11)	(12)
	CAR (-1,1)	CAR (-1,1)	CAR (-1,1)	CAR (-1,1)	ΔEPSG	ΔEPSG	ΔEPSG	ΔEPSG	ΔROA	ΔROA	ΔROA	ΔROA
DUALITY	0.2581**	0.2759**	0.3162**	0.2318*	0.2839***	0.3302***	0.3146**	0.3858***	0.2197**	0.1846*	0.0759	0.1701
	(2.15)	(2.24)	(2.08)	(1.91)	(2.89)	(3.32)	(2.29)	(3.22)	(2.15)	(1.85)	(0.53)	(1.22)
STATECAP	0.0332	0.0273	0.0473	0.1314	-0.0685	-0.0560	-0.1484	-0.1819	-0.0834	-0.0463	-0.0266	-0.107
	(0.38)	(0.31)	(0.54)	(1.22)	(-0.65)	(-0.48)	(-1.23)	(-1.48)	(-0.74)	(-0.41)	(-0.19)	(-0.69)
DEALTYPE	0.0418	0.0353	0.0225	0.0431	-0.0271	-0.0057	0.0466	-0.0004	0.0307	-0.0282	0.0074	-0.018
	(0.51)	(0.43)	(0.27)	(0.5)	(-0.39)	(-0.08)	(0.72)	(-0.01)	(0.30)	(-0.29)	(0.07)	(-0.17)
ACQUIRED	-0.1535*	-0.1419	-0.1450*	-0.1473	-0.1107	0.0002	-0.1229	-0.0903	0.0768	0.0791	-0.0326	0.0763
	(-1.73)	(-1.56)	(-1.67)	(-1.45)	(-1.09)	(0.00)	(-1.52)	(-1.17)	(0.81)	(0.79)	(-0.38)	(0.80)
TOEHOLD	0.0061	-0.003	-0.0014	-0.0571	0.1793*	0.1260	0.1791**	0.1422	-0.0884	-0.1074	-0.0406	-0.083
	(0.07)	(-0.03)	(-0.02)	(-0.68)	(1.87)	(1.32)	(1.99)	(1.65)	(-0.84)	(-1.00)	(-0.40)	(-0.77)
OCF	0.0002	-0.0087	0.0009	0.0353	-0.0380	-0.1300	-0.0737	-0.1388	0.1344	0.1000	0.1095	0.0899
	(0.00)	(-0.08)	(0.01)	(0.42)	(-0.35)	(-1.32)	(-0.70)	(-1.29)	(1.18)	(0.98)	(1.11)	(0.93)
ROA	0.0328	0.0262	0.0708	-0.004	-0.262**	-0.1516	-0.2792***	-0.2825*				
	(0.37)	(0.31)	(0.81)	(-0.04)	(-2.04)	(-1.29)	(-2.09)	(-1.90)				
SIZE	0.1684	0.1022	0.1551	0.0925	-0.2081	-0.2838***	-0.311***	-0.269***	0.0344	-0.1173	-0.1559	-0.133
	(1.29)	(1.07)	(1.59)	(0.94)	(-1.52)	(-2.86)	(-3.21)	(-2.85)	(0.23)	(-1.21)	(-1.55)	(-1.06)
LEVERAGE	0.0154	-0.0037	0.0097	-0.0221	0.2083**	0.0957	0.1081	0.1180	-0.1710*	-0.0590	-0.0870	-0.092
	(0.20)	(-0.05)	(0.14)	(-0.28)	(2.08)	(0.94)	(1.30)	(1.08)	(-1.76)	(-0.66)	(-0.98)	(-0.94)
TOBINSQ	-0.0707	0.0012	-0.0974	0.0321	0.2448**	0.2480**	0.2940***	0.3054**	-0.1420	0.0563	0.0153	-0.131
	(-0.59)	(0.02)	(-0.79)	(0.25)	(2.36)	(2.56)	(3.09)	(2.51)	(-1.02)	(0.72)	(0.21)	(-0.94)
TARGETLIST	0.0583	0.0693	0.0791	0.0847		0.0358				0.2488		
	(0.49)	(0.58)	(0.66)	(0.67)		(0.28)				(1.63)		
TARGETSOE	-0.1382	-0.1409	-0.1387	-0.1257		0.2386				-0.0557		
	(-1.22)	(-1.24)	(-1.28)	(-1.05)		(1.50)				(-0.33)		
BOARDSIZE	-0.0383				-0.1507				-0.1105			
	(-0.39)				(-1.01)				(-0.88)			
AUDITOR	-0.061				-0.180**				-0.0109			
	(-0.62)				(-2.01)				(-0.08)			

(continued)

Table 8.12 (continued)

	(1)	(2)	(3)	(4)	(5)	(6)	(7)	(8)	(9)	(10)	(11)	(12)
	CAR (-1,1)	CAR (-1,1)	CAR (-1,1)	CAR (-1,1)	ΔEPSG	ΔEPSG	ΔEPSG	ΔEPSG	ΔROA	ΔROA	ΔROA	ΔROA
NON-EXECUTIVE	-0.0161 (-0.24)				0.217*** (2.77)				-0.0808 (-0.78)			
CEOOWN			0.0304 (0.31)				-0.1320 (-1.47)				0.1484 (1.20)	
CEOAGE			-0.0754 (-0.82)				0.3041** (2.39)				0.0207 (0.18)	
CEOGENDER			0.0906 (1.23)				0.0484 (0.63)				-0.1066 (-0.98)	
CEODEGREE			-0.0835 (-1.01)				0.1353 (1.48)				0.0683 (0.68)	
INSIDERS				0.2212* (1.76)				-0.1717 (-1.44)				0.0744 (0.62)
DOMESTIC				-0.0201 (-0.21)				0.2362*** (3.18)				0.0443 (0.39)
FOREIGN				-0.0469 (-0.48)				-0.0107 (-0.08)				0.1385 (1.21)
Industry fixed effect	Yes	Yes	Yes	Yes	Yes	Yes	Yes	Yes	Yes	Yes	Yes	Yes
Year fixed effect	Yes	Yes	Yes	Yes	Yes	Yes	Yes	Yes	Yes	Yes	Yes	Yes
N	183	181	187	174	117	120	121	113	111	114	115	108
Adj; R-sq	0.004	0.006	0.011	0.02	0.230	0.213	0.221	0.231	0.063	0.071	0.039	0.059

This table presents robust regression results for the sample of 188 mergers and acquisitions between 2004 and 2013 in Vietnam. For Models (1)–(4), the dependent variables are CAR(-1, 1); Models (5)–(8), ΔEPSG; and Models (9)–(12), ΔROA. Beta coefficient estimates are standardised. *T-values* are reported in parentheses. ***, ** and * stand for statistical significance at the 1%, 5% and 10% respectively. Year dummy and industry dummy coefficients are suppressed for brevity

As argued by Peng et al. (2007), with the presence of the state in the firm, the CEO is under political pressure to perform. Regardless of the current level of government ownership, SIEs have their origins as being a majority government-controlled entity, and the leadership of these SIEs is headed by leaders who still have profound political and communist party roots. These leaders are expected to act as good stewards of the state's asset under their management. This, in other words, is due to the political risk of not heeding party ideologies and objectives or failing to meet targets set by local governments, as evident in China (Li & Zhou, 2005; Li & Qian, 2013).

Alternatively, the CEO may be interested in advancing his/her political career, for which a good track record of being a good steward of state asset is quite important, which supports the relevance of the stewardship argument here.

Additionally, for SIEs, their CEOs have likely assumed the management position long before equitisation. These long-serving CEOs benefit their firms with their networking and connections (Engelberg et al., 2013), especially political connections in highly regulated markets (Chen et al., 2011; Mitchell & Joseph, 2010).

Furthermore, emerging market firms might choose the CEO duality structure to leverage their leadership expertise. CEO duality helps business save on their search for leaders given the level of talent scarcity in Vietnam, which is even more so for the state-owned sector. Under conditions of resource scarcity, CEO duality could be a way for firms to enhance unified leadership while economising on communication and compensation costs (Peng et al., 2007). Even in a developed market context, in Australia, Christensen et al. (2013) show that while splitting the titles is good for large Australian companies, small listed firms indeed benefit from CEO duality.

Lastly, the positive impact of CEO duality on organisational outcomes among firms with state shareholding suggested that CEO duality could help these firms to re-balance the board against the power of non-executive directors representing the state interests on the board. A powerful CEO with a motivation to be a good steward of firm value will minimise possible political interference of the state on firms' decisions and, hence, reduce principal costs of the state shareholder.

We were mindful of the potential endogeneity of research on corporate governance and corporate performance, which is highlighted as "a serious methodological problem" by Iyengar and Zampelli (2009), especially when the predictor variable is a dummy. Robustness checks to confirm the impact of *DUALITY* included the two-stage least squares regression analysis with an instrumental variable (Ramdani & Witteloostuijn, 2010) and the propensity score matching technique (PSM) (Campello et al., 2010; Saunders & Steffen, 2011). We also used principal components analysis (PCA) to ensure that our results were not biased due to the design of non-parsimonious models with a relatively small sample size.[7] PCA results confirmed the positive impact of *DUALITY* on *CAR(-1, +1)* and *ΔEPS* and its insignificant impact on *ΔROA* from the OLS regressions, which was consistent with OLS and PSM analysis.

8.3   CHAPTER CONCLUSION

This chapter has presented empirical evidence that state control via the level of regulation applicable to the industry of the firm has a certain bearing on the firm's M&A performance. In brief, state control matters for firms, and what matters is the way they are regulated. Firms in regulated industries are disadvantaged; however, those with the state as the largest shareholder do not seem to bear such an impact. In the context of a transitioning market where competition is being introduced into regulated industries via privatisation, policies change to respond to new market conditions. Thus, regulatory risk is considerable (Helm & Jenkinson, 1997). Firms that have the state as the largest shareholder develop better capabilities in managing their regulatory risk. The interaction between regulation and state ownership shows that firms should understand their constraints and adapt to the environment.

This chapter has also reported our findings regarding how corporate governance structure, CEO duality, affects firms' M&A performance in Vietnam. CEO duality was positively related to shareholders' abnormal returns upon M&A announcement and post-M&A firm growth, in line with the stewardship theory.

The development context of Vietnam during the study's time frame from 2004 to 2013 helps explain why the benefits of CEO duality could outweigh its potential agency costs. In young and growing emerging markets like Vietnam at the beginning of the century, CEO duality might indeed be advantageous under conditions of absent anti-takeover provisions in the legal system and leadership resource scarcity. Firms with CEO

[7] Please see Pham, N. (2015) for the detailed robustness check analysis.

duality, therefore, can leverage their managerial and leadership expertise. Additionally, under the monitoring pressure of institutional forces such as the Supervisory Board and local communist party committees, the CEO may have less incentive to make opportunistic and self-serving M&As at the expense of shareholders. For firms with the state capital, CEO duality may empower the CEO to re-balance the board against the power of political directors representing the state interests, mitigating principal costs of principal-principal conflict. For small emerging market firms, CEO duality could be a way to achieve optimal governance with less sophisticated structures.

However, it should be noted that as markets develop and corporate governance practices evolve, a corporate structure of the past, such as CEO duality, may no longer be the best practice in the future.

REFERENCES

Agrawal, A., & Knoeber, C. R. (2001). Do Some Outside Directors Play a Political Role? *Journal of Law and Economics, 44*(1), 179–198.

Bartholdy, J., Olson, D., & Peare, P. (2007). Conducting Event Studies on a Small Stock Exchange. *The European Journal of Finance, 13*(3), 227–252.

Becker-Blease, J. R., Goldberg, L. G., & Kaen, F. R. (2007). Mergers and Acquisitions as a Response to the Deregulation of the Electric Power Industry: Value Creation or Value Destruction? *Journal of Regulatory Economics, 33*(1), 21–53.

Boudier, F., & Lochard, J. (2013). How do Cross-Border Mergers and Acquisitions Answer to Deregulation in Services? *The World Economy, 36*(11), 1424–1441.

Cai, Y., & Sevilir, M. (2012). Board Connections and M&A Transactions. *Journal of Financial Economics, 103*(2), 327–349.

Campa, J. M., & Hernando, I. (2004). Shareholder Value Creation in European M&As. *European Financial Management, 10*(1), 47–81.

Campello, M., Graham, J. R., & Harvey, C. R. (2010). The Real Effects of Financial Constraints: Evidence from a Financial Crisis. *Journal of Financial Economics, 97*(3), 470–487.

Chan, W., & Emanuel, D. (2011). Board Governance and Acquirers' Returns: A Study of Australian Acquisitions. *Australian Journal of Management, 36*(2), 174–199.

Chen, C. J. P., Li, Z., Su, X., & Sun, Z. (2011). Rent-seeking Incentives, Corporate Political Connections, and the Control Structure of Private Firms: Chinese Evidence. *Journal of Corporate Finance, 17*(2), 229–243.

Christensen, J., Kent, P., Routledge, J., & Stewart, J. (2013). Do Corporate Governance Recommendations Improve the Performance and Accountability of Small Listed Companies? *Accounting & Finance*, n/a-n/a.. https://doi.org/10.1111/acfi.12055

Claessens, S., Feijen, E., & Laeven, L. (2008). Political Connections and Preferential Access to Finance: The Role of Campaign Contributions. *Journal of Financial Economics, 88*(3), 554–580.

Claessens, S., & Yurtoglu, B. B. (2013). Corporate Governance in Emerging Markets: A Survey. *Emerging Markets Review, 15*(0), 1–33.

Coeurdacier, N., De Santis, R. A., & Aviat, A. (2009). Cross-border Mergers and Acquisitions and European Integration. *Economic Policy, 24*(57), 55–106.

Corrado, C. J., & Truong, C. (2008). Conducting Event Studies with Asia-Pacific Security Market Data. *Pacific Basin Finance Journal, 16*(5), 493–521.

Crain, W. M., & Hopkins, T. D.. (2001). *The Impact of Regulatory Costs on Small Firms*. U.S. Small Business Administration, Office of Advocacy. www.sba.gov/advo/research/rs207tot.pdf

Desai, A., Kroll, M., & Wright, P. (2003). CEO Duality, Board Monitoring, and Acquisition Performance: a Test of Competing Theories. *Journal of Business Strategies, 20*(2), 137–156.

Elton, E. J., & Gruber, M. J. (1971). Valuation and the Cost of Capital for Regulated Industries. *Journal of Finance, 26*(3), 661–670.

Engelberg, J., Gao, P., & Parsons, C. A. (2013). The Price of a CEO's Rolodex. *Review of Financial Studies, 26*(1), 79–114.

García-Canal, E., & Guillén, M. F. (2008). Risk and the Strategy of Foreign Location Choice in Regulated Industries. *Strategic Management Journal, 29*(10), 1097–1115.

Helm, D., & Jenkinson, T. (1997). The Assessment: Introducing Competition into Regulated Industries. *Oxford Review of Economic Policy, 13*(1), 1–14.

Hillman, A. J. (2005). Politicians on the Board of Directors: Do Connections Affect the Bottom Line? *Journal of Management, 31*(3), 464–481.

Holburn, G. L. F., & Vanden Bergh, R. G. (2008). Making Friends in Hostile Environments: Political Strategy in Regulated Industries. *Academy of Management Review, 33*(2), 521–540.

IFC. (2010). *Corporate Governance Manual*. Hanoi International Finance Corporation.

IFC. (2012). *Vietnam Corporate Governance Scorecard*. International Finance Corporation.

Iyengar, R. J., & Zampelli, E. M. (2009). Self-Selection, Endogeneity, and the Relationship between CEO Duality and Firm Performance. *Strategic Management Journal, 30*(10), 1092–1112.

Jorgenson, D. W., & Handel, S. S. (1971). Investment Behavior in US Regulated Industries. *The Bell Journal of Economics and Management Science, 2*(1), 213–264.

Joskow, P. L., & Noll, R. G. (Eds.). (1981). *Regulation in Theory and Practice: An Overview.* The MIT Press.

Joskow, P. L., & Rose, N. L. (Eds.). (1989). *The Effects of Economic Regulation* (Vol. II). Elsevier Science Publishers B. V.

Kim, E. H., & Lu, Y. (2011). CEO Ownership, External Governance, and Risk-taking. *Journal of Financial Economics, 102*(2), 272–292.

Lambert, R. A. (1983). Long-Term Contracts and Moral Hazard. *The Bell Journal of Economics, 14*(2), 441–452.

Li, H., & Zhou, L.-A. (2005). Political Turnover and Economic Performance: the Incentive Role of Personnel Control in China. *Journal of Public Economics, 89*(9–10), 1743–1762.

Li, J., & Qian, C. (2013). Principal-principal Conflicts Under Weak Institutions: A Study of Corporate Takeovers in China. *Strategic Management Journal, 34*(4), 498–508.

Martin, A. D., Nishikawa, T., & Williams, M. A. (2009). CEO Gender: Effects on Valuation and Risk. *Quarterly Journal of Finance and Accounting, 48*(3), 23–40.

Masulis, R. W., Wang, C., & Xie, F. E. I. (2007). Corporate Governance and Acquirer Returns. *The Journal of Finance, 62*(4), 1851–1889.

Mitchell, H., & Joseph, S. (2010). Changes in Malaysia: Capital controls, prime ministers and political connections. *Pacific-Basin Finance Journal, 18*(5), 460–476.

OECD. (2015). *G20/OECD Principles of Corporate Governance.* OECD Publishing. https://doi.org/10.1787/9789264236882-en.

OECD. (2016). *State-Owned Enterprises as Global Competitors: A Challenge or an Opportunity?* OECD Publishing.

Parker, D. (2003). Performance, Risk and Strategy in Privatised, Regulated Industries. *International Journal of Public Sector Management, 16*(1), 75–100.

Peng, M. W., Zhang, S., & Li, X. (2007). CEO Duality and Firm Performance during China's Institutional Transitions. *Management and Organization Review, 3*(2), 205–225.

Pham, N. (2015). *The Impact of the State on M&A performance: an Empirical Study on Vietnam.* Thesis, Department of Finance. Melbourne, Australia, La Trobe University. PhD.

Pham, N., Oh, K. B., & Pech, R. (2015). Mergers and Acquisitions: CEO Duality, Operating Performance and Stock Returns in Vietnam. *Pacific-Basin Finance Journal, 35*, 298–316. https://doi.org/10.1016/j.pacfin.2015.01.007

Ramdani, D., & van Witteloostuijn, A. (2010). The Impact of Board Independence and CEO Duality on Firm Performance: A Quantile Regression Analysis for Indonesia, Malaysia, South Korea and Thailand. *British Journal of Management, 21*(3), 607–627.

Saunders, A., & Steffen, S. (2011). The Costs of Being Private: Evidence from the Loan Market. *Review of Financial Studies*. https://doi.org/10.1093/rfs/hhr083

Singal, V. (1996). Airline Mergers and Competition: An Integration of Stock and Product Price Effects. *The Journal of Business, 69*(2), 233.

Srivastava, R., & Prakash, A. (2014). Value Creation through Cross-border mergers and Acquisitions by the Indian Pharmaceutical Firms. *Journal of Strategy and Management, 7*(1), 49–63.

State Securities Commission of Vietnam & IFC. (2019). *Vietnam Corporate Governance Code of Best Practices for Public Companies in Vietnam* (1st ed.).

CHAPTER 9

Model Building and Concluding Thoughts

We now need to systematically consolidate the findings presented in Chaps. 6, 7 and 8 of this book. The chapters have addressed different corporate features and institutional factors affecting Vietnamese firms' M&As. According to the research methodology explained in Chap. 5, subsequent to the qualitative and quantitative studies in the exploratory mixed-methods design (QUAL → QUAN → MODEL BUILDING), the next step is model building. The thread that weaves all these findings together is the underlying theoretical model proposed at the end of Chap. 4. In the theoretical model, we integrate the agency theory and the theory of political behaviour of state firms to provide a perspective to understand how state ownership, state control and corporate governance structure influence firms' performance, in this case, Vietnamese firms' M&A performance.

In the quantitative study, the performance of an M&A is assessed based on (1) the shareholder wealth generated—the wealth impact, measured by the cumulative abnormal returns upon the event announcement; (2) the change in earning growth $\Delta EPSG$—*the growth impact*; and (3) the change in return on assets ΔROA post-M&A—*the efficiency impact*.

It is necessary to revisit the M&A model to understand if these factors significantly impact the firm and how they interact. The model can serve as a contextualised theoretical framework to study corporate performance in emerging markets.

© The Author(s), under exclusive license to Springer Nature
Singapore Pte Ltd. 2021
N. Pham, K.-B. Oh, *State on Board!*,
https://doi.org/10.1007/978-981-16-3525-0_9

This chapter starts with a summary of the significant findings, followed by the presentation of the theoretical model. We highlight the links and dynamic interactions among the key findings and discuss the practical implications of the results. A practical model derived from these findings will also be introduced to offer investors and practitioners a point of reference or enrich their toolbox. This chapter will end with some concluding thoughts about the contents of the book.

9.1   Major Findings

Institutional factors mattered. State ownership and state control impacted firm performance negatively. Boards structured with CEO duality delivered better performance in M&As.

The qualitative study provided us with an essential understanding of M&A activity in Vietnam as an emerging market in general and the issues involving M&A of SIEs in particular. The in-depth interviews with M&A professionals and corporate managers have resulted in valuable insights into those factors that are perceived to be relevant to the M&A performance of Vietnamese firms. In other words, Chap. 6 has provided the initial but valuable qualitative evidence that reinforces the hypotheses in this study that institutional factors matter. Figure 9.1 depicts the links and

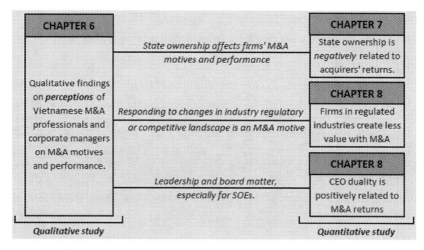

Fig. 9.1   The QUAL-QUAN links among the chapters

complementarities between qualitative and quantitative findings among the chapters.

The in-depth interviews have shown us that Vietnamese SIEs and non-SIEs differ vastly in terms of M&A motives and performance. This is a point that foreign investors should note when searching for joint venture partners in emerging markets in terms of coherence of strategic direction. This finding is reported in Chap. 6. SIEs are generally driven by the political and economic policies of the government. Evidence has confirmed that M&A could be a vehicle for SIEs to implement policies such as those to reform the Vietnamese state-owned sector and financial markets. Non-SIEs are less subject to political interference, and their M&A decisions are thus expected to be more commercially and economically driven. The in-depth interviews also uncovered the issue of principal costs of the state shareholder and some insightful discussions on the possible behaviour of the state shareholder that potentially gives rise to such costs. These include marginalising minority investors in decision-making, the moral hazard of easy access to capital, term-bound thinking, rent-seeking business mindset and favour-granting attitude. Board participation is the channel through which the state extends its influence on the firm. This qualitative evidence points to the negative impact of state ownership, consistent with the finding from the quantitative study reported in Chap. 7. We found that firms having the government as the largest shareholder were associated with lower M&A performance than their non-SIEs counterparts. It should be noted that having the government as the largest shareholder does not necessarily mean that state ownership is beyond 50%.

In terms of the motivations for M&A revealed by the respondents, Vietnamese firms conduct M&A to acquire strategic assets that are critical or strategic for them to remain competitive in or to enter into a particular industry in response to the changing competitive and regulatory landscape. This response supports the hypothesis that industry regulation is one of the crucial drivers of M&A, and in Chap. 8, we emphasise that this underpins the need to conduct an empirical analysis of industry regulation as a significant predictor. Additionally, the analysis presented in Chap. 8 drills down to the interaction between state ownership at the firm vis-à-vis industry regulation and provides some interesting findings pertaining to the benefit of related deals in a regulated industry. Here, we find that firms with the state as the largest shareholder bear the less negative impact of being in a regulated industry than other firms in the same industry.

In terms of corporate governance structure, we examined if firms with CEO duality, having the CEO as the same person as the Chairman of the Board, do well at their M&As. We find that CEO duality had a strong positive impact on firms' M&A returns and growth performance, supporting the stewardship theory. The impact of CEO duality was more profound for firms with state capital than those without. The reported positive impact of CEO duality suggests that Vietnamese CEOs are expected to be a steward of corporate assets, on behalf of the state as well as other shareholders, rather than utilising the assets for their personal gain. This is not surprising, especially for CEOs of SIEs, as they are often motivated by political ambitions, for which a demonstration of good stewardship for state assets is critical (Li & Qian, 2013). It is common for Vietnamese business leaders to join politics, for example, by becoming a member of the Vietnamese National Assembly for this purpose. If stewardship motivation is true, it is unlikely that these CEOs will act opportunistically to harm the value of their firms, similar to what is found in China (Peng et al., 2007). Pressure for Chinese firms to perform also comes from the fact that the turnover of provincial leaders depends on local economic performance (Chen et al., 2005).

The positive association of CEO duality on acquirer returns for SIEs suggests that the market prefers these firms to have CEO duality for a number of reasons. Firstly, CEO duality empowers the CEO to mitigate or neutralise the political power of the state shareholder representatives on the Board of Directors. As we have argued in Chap. 4, firms with the state as a shareholder may be subject to principal costs associated with the state shareholder because, in many SIEs, the state representatives dominate board seats (Su et al., 2008). For SIEs in which the CEO is not the chairman, a representative of the state will likely be. Therefore, having the COE as the Board Chairman helps put less power in the hands of state representatives. In other words, CEO duality is a way to mitigate principal-principal conflict between the state and other shareholders and thus reduce principal costs.

Second, CEO duality is a less sophisticated structure that allows firms to economise on communication and compensation costs under a resource-constrained environment and leverage leadership expertise in an institutionally transitioning market (Peng et al., 2007). Overall, the positive impact of CEO duality on organisational outcomes we measured could imply that the benefit of CEO duality in mitigating principal costs and other economic benefits under this structure outweighed the potential agency costs it may have caused.

It should be noted that most market regulators and investors now are pushing companies to avoid CEO duality, including Vietnam. Vietnam's new Law on Enterprise (2020) does not allow public companies and state-controlled joint-stock companies to have one person acting both as the CEO and as the chairman. The positive impact of CEO duality identified by this study does not imply that CEO duality is a best practice. Our findings were related to M&A transactions of listed firms in Vietnam from 2004 to 2013, the early development of the two stock exchanges in Vietnam. Given the market context at that time, our findings suggest that in an institutionally constrained but transitioning environment, the corporate governance structure of firms may not work best if it is unnecessarily sophisticated. As markets develop, firms grow in scale and size and investors become more professional, the corporate governance structure of the firm will also need to evolve towards better board independence.

9.2   MODEL BUILDING

9.2.1   *The Theoretical Model*

The following theoretical model puts the findings from the preceding chapters into perspective. This model represents an institutional framework to study corporate decisions and governance in an emerging market context. By emphasising the importance of institutional forces embedded in the business environment, this research has found a robust theoretical ground to explain the empirical observation in Vietnam. The factors examined in this research are state ownership, regulatory control and corporate governance structure. The common thread among these factors is clearly related to the state's overwhelming role in the economy, which is a typical feature of the Vietnamese market. As an owner, the state directly influences corporate strategy through its voting power in firms, whereas through industry regulation, the state oversees the development of industry and regulates firms' activities. In both of these roles, the state exerts a negative rather than positive impact on firms' performance and reduces shareholder wealth. From an agency perspective, the negative effect of the state could be linked to the inefficiency of the double agency model of state capital management in which the state delegates the management of state capital to an SCMA who, in turns, delegates the responsibilities to the state capital representative. Consequently, the multiple agency layers of the model plus the lack of ownership incentives of the representative give rise to agency costs and principal costs of SIEs.

The heavy presence of the state in the current economy could be traced back to the previous economic structure of the market before Doi Moi in 1986, which was a centrally planned economy or alternatively known as a command economy. During the time of a centrally planned economy, all major economic decisions were controlled by the government. Economic development was planned centrally with periodic overall growth targets, which were allocated to each industry or province. All major economic units and resources were owned by the state. Industries were heavily regulated to allow resources to be allocated to prioritised sectors (Cheong et al., 2010). The role of the state as observed today in the economy is inherited from the previous command economy, discussed in Chap. 3 as an example of the theory of path dependence (Bebchuk & Roe, 2000). This link is demonstrated in Fig. 9.2.

The third component of this theoretical model is corporate governance. Despite being a firm-level factor, the CEO duality feature in corporate governance examined in this study is deeply rooted in the Vietnamese market's institutional setting. As argued earlier, the prevalence of CEO duality among firms is grounded on the political ideology or dogma of centralised power in a single-party system under the Communist Party of Vietnam and the entrenched duality practice among state-owned firms. This is, again, evidence of the path dependence theory. In this model, CEO duality has a positive impact on firms' M&A performance, indicating that a less sophisticated structure could be more effective or optimal for emerging market firms in order to adapt to an institutionally constrained environment.

One should interpret the findings regarding the positive impact of CEO duality on Vietnamese firms' M&A performance within the study time and market context. The study was conducted at the infancy time of the stock market in Vietnam, from 2004 to 2013. The findings reflect what was suitable for the firms during that environment. The market was constrained in leadership talent and capital, and firms were relatively small. CEO duality could benefit the firm as it is an economical option for the firm to leverage its leadership talent. However, nowadays, CEO duality is no longer considered a good practice by both regulators and investors due to board independence concerns.

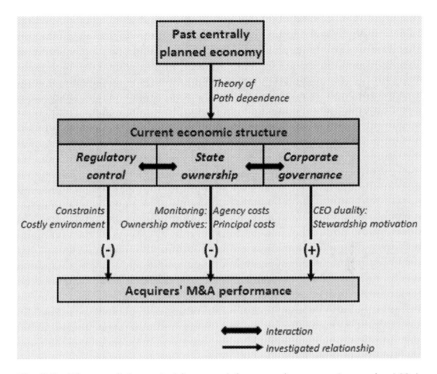

Fig. 9.2   The overall theoretical framework for research on emerging market M&A

It should be reminded that it is not just the components but also the interactions among these components that create the model. As discussed earlier, the interaction between state ownership and industry regulation reduces the negative impact on firms operating in a regulated industry. Similarly, CEO duality is seen as a positive factor that helps mitigate the principal problem of state ownership.

9.2.2   The Practical Model

The Four-Quadrant Model
We have seen that an M&A decision of a firm could be driven by various factors. If state ownership is involved, a firm's M&A could possibly be driven more by political and social concerns than its commercial viability. A politically motivated corporate decision under the influence of the state

shareholders may put other private shareholders at risk, especially when they are the minority. Here, we propose a practical model that assists corporate executives with their decision-making regarding decisions that could involve non-commercial motivations.

Figure 9.3 illustrates the four-quadrant M&A project evaluation model—*the four-quadrant model* in short. When a firm considers a project, it should evaluate both the commercial profitability and the project's non-commercial or societal value (such as community and environmental benefits). Its commercial viability could be evaluated using our model variables, including shareholder returns—*wealth impact*; earning growth—*growth impact*; and ROE/ROA—*profitability/efficiency impact*. We have explained in our model how these variables should be measured.

The firm should also appraise the societal value of the project, which could carry even more weight under the pressure of the state shareholder.

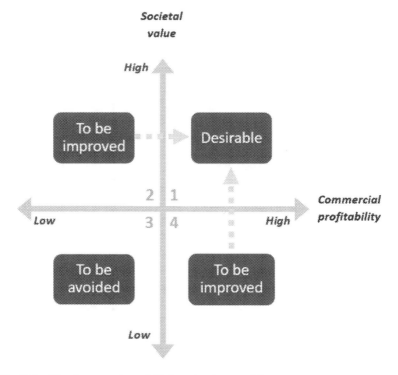

Fig. 9.3   The four-quadrant M&A evaluation model

Societal value is about how the project can benefit society. It can include, but not limited to, employment, social security and stability, diversity, environment and other benefits to the communities.

In the first quadrant, desirable projects are when the deliverable commercial profitability and societal value are both positive. So, embarking on such projects will serve both the state shareholder and other shareholders. There are other situations when a project is not that desirable. In Quadrant Two, a project may be good for society, for example, from the perspective of the state shareholder, but will not be profitable to the firm. Examples of those projects are when a firm has to acquire another loss-making firm under the pressure/direction of the government. The societal benefit, in this case, is reduced unemployment and preservation of state capital. However, the acquisition is not profitable to the firm on its financial metrics. If the firm can restructure the project's terms and conditions to improve the profitability of the project, it could be moved to Quadrant One and thus be accepted. If the project is still not viable to the firm, it should be undertaken by other firms that may have better synergies or capacity to realise its value. In many cases, such a type of project could be financed by the government's state budget and social impact investors.

Projects in Quadrant Three should be avoided as they would bring no benefits to both the firm and society. An example of this type of project is when a firm considers additions to an existing loss-making coal mining project due to sunk costs already committed to the project, which is not uncommon, especially among SIEs. This project would mean a further loss of state capital, environmental cost and loss to the firm.

Lastly, projects in the fourth quadrant may look good financially to the firm but not to the society, say due to certain environmental, social or governance (ESG) concerns. These projects are to be improved in terms of how they should benefit society. The firm can incorporate non-financial ESG criteria and metrics in evaluating the project. If the firm can improve on the ESG aspects of a project to move it to Quadrant One, it should be accepted.

The four-quadrant model is very primitive at this stage, as there are still questions to be answered about how best to measure the commercial and societal value of a project. There is room for further theoretical development about firms' strategies to move a project to the desirable quadrant. However, the model could serve as a good starting point of reference for corporate decision-makers and investors in evaluating a project, especially for firms with mixed ownership and diverse commercial and non-commercial motivations.

The Emerging Market Mergers and Acquisitions: EMMA Model
From the study, we also build the second applied model for emerging market mergers and acquisitions, the "EMMA" model. The model integrates all qualitative and quantitative findings in this research to produce a recommended framework of important M&A factors that decision-makers will find helpful.

This model could serve as a tool for deal structuring and risk management. While emerging markets are generally perceived to be "high risk, high return", the risks with M&A here are not necessarily unmanageable. Risk arises from the uncertain and the unknown. By bringing these important factors to light, the model hopefully can draw the attention of decision-makers to these issues to minimise unexpected or unfavourable outcomes.

The purpose of the model is not to list all popular must-ticks on a deal checklist. Rather, the focus of the model is on factors representing the typical characteristics of M&A involving emerging market firms. This model is applicable for both domestic M&A between emerging market firms and cross-border M&A involving an emerging market target. As all components of this model start with a P, EMMA could be referred to as the 5Ps of emerging market M&A, illustrated in Fig. 9.4.

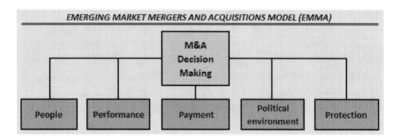

Fig. 9.4   The 5P emerging market mergers and acquisitions model

PEOPLE
• Leadership and board structure
• Owners and managers:
    – *Who are they?*
    – *What do they know?*
    – *Who do they know?*

The first *P* of EMMA is *People*. For a merger or an acquisition to be successful, management and board leadership of both acquirer and target firms are essential with regard to who they are, what they know and who they know. Regarding the acquiring firm, as it can be inferred from Chap. 8, certain models of board structure can make the decision-making process more effective. Although CEO duality is no longer a structure that is encouraged, especially for listed firms, the implication of the findings is that a strong and powerful CEO is needed for a good business. In Vietnamese firms where political pressure overwhelms, a strong CEO and a strong board will be able to mitigate the principal costs of political equity ownership and leverage the firm's leadership skills and connections.

For SIEs, the interviews also reveal that leaders of SIEs need to transform their firms from a rent-seeking to a value-creating business model to deliver wealth for shareholders. Regarding a target firm, it is critical for an acquirer to understand the backgrounds, motivations and expectations of the owners and managers of the target.

As discussed, in Vietnam, the shareholding structure is not widely dispersed. Vietnamese firms commonly have block-shareholders who typically are either the state shareholder or families. The shareholding, however, is not always as transparent as it should be. The due diligence check of a potential target should pay special attention to this issue so that the acquirer can better appreciate the needs and motivations of the target owners in a deal. Broadly, this could contribute to the relational capital, which is a part of the intellectual capital of a firm. It could be related to customers, partners, political connection for regulatory privileges or connection with banks for easier access to finance. The analysis of the target should evaluate how these relationships support the business or constrain the business and whether it will continue after the change of ownership.

> ## PERFORMANCE
> - Financial performance of both acquirer and target
> - Synergies
> - Strategic fit
> - Valuation methods and inputs

The second *P* in EMMA refers to *Performance* of both the acquiring and target firm, covering both current and potential performance. A key question in a deal is always how to assess the performance of a target firm and its value. As the interviews with M&A professional have shown, Vietnamese firms are attractive for their access to an excellent local consumer market. However, the assessment of growth opportunity after acquisition should take into account the potential competition from neighbouring markets because Vietnamese consumers with a high disposable income actually prefer overseas service providers. Synergies should also be considered. Chapter 6 shows that typical synergies in Vietnamese deals are operational, marketing, financial and management. There are also various issues to consider in the valuation process, such as the illiquid stock market, lack of comparable firms and distorted cost of capital information. Acquirers need to be aware of certain hidden performance issues relating to taxes and accounting policies.

PAYMENT
- Payment plan (means, currency, payment structure and conditions)
- Other parts of the payment

The third *P* in EMMA is *Payment*. The payment plan should always be carefully considered. The M&A professional respondents indicated that most of the deals in Vietnam have a simple payment plan, with cash being the main medium of payment. The use of an escrow account or an earn-out agreement is advisable; however, the cultural interpretation of such agreement should be noted. An earn-out agreement or a staged payout plan should clearly specify the payments contingent on the target satisfying an agreed-upon milestone. The milestone could be performance-based such as profitability or cash flow.

However, it is more advisable for the milestone to be activity-based such as successfully transferring the title of a strategic asset to the acquirer, obtaining regulatory approval for opening new outlets or launching a new product. This is critical to an emerging market deal as expected post-deal transactions may not happen according to plan due to political risks and many other external factors.

Considerations should also be given to other parts of financial and non-financial payments such as fee-based consulting contracts and employment contracts to target owners and managers to utilise their experience and relationship. The acquirer is also advised to understand the bargaining culture to negotiate payment options wisely.

POLITICAL ENVIRONMENT
- SIEs and political influences
- Industry regulations
- Market regulations
- Legal risks
- Transparency issues
- Corruption risks

Deals in emerging markets are subject to a high level of political risk, which gives rise to the fourth *P* of the model, the *Political environment*. Firstly, for the state-owned sector, the respondents said that SIEs are subject to political interference, and their M&A may not be driven by only economic objectives, which could explain the negative wealth performance of SIEs' M&A reported in Chap. 6.

This finding highlights the detriment to shareholder value of SIE's M&A and therefore recommends SIEs to carefully consider the economic value of each acquisition.

At the industry level, according to Chap. 8, the level of regulation in an industry is associated with lower M&A returns, suggesting that firms in regulated industries should not consider M&A unless they are substantially owned by the state. We also find that regulated firms do not perform well when they acquire a firm in an unrelated industry.

At a macro level, a variety of market regulations are applied in Vietnam, including the daily price limit of the capital market, managed float management in the foreign exchange rate market and interest rate caps in the money market. Government regulations cause market imperfections that may distort transaction prices and cost of capital for firms, affecting deal valuation and payment. These policy risks need to be considered and addressed by proper risk management strategies such as interest rate and foreign exchange rate hedging.

Furthermore, legal risks due to changes in conditions for conditional business activities and legal restrictions for foreign-invested businesses, for example, could also be significant in an emerging market deal. Other factors such as the delay in IPO process, prolonged waiting time from IPO to listing stocks on an organised exchange, market illiquidity on the UPCoM and the trend in state capital investment and divestment, among others, are all critical for investors when evaluating an exit strategy. As our analysis highlights, it is not the existence of these rules and regulations that matter; rather, the risk lies in the inconsistency or lack of transparency in their application.

Lastly, a lack of transparency and the reliance on connections for privileges may lead to possible corruptive behaviour. It is a real challenge but a must for an acquirer to verify if a prospective target is free from corruption; otherwise, the acquirer will be at risk of violating anti-corruption laws when acquiring a corruptive target.

> PROTECTION
> - Due diligence
> - The use of deal insurance purchase
> - Foreign exchange risks and hedging costs
> - Other risk management strategies

The last *P* in the model is *Protection*, which focuses on how firms should manage risks in emerging market M&A. Firms are advised to use M&A professional services for due diligence regarding financial, legal and tax audits to avoid commercial and legal risks. Some large deals may find it beneficial to employ an intelligence firm to obtain better market and corporate information for better evaluation of the target.

Moreover, although the use of deal insurance purchase has not been popular in the Vietnamese market, some M&A professionals have started recommending it to large clients such as representations and warranties insurance. Hedging by foreign exchange and interest rate derivatives could be used for transaction risk management. Lastly, other risk management strategies may include structured payments.

In summary, the 5P EMMA model draws the attention of decision-makers to important factors concerning M&A in emerging markets where the institutional environment is weak and corporate governance mechanisms to protect shareholders are limited. This is by no means an exhaustive list. Instead, it is a risk-focused framework that should help firms avoid risky value-destroying acquisitions.

The key message is that M&A value should be sought by identifying the acquirer's own people and performance strengths and weaknesses and those of the target, working out an effective payment plan, understanding the political environment of both firms and employing necessary protective measures for risk management.

Due Diligence Recommendations for Private Investors to Invest in Mixed-Ownership SIEs

The World Bank (2014) recognises the corporate governance challenges of SIEs with mixed ownership. If the government ownership is at a minority level, the state shareholder may not be incentivised to spend resources for stewardship responsibilities with the portfolio companies. For SOEs in which the government is a controlling shareholder, the interest of the state shareholder may not be aligned with that of minority private shareholders. In such cases, the state, as the ownership entity, may have unreasonable demands on the firm, which can cause principal costs to the firm. Private shareholders will have the confidence to invest if they can be assured that the SOE has good corporate governance for equitable treatment of all shareholders.

Before embarking on an investment in an emerging market SIE, private investors must understand the legal environment governing state ownership in the country. It is also crucial for private investors to review the state shareholder's practice and reputation as a business owner. For investors adopting this fundamentally top-down approach, the World Bank's country-level toolkit for reviewing the corporate governance framework of the state-owned sector could be a good source of reference (World Bank, 2014).

Based on the experience in the market and our research findings, we prepare the following recommendations for a number of corporate governance issues that a *private sector investor* should have in its due diligence work on a target SIE. This is, by no means, to replace the usual due diligence of the investor. Instead, these are essential points to evaluate the impact of the state capital on a firm's valuation and risk for their safeguard.

Factors	Possible risk/impact of state ownership
State ownership rationale and objectives	• The state ownership motives • Investment/divestment intention • The investment horizon of the state owners (the classification as to whether the firm belongs to the long-term/medium- or short-term list for government ownership)
State capital management	• State capital management agency • She voting right of the state capital and any other special rights/arrangement in place • State ownership representative at the firm (term)
Required performance of state capital	• The performance target in terms of return on capital, ROE, ROA and so on of the state owners • The state shareholder's preference of dividends to growth?
Future investment/divestment plan of the state shareholder	• The plan for state ownership in the industry • Future divestment/investment plan of state ownership at the firm • The timing of state investment/divestment • Observation of past divestment of state capital of firms in the same industry/sector (any liquidity issues, price impact) • The state owner's preference to divest (who does the state owner sell to? Is there a preference for public investors or strategic investors?) • The performance of similar state-divested firms in the past
Board composition, nomination, performance evaluation and compensation	• The size of the board and board independence level • Directors' term • Diversity, skills and experience matrix • Director nomination and CEO appointment (by BOD or a higher authority sign-off?) • The management and board compensation structure • The representative(s) of the state shareholder on the board: Number, skills and experience, contribution to the overall skills matrix of the board, their past participation in board discussion, the term for directorship, remuneration of the state representative and performance evaluation of their role
Board risk management and oversight function (board sub-committees)	• The board's committees and the independence level of the committees • The participation of the state representative in these committees • The state's influence on each committee • The risk appetite of the state shareholders and risk-taking guidelines from the state owners • The state owner's risk communication to the SIE • Risk audit at the government owner level • Risk audit at the SIE level • The oversight of related party transaction at the SIE

(continued)

(continued)

Factors	Possible risk/impact of state ownership
CEO and senior management	• Education and professional background • Political background and connection • Any past integrity, reputational controversy or future risk • Shareholding, including ownership of related parties • Management compensation structure (long-term and short-term incentives)
Capital structure	• The current capital structure of the firm (debt/equity) • Sources of its debt and equity • State capital's effect on the firm's capital structure and its cost of capital • Access to any preferential financing thanks to state ownership status (If yes, how has that preferential financing information been factored into the current valuation of the firm?) • Possible impact on capital structure and cost of capital if state ownership discontinues (to what proportion of debt? Equity? By how much?)
Other shareholders	• Other large shareholders of the firm • Diversity among corporate shareholders, government owners, financial institutions, family or related shareholders and the public shareholders • The current level of foreign ownership? (Up to/near the limit of foreign ownership? Who are these foreign investors? Passive or active investors? Do they seek to engage with the firm to improve the firm's corporate governance?) • Whether the other large shareholders are active to re-balance against the interest of the state owner in case of adversity
Business activities	• Main business activities of the firm, • The firm's market position • How does state ownership/the SIE status support the firm in its business activity? Any advantages in accessing markets such as government guarantees, obtaining a licence, securing contracts and so on? To what extent? • If yes, what proportion of revenue/profits could be affected if state capital discontinues? • Risk of political interference (past incidences of altered contracts, directed contracts, directed lending, M&A, etc.) • Risk of corruption and bribery

Central to this due diligence is the question of how the state-owned status has affected the firm in its main business activities, financing, governance and cost of capital and whether such impact has been factored into the valuation of the firm. Preferential funding from state-owned banks, privileged access to information, tax concessions and subsidies, grants and supports, exemption from regulations and price subsidies are among the examples of advantages that an SIE may enjoy. However, these preferential treatments are not sustainable and should not be the core value of the firm. It is essential to know how the firm will be impacted if state ownership discontinues.

The implications of the theoretical model and the practical models and recommendations will be discussed next.

9.3   IMPLICATIONS

9.3.1   Theoretical Implications for Research

The empirical evidence from this research confirms that institutional factors matter and should be included in the design for emerging market research. These findings suggest a number of important implications for theory development. First of all, this research responds to the need to develop new theories that capture the essence of the roles of the state in an emerging market context. This task is even more challenging given the transitional nature of emerging markets, as existing theories may become out of context. This research, therefore, integrates agency theory (Jensen & Meckling, 1976) and political theory (Shleifer & Vishny, 1994) to form a perspective that reflects both the political and commercial interests of the state shareholder. In this book, we have presented a fundamental rethinking of agency theory to account for the presence of the state as a shareholder in a firm along the key dimensions: its motivation, behaviour, structure, the channel of corporate impact and the resulting principal-principal conflict between the state shareholder and other shareholders. The inclusion of the state shareholder and the consideration of its non-commercial ownership motivation timely extend the classic agency theory by converting the dichotomous agency problem between managers (agent) and shareholders (principal) into a multi-polar problem between managers and multiple shareholders.

Secondly, from an agency perspective, this research has put forward a new insightful concept of *principal costs* of the state shareholder. The introduction of this term reflects a needed focus on the responsibility and accountability of the principal rather than the traditional scrutiny on managers, a novel approach that could facilitate further theorisation and empirical corporate finance research in markets where the state still plays a dominant role in the economy. The issue has become increasingly relevant as SIEs are expanding via M&A even beyond the local economy.

Thirdly, from a methodological standpoint, the insights gained from the in-depth interviews in the qualitative phase of this research have demonstrated the value of an underexplored method in finance. Interviewing allows us to understand the underlying behavioural motivations and factors driving individual decisions, which are generally not apparent or possible with secondary data research. Furthermore, this research suggests examining M&A performance or any other corporate issues from various perspectives, including firm's internal measurement based on management assessment (from interviews and surveys), financial ratios and market's view based on stock returns. Combining secondary data and qualitative results provides a meaningful triangulation that enhances the validity and reliability of the conclusions claimed (Baker et al., 2011; Percival, 1993).

9.3.2   Policy Implications

The findings from this research raise important policy considerations for Vietnam and other emerging markets to develop a more supportive and conducive institutional environment. Although a negative impact of state ownership on organisational outcomes has been documented regarding state ownership, this research does not necessarily argue for demolishing the state's presence as a shareholder. Instead, by pointing out that the crux of principal costs of the state shareholder is the inefficiency of the double agency model of state capital management, we recommend the following courses of actions for Vietnamese and emerging market policymakers to improve the efficiency of state capital:

- To improve the separation between the state's ownership function and other function by professionalising state capital management;
- To reduce the number of agency layers in state capital management;
- To empower the state capital management agencies to make investment decisions and, at the same time, increase the transparency and accountability of their decisions;
- To incentivise the state capital representatives to more effectively exercise ownership rights and responsibilities at firms;

- To minimise detrimental behaviours of the state shareholder such as marginalising minority investors, moral hazards in capital management and "term-bound" thinking, rent-seeking and favour-granting mindsets; and
- To provide mechanisms that ensure the interest of non-state shareholders is considered in firms' decision-making.

These suggestions are in line with the guidance of the new Law on Enterprise (2020) and the Corporate Governance Code of Best Practices (2019) in Vietnam. All offer timely assistance to the Vietnamese government with its current commitment to reform the state-owned sector.

Regarding regulatory control, the evidence presented in this book has revealed that M&As by Vietnamese firms in regulated industries does not create wealth. This is possibly due to the higher level of constraints they face. Policymakers, therefore, should consider how firms are disadvantaged by regulation as it will affect the competitiveness of Vietnamese firms in competing with those from a more liberal and supportive regulatory environment. Furthermore, we have also documented that firms in which the state is the largest shareholder bear less of the negative regulatory impact, suggesting that a genuinely desirable level playing field between state-owned and private firms has yet to be attained.

9.3.3   Practical Implications

The theoretical and practical models proposed in this book could be a useful analytical tool for investors, businesses and practitioners for M&A involving emerging market firms. The theoretical model draws the attention of decision-makers to the possible impacts that institutional factors may have on organisational ramifications and outcomes, the understanding of which is critical for having value-creating M&A (Fan et al., 2011; Kearney, 2012). Firms need to consider the possible constraints resulting from their ownership structure, regulatory environment and leadership in an emerging market when planning their M&A strategies. Extra care should be taken for cross-border M&As when firms are not familiar with the institutional forces of a new environment.

As emerging market SIEs have been both attractive targets and globally active acquirers, it would be beneficial for firms and investors in other emerging and developed markets to understand the implications of having the state shareholder. Besides being aware of the possible agency and principal costs of having the state shareholder, emerging market firms, especially SIEs, should direct their effort towards developing corporate mechanisms that minimise principal-principal conflict and other agency concerns to maximise firm value. This could be achieved by, for example, ensuring that the board is not politically driven to serve only the interest of the state and but that minority shareholders' interest is also represented and considered on boards.

The practical four-quadrant model and the 5P EMMA model offer a simplified but systematic framework for firms to design their M&A strategy, especially for emerging market firms with the state capital, as their M&A projects could have different political, social and commercial motivations. While the model needs to be developed further, it can still be useful for firms and shareholders in evaluating M&A projects and make an informed decision for effective voting.

The research we present in this book has also demonstrated a multi-dimensional approach to conducting an ex-post evaluation of M&A performance that assesses the wealth, efficiency and growth impacts of a merger or an acquisition, that is, *CARs*, *ΔROA* and *ΔEPSG*, respectively. On the one hand, this approach allows for both an internal (operating performance) and external assessment (stock returns). On the other hand, it examines M&A performance in terms of short-term shareholder returns as well as long-term operating improvement. Consequently, this approach could be utilised by firms in evaluating their M&A performance to facilitate organisational learning and development of future M&A strategy.

9.3.4   *Limitations*

A number of limitations should be noted regarding the research we presented in the book. Firstly, the caveats associated with the qualitative study should be acknowledged regarding the sampling method. As discussed in Chap. 5, the sample for the interviews was recruited by a non-random, purposive sampling method, which may introduce sample selection bias towards certain types of firms, industry sectors, locations and size (King, 2004; Kvale & Brinkmann, 2009).

The sample was later expanded by a snowball sampling technique in which current participants introduced potential future participants. If the sample was biased, then the snowball sampling would likely worsen the problem.

An observable bias of this research is that the sampled firms are relatively small in size and mainly located in the two largest cities of Vietnam. Additionally, the sample is dominated by private firms rather than SIEs and listed firms. As the research focuses on comparing SOEs and non-SOEs, an ideal sample would have a balanced number of the two groups, which was impossible as access to SIEs was very limited. Nevertheless, the quantitative study that covers a larger number of SIEs and firms of various sizes could reduce these biases.

The quantitative study, however, carries its owns limitations. First, the study was based on 188 M&A of listed Vietnamese firms, a relatively small sample compared to the number of variables included in each model. As the chance that significant differences will be missed is higher for small samples, it is more challenging to find significance (Wooldridge, 2002).

Secondly, there are particular challenges with event study methodology in terms of the choice of the prediction model, selections of the estimation and event windows, infrequent trading and event clustering. This research uses the market model as the prediction model, according to Fama et al. (1969) and Brown and Warner (1980). Despite its popularity, the method is criticised for producing too low returns and inflating abnormal returns, especially for small firms (Banz, 1981). Considered alternatives include the different variants of the asset pricing models such as Fama-MacBeth residuals and the Mean Adjusted Returns method (Brown & Warner, 1980), each of which has its own limitations. Indeed, Brown and Weinstein (1985) do not find any advantages of the factor models over the simple market model.

In terms of the estimation window and event time window choices, there is no definite rule, and discretion belongs to the researcher. While longer estimation windows could potentially improve accuracy as they provide larger samples of returns, there is a risk of structural breaks due to noise events, which should not be ignored in emerging markets.

Similarly, the decision of the event window also represents a trade-off between more extended periods for processing information and capturing information leakages and possible confounding events. Moreover, event studies on small stock exchanges, such as the Vietnamese exchanges, have constantly been scrutinised because there are many infrequently traded stocks (Maynes & Rumsey, 1993). For small stock markets, it is difficult to consistently detect small abnormal returns unless the sample only contains thickly traded stocks (Bartholdy et al., 2007). The remedies are to use trade to trade returns rather than daily returns and to separate thinly traded stocks from those that are not (Bartholdy et al., 2007), which is not possible in this research because trading data for Vietnamese firms are not available.

Another recommendation for small stock markets is to use non-parametric tests instead of parametric ones (Bartholdy et al., 2007; Corrado & Truong, 2008). Other problems of conducting event studies in small stock markets include information leakages and insider trading, event-induced variance, unknown event announcement time and noisy events or clustering events (Bartholdy et al., 2007; Bhattacharya et al., 2000; Masulis et al., 2007).

Thirdly, endogeneity is potentially a fundamental problem of research that aims to establish causal links among ownership—governance—performance (Imbens & Wooldridge, 2009). As corporate governance structure is endogenous to the firm, this research used instrumental variable estimation and propensity score matching analysis for robustness check for the result reported in Chap. 8.

Similarly, it could be argued that state ownership is not an exogenous factor to the firm because the decision of the State to privatise a firm or to invest state capital in a firm could depend on its performance (Firth et al., 2012). Whether regulation is a totally exogenous factor is also a question of concern, which has not been fully addressed by this research.

Furthermore, as M&A is a firm's decision, there is also a concern of sample selection bias (Ahern, 2009). The challenge for studies on corporate events is that we can only work with the outcome of the choice made as the outcome of the choices not made is not observable (Tucker, 2010). The solution would be to compare an acquirer with its own "no acquisition" hypothetical self by an experimental design or to expand the sample to include non-acquiring firms that are fully matched to be control firms for comparison, both of which are not practical in our research context. That would be ideal!

9.3.5   Implications for Future Research

Our research opens up several exciting avenues for future research, not only in M&A but also in other corporate decisions and corporate governance aspects of emerging market firms. Firstly, it would be interesting to see if the theoretical framework can apply to other emerging markets. Secondly, this book has raised the controversial issues of agency costs and principal costs of the state shareholder in emerging market firms. For the debate to move forward, a better understanding of these concepts and their dimensions needs to be developed. The discussion of the behaviours of the state shareholder that possibly lead to principal costs in this book, though insightful, is preliminary. Further, future research could focus on exploring each of these issues in more depth, either qualitatively or quantitatively.

Furthermore, as emerging market states are using SOEs as a vehicle to reach global marketplaces via M&A (Chen & Young, 2010; Jongwanich et al., 2013), this research could be expanded to examine if the agency issues are extended overseas, especially when these SOEs have a presence in more developed markets with better institutional protection of shareholder interest and regulatory constraint.

Lastly, more research on the dynamism of institutional factors is needed because the layers and multiple aspects of institutional pressure facing emerging market firms are not static over time due to liberalisation and institutional transition progress (Peng, 2003). The influence of the government via business ownership and industry regulations will change and so will firms' responses to institutional developments.

9.4   CONCLUDING THOUGHTS

The tremendous growth of emerging market SOEs in recent years, both at home and abroad, has led us to wonder if we have fully understood their motivations, behaviour and performance. The agency theory alone would not be sufficient to explain an SOE's political, social and other drives as well as burdens instilled on it by the state shareholder. The presence of state capital at the firm introduces further complexities. It induces externalities to the agency theory due to the state capital representative's role at the firm and the existence of the state capital management agency.

We have incorporated new elements into agency theory to widen its application and enhance its stance in a political and institutional context. These new elements include more layers of the agency relationship and the concept of principal costs. Therefore, we contribute to the development of agency theory by making it a more relevant theoretical foundation for further theorisation in emerging markets. Standing on the shoulders of giants allows us to see the far, but it is essential not to lose sight of the near. Robust theories that are locally relevant are truly needed now in studies on emerging markets.

A note of caution must be added that the negative impact of state ownership on Vietnamese firms' M&A outcomes is different from what is observed in China (Bhabra & Huang, 2013) and, therefore, may vary for other emerging markets. The findings from our research again raise the question of why efforts to improve the efficiency of state capital in Vietnam have resulted in so little success. The privatisation process has produced a new type of hybrid firm with both state and private capital; yet, the mechanisms for the state and private owners to co-reside productively in a business have not been timely developed. The process of equitisation in Vietnam has been much slower than planned. Business performance and governance post-equitisation have not been promising, reducing the confidence of private sector investors. So even though access to the capital market is wide open, many Vietnamese SOEs are caught in a circle of capital inadequacy and low efficiency.

Much could be learned from the experience of China in recent years where the Chinese government has successfully used SOEs as an economic power engine domestically and to expand its control over resources globally via outward M&A. It seems that despite the common market system with socialist characteristics between the two countries, the divergence in institutional reform policies and progress has led to different resources, capabilities and priorities of SOEs and hence also different outcomes.

References

Ahern, K. R. (2009). Sample Selection and Event Study Estimation. *Journal of Empirical Finance, 16*(3), 466–482.

Baker, H. K., Singleton, J. C., & Veit, E. T. (2011). *Survey Research in Corporate Finance: Bridging the Gap between Theory and Practice*. Oxford Scholarship.

Banz, R. W. (1981). The Relationship between Return and Market Value of Common Stocks. *Journal of Financial Economics, 9*(1), 3–18.

Bartholdy, J., Olson, D., & Peare, P. (2007). Conducting Event Studies on a Small Stock Exchange. *The European Journal of Finance, 13*(3), 227–252.

Bebchuk, L. A., & Roe, M. J. (2000). A Theory of Path Dependence in Corporate Ownership and Governance. *Stanford Law Review, 52*(1), 127.

Bhabra, H. S., & Huang, J. (2013). An Empirical Investigation of Mergers and Acquisitions by Chinese listed companies, 1997–2007. *Journal of Multinational Financial Management, 23*, 186–207.

Bhattacharya, U., Daouk, H., Jorgenson, B., & Kehr, C.-H. (2000). When an Event Is Not an Event: The Curious Case of an Emerging Market. *Journal of Financial Economics, 55*(1), 69–101.

Brown, S. J., & Warner, J. B. (1980). Measuring Security Price Performance. *Journal of Financial Economics, 8*(3), 205–258.

Brown, S. J., & Weinstein, M. I. (1985). Derived Factors in Event Studies. *Journal of Financial Economics, 14*(3), 491–495.

Chen, Y., Li, H., & Zhou, L.-A. (2005). Relative Performance Evaluation and the Turnover of Provincial Leaders in China. *Economics Letters, 88*(3), 421–425.

Chen, Y. Y., & Young, M. N. (2010). Cross-Border Mergers and Acquisitions by Chinese Listed Companies: A Principal–principal Perspective. *Asia Pacific Journal of Management, 27*(3), 523–539.

Cheong, K.-C., Pham, D. M., & Nguyen, T. (2010). *From Low-Income to Industrialised: Vietnam in the Next Decade and Beyond.* Vietnam Academy of Social Sciences.

Corrado, C. J., & Truong, C. (2008). Conducting Event Studies with Asia-Pacific Security Market Data. *Pacific Basin Finance Journal, 16*(5), 493–521.

Fama, E. F., Fisher, L., Jensen, M. C., & Roll, R. (1969). The Adjustment of Stock Prices to New Information. *International Economic Review, 10*(1), 1–21.

Fan, J. P. H., Wei, K. C. J., & Xu, X. (2011). Corporate Finance and Governance in Emerging Markets: A Selective Review and an Agenda for Future Research. *Journal of Corporate Finance, 17*(2), 207–214.

Firth, M., Malatesta, P. H., Xin, Q., & Xu, L. (2012). Corporate Investment, Government Control, and Financing Channels: Evidence from China's Listed Companies. *Journal of Corporate Finance, 18*(3), 433–450.

Imbens, G. W., & Wooldridge, J. M. (2009). Recent Developments in the Econometrics of Program Evaluation. *Journal of Economic Literature, 47*(1), 5–86.

Jensen, M. C., & Meckling, W. H. (1976). Theory of the firm: Managerial Behaviour, Agency Costs and Ownership Structure. *Journal of Financial Economics, 3*(4), 305–360.

Jongwanich, J., Brooks, D. H., & Kohpaiboon, A. (2013). Cross-border Mergers and Acquisitions and Financial Development: Evidence from Emerging Asia. *Asian Economic Journal, 27*(3), 265–284.

Kearney, C. (2012). Emerging Markets Research: Trends, Issues and Future Directions. *Emerging Markets Review, 13*(2), 159–183.

King, N. (Ed.). (2004). *Using Interviews in Qualitative Research.* Sage Publications.

Kvale, S., & Brinkmann, S. (2009). *Interviews: Learning the Craft of Qualitative Research Interviewing.* SAGE Publications, Inc.

Li, J., & Qian, C. (2013). Principal-principal Conflicts under Weak Institutions: A Study of Corporate Takeovers in China. *Strategic Management Journal, 34*(4), 498–508.

Masulis, R. W., Wang, C., & Xie, F. E. I. (2007). Corporate Governance and Acquirer Returns. *The Journal of Finance, 62*(4), 1851–1889.

Maynes, E., & Rumsey, J. (1993). Conducting Event Studies with Thinly Traded Stocks. *Journal of Banking & Finance, 17*(1), 145–157.

Peng, M. W. (2003). Institutional Transitions and Strategic Choices. *The Academy of Management Review, 28*(2), 275–296.

Peng, M. W., Zhang, S., & Li, X. (2007). CEO Duality and Firm Performance during China's Institutional Transitions. *Management and Organization Review, 3*(2), 205–225.

Percival, J. (1993). Why Don't We Just Ask Them? *Finance Practice and Education, 3*(2), 9–9.

Shleifer, A., & Vishny, R. W. (1994). Politicians and Firms. *The Quarterly Journal of Economics, 109*(4), 995–1025.

Su, Y., Xu, D., & Phan, P. H. (2008). Principal–Principal Conflict in the Governance of the Chinese Public Corporation. *Management and Organization Review, 4*(1), 17–38.

Tucker, J. W. (2010). Selection Bias and Econometric Remedies in Accounting and Finance Research. *Journal of Accounting Literature, 29*, 31–57.

Wooldridge, J. M. (2002). *Econometric Analysis of Cross Section and Panel Data.* MIT Press.

World Bank. (2014). *Corporate Governance of State-Owned Enterprises: A Toolkit.* World Bank. https://doi.org/10.1596/978-1-4648-0222-5